PLEASE EXPLAIN

Anna Broinowski is an author and filmmaker who has been tracking the illicit, subversive and bizarre since her 1995 film on the Japanese cultural underground, *Hell Bento!!*

Her films include *Aim High in Creation!* (about the North Korean propaganda film industry), *Forbidden Lie$* (about hoax author Norma Khouri), *Helen's War* (about anti-nuclear campaigner Dr Helen Caldicott), *Sexing the Label* (about queer Sydney in the 1990s) and *Pauline Hanson: Please Explain!*, which screened on SBS in 2016.

They've won stuff, including three AACTAs, a Walkley, the Rome Festival Cult prize, Best Film at Silverdocs USA, a NSW Premier's Literary Award, the Writer's Guild of America Best Nonfiction Screenplay and a Russian Film Critics' prize shaped like an elephant.

After covering Kim Jong Il in her first book, *The Director is the Commander*, and Senator Pauline Hanson in this one, Anna is looking forward to not writing about politicians for a while.

PLEASE EXPLAIN

The Rise, Fall and Rise Again of Pauline Hanson

ANNA BROINOWSKI

VIKING
an imprint of
PENGUIN BOOKS

VIKING
UK | USA | Canada | Ireland | Australia
India | New Zealand | South Africa | China

Penguin Books is part of the Penguin Random House group of companies whose addresses can be found at global.penguinrandomhouse.com.

First published by Penguin Random House Australia Pty Ltd, 2017

1 3 5 7 9 10 8 6 4 2

Text copyright © Anna Broinowski 2017

The moral right of the author has been asserted.

All rights reserved. Without limiting the rights under copyright reserved above, no part of this publication may be reproduced, stored in or introduced into a retrieval system, or transmitted, in any form or by any means (electronic, mechanical, photocopying, recording or otherwise), without the prior written permission of both the copyright owner and the above publisher of this book.

Please note that every effort has been made to contact copyright holders. Anyone with an outstanding claim should contact the publisher.

Cover design by Alex Ross © Penguin Random House Australia Pty Ltd
Text design by Samantha Jayaweera © Penguin Random House Australia Pty Ltd
Cover photograph © Emma Phillips, 2016
Typeset in Adobe Garamond Pro by Midland Typesetters, Australia
Colour separation by Splitting Image Colour Studio, Clayton, Victoria
Printed and bound in Australia by Griffin Press, an accredited ISO AS/NZS 14001 Environmental Management Systems printer.

National Library of Australia
Cataloguing-in-Publication data:
Broinowski, Anna, author.
Please explain : the rise, fall and rise again of Pauline Hanson / Anna Broinowski.
9780143784678 (paperback)
Subjects: Hanson, Pauline (Pauline Lee)
Women politicians – Australia.
Political parties – Australia.
Australia – Politics and government.
Australia – Race relations.

penguin.com.au

May you live in interesting times.
—Old Chinese curse

CONTENTS

Prologue		1
Chapter 1	She's fed up, and she's back	7
Chapter 2	I don't like it!	37
Chapter 3	The fish and chip shop	64
Chapter 4	The Member for Oxley	83
Chapter 5	The maiden speech	111
Chapter 6	Please explain?	139
Chapter 7	The rise of One Nation	167
Chapter 8	The fall of Pauline	202
Chapter 9	Rock bottom	235
Chapter 10	The rise of Senator Hanson	267
Epilogue		302
Acknowledgements		310

Prologue

I first met Pauline Hanson on a hot January morning in 2009. She was staying in Sylvania Waters: the Sydney suburb that spawned Australia's first reality TV star, tough-talking nouveau riche battler Noeline Baker.

It was 9 a.m. on a Sunday but Hanson answered the door dressed for a cocktail party, in head-to-toe white with matching stilettos and pearls. At fifty-four, she was trim and impeccably made-up, her muscled hands the only evidence of the years of hard labour she'd put into her Ipswich fish and chip shop, before her incendiary views on Asians and Aborigines catapulted her into federal politics.

'Wow, you're even more of an icon in 3D,' I blurted before I could stop myself.

Hanson has undeniable X factor; she's more of a force field than a human being. She glared at me with her astonishingly wide-set aquamarine eyes and let us in.

After thirteen years of being derided by progressive commentators, multicultural academics, angry protesters and her political enemies as an uneducated, racist redneck, Hanson was no fan of the 'elitist' media. She was intensely wary about the feature film my producers and I wanted to make about her incredible journey – from working single mother to Australia's most notorious independent politician, followed by imprisonment for electoral fraud and subsequent redemption as a TV celebrity on *Dancing with the Stars*.

But Hanson was flattered that Cate Blanchett was interested in playing her, and liked the idea of her political legacy being immortalised on the big screen. A strident critic of what she calls the 'boys' club' ever since former prime minister Tony Abbott kickstarted the legal proceedings that eventually saw her jailed, Hanson – who swears she's no feminist – agreed with me that had she been a male politician, a film about her story would already have been made.

We began to talk, and Hanson was frosty and monosyllabic. But when I told her I was a pro-refugee, pro-environment, pro-reconciliation leftie who had grown up in Asia and disagreed with almost everything she said, she decided to trust me. Hanson prides herself on being a straight talker and values honesty in others. She took me down to the Sylvania Waters boat club, ordered the fish and chips, and began to tell me about her life.

She was going through a tough time. She'd recently split with her latest beau, 49-year-old country-and-western singer Chris Callaghan, and was recovering from her failure to win a Senate seat in the 2007 federal election, while struggling to fight a new campaign for the Queensland seat of Beaudesert.

'Politicians have to do the right thing. People are dying,' Hanson told me later that night as we sat around the pool nursing Ginger Bitches, her favourite tipple of Bundy and dry. Then she started to cry. 'When you are in politics, you have to make tough decisions and don't let emotion get in the way.'

Hanson was considering doing a Channel 7 reality TV dating show, to find herself a new husband. 'I am open to offers. I would dearly love to meet someone who I can spend the rest of my life with and have that companionship with,' she'd told the *Daily Telegraph*.

The TV show never happened, and Hanson went on to lose in Queensland, her fifth attempt to win political office since losing her federal seat in 1998.

On that muggy evening in Sylvania Waters in 2009, neither of us dreamt that seven years later, after eight failed election campaigns, Hanson would be back in federal parliament.

Now it's 2017, and Pauline Hanson, after eighteen years in the political wilderness, is serving a six-year term in the federal Senate. She's enjoying new relevance and power as the head of her resurgent populist far-right party, One Nation.

And I am in recovery from a gruelling shoot following Hanson's 'Fed Up' campaign tour around the pubs, clubs and main streets of rural Queensland. When our feature film stalled, I translated my years of research and access to Hanson into an SBS documentary. It was initially intended to examine Hanson's impact on multicultural Australia in the 1990s. But in filming it, I had a front-row seat to the grassroots campaign that finally delivered Hanson back to power.

Pauline Hanson: Please Explain! went to air on Sunday night, 31 July 2016. Hanson announced on social media 'an exclusive behind the scenes (director's cut) of my reaction to tonight's SBS screening of my political career', and live-streamed herself watching the film on Facebook.

No fewer than 113 774 followers logged in to Hanson's strange, postmodern echo chamber, happy to watch their icon sitting on a grey couch doing nothing for seventy-two minutes – while over half a million Australians tuned in to the documentary itself.

Hanson had shared the intimate details of her life with me. Now the intense highs and lows of the two-decade political quest that cemented her place as Australia's most polarising powerbroker were exposed to her enemies and followers alike.

In the film, Professor Marcia Langton, former New South Wales MLC Helen Sham-Ho and newly elected federal MP Linda Burney excoriated Hanson for the damage she inflicted on Indigenous and multicultural Australia in the 1990s. Her former spin doctors, John Pasquarelli and David Oldfield, both claimed credit for her extraordinary pull with disenfranchised blue-collar voters. Former prime minister John Howard, from his lofty office in Sydney's CBD, denied Hanson had any impact on his hardline stance against refugees, his refusal to apologise to the stolen generations, and the punitive Indigenous policies of his four-term reign. Flicking his hand as if to wipe Hanson off the screen, Howard dismissed the yet-to-be elected senator as 'an irrelevance on the political scene'.

Hanson sat through the film, bright-eyed and silent – breaking into laughter only when Marcia Langton called her 'a halfwit' and a man in Hong Kong said she was crazy. She groaned in disgust each time her alleged former lover David Oldfield appeared, but seemed to enjoy the archival montages of her awkward younger self railing against the establishment for the first time.

I didn't watch the film; I watched Hanson watching it. We'd developed a combative, frank and oddly affectionate relationship during our time on the road. We'd traipsed through stockyards and country fetes together, shared counter lunches and home-cooked curries, clambered up the cyclone-smashed dunes of Great Keppel Island, traded intimacies over Ginger Bitches, and brawled for weeks through the crystal-clear lens of my camera.

Thanks to our political differences, our relationship stopped shy of friendship. But it mattered to me what she thought.

When the credits rolled, Hanson looked drained but calm.

'My final take out is if you believe in something, have the guts to do it,' she said to her Facebook fans. 'I'm still here, and I'll keep doing it as long as you want me to.'

The screen filled with emoticon confetti – mostly love hearts. There were a few angry devil faces too. The live comments feed was already into the thousands. Apart from the usual social media non sequiturs: 'give us a dab, Pauline'; sexual proposals: 'My shaft aches for you – are you red down below as well?'; and a few demands that Hanson 'go back to the fish shop, you racist!', the comments were overwhelmingly positive. Many said simply, 'Pauline for PM'.

Hanson kept staring at her Facebook fans through the camera, unblinking, until James Ashby, her chief of staff, decided to turn it off.

My ethical test of whether you've betrayed a documentary subject's trust is simple: they may not like your film, but if they'll still sit down and have a beer with you once they've seen it, you've passed.

Later that night, I rang Senator Hanson at her farm outside Ipswich. 'Yes, I'll still have a drink with you,' she said a little stiffly. Then she abruptly handed her phone to James Ashby and went off to have a shower.

Who the irascible, unique and resilient woman behind the Hanson phenomenon is, what drives her, how she has shaped Australia, and what we can do about it are questions that have obsessed me ever since Pauline and I ate fish and chips in Sylvania Waters in 2009.

In attempting to answer them, I am not endorsing Hanson's views, nor am I giving her an uncritical platform. I am deliberately engaging with the debate that the majority of tolerant Australian voters, on all sides of politics, refused to directly engage with the first time Hanson divided Australia, in the 1990s.

In 2001, journalist Margo Kingston, in her raw and brilliant account of Hanson's botched 1998 federal election campaign, *Off the Rails*, issued a prescient warning:

> Alienation is a dangerous thing, better to have her in parliament as the token voice representing the rednecks rather than leave them outside the political process and have them grow far more dangerous. The asset she's got is she's not evil, she's ignorant. If she goes down and the establishment thinks she's the problem not the symptom, the next Pauline Hanson could be more clever, tougher to crack, far more dangerous.

Hanson Mark 2 is cleverer, and definitely tougher, than Mark 1. She has always been a symptom, and not the cause, of the bigotry, fear and guilt boiling beneath that sunny confection we call the Australian dream.

Whether Senator Hanson, over the next six years, also proves more dangerous is up to us.

Chapter 1
She's fed up, and she's back

If Donald Trump's got a chance, Pauline's got a chance.
—Broadcaster Alan Jones, interview, December 2015

'Are you happy to see us?' I ask Pauline Hanson as she climbs into our camera van on the last day of our shoot in December 2015.

'No,' she shoots back, crossing her kitten heels and smoothing her block-print frock, pouting at our laconic cameraman, Luke. 'Didn't miss you at all. Didn't miss the camera.'

I've spent a year filming Hanson on the hustings, driving her to tears, frustration and rage with my dogged questions about her incendiary political career. I've learnt she is most cooperative when distracted with something pleasant: Luke, as well as being a brilliant cinematographer, is surfer-hottie gorgeous.

'We've got every state covered for Senate candidates. It's going to be a big campaign, there's much work to be done.' Hanson ignores me and flashes Luke a conspiratorial smile. She's been up till midnight drinking with a prospective candidate for her revamped ultra-nationalist party, Pauline Hanson's One Nation. She won't tell us who.

'What did you have for breakfast?' Phil the sound guy wants to know, checking his levels. Each morning, Phil peers into Hanson's décolletage to velcro a radio mic to her bra. Hanson, who has run the celebrity gamut from *Who Wants to Be a Millionaire* and *This Is Your Life* to a year-long stint in a sailor suit doing cabaret hits with musical hoofer Todd McKenney, tolerates Phil's physical intrusions with the pragmatism of a seasoned star.

When she's in a good mood, she'll do a little chest shimmy, playfully trying to dislodge the tape Phil has carefully hidden beneath whatever form-fitting frock she's chosen for the day. Today is definitely a good-mood day.

'I haven't had brekkie. I can't eat this time of the day. That's why I have a big lunch,' says Hanson, shimmying – as Phil, headphones on, winces at the sound of his mic scraping against polyester.

Hanson contentedly powders her nose in front of a rose-gold compact, and we veer around one of Canberra's endless roundabouts towards Parliament House. We're shooting some portraits of Hanson on her old political stomping ground for our SBS documentary about her explosive years in the spotlight, from 1996 to 2004. It will air in 2016, the twentieth anniversary of her maiden speech.

That speech solidified Hanson's reputation as Australia's most controversial independent politician, rocketing her from pariah MP to household name. When she stood in the near-deserted House of Representatives on 10 September 1996 to announce, in her trademark quaver, that Australia was 'in danger of being swamped by Asians', and that 'if I can invite whom I want into my home, then I should have the right to have a say in who comes into my country', the mainstream media ignored or attacked her, and Labor and Liberal politicians, terrified of guilt by association, ran for cover.

But the parliament switchboard melted down with calls and faxes from Australians across the country, congratulating Hanson on 'having the guts' to say what they were thinking. Hanson, shunned by the major parties and political commentators, was an instant sensation on the chat-show circuit, showered with marriage proposals and flowers.

Two years later, Hanson's fledgling One Nation won an unthinkable eleven seats in the Queensland election, routing the Liberal and National vote and handing power to Labor. First-term Liberal prime minister John Howard moved swiftly to preference One Nation last in the federal election, and, on 3 October 1998, Hanson's meteoric rise was over almost as quickly as it had begun. One Nation won a single Senate seat, and Hanson was unceremoniously ousted from the lower house.

In 2015, she had not held a political office for seventeen years.

Hanson had tried and failed to get back into power eight times since 1998 – running variously as a One Nation or independent candidate in a string of state and federal elections. At best, the media portrayed her as dedicated but doomed: a deluded serial candidate who couldn't quite move on from her glory days. At worst, she was seen as a political mercenary – cynically pursuing the lucrative electoral funding up for grabs each time a candidate won over 4 per cent of the vote.

'The interesting thing about Pauline Hanson is . . . she knows she's going to get more than 4 per cent . . . which means she gets a big cheque at the other end. I don't think she has the belief she had in the '90s, I think it's like, "Hey, time for a pay day",' says One Nation's former webmaster, Scott Balson.

In 1997, the future-focused Balson made Hanson Australia's first cyber politician, setting up a digital newsfeed to run 'honest' stories to counter the negative coverage of Hanson and One Nation in the analogue press. Balson and Hanson fell out in 1999, when he suggested that One Nation was not the financially transparent entity its members had been led to believe it to be.

'I don't think she ever believed she'd get a seat . . . She just wants that 4 per cent cap so she gets that cheque. I know she's received about two hundred thousand each time she's run. Seven or eight [elections] adds up to a huge amount of money,' Balson coolly observes.

Hanson, always up for a scrap, bristles at the accusation. 'What absolute rubbish. The perception that you run and get all this money is ridiculous. In Queensland you have to show receipts. Federally you do, but the money goes to the party, it's not your money. So people have no idea what it costs you to run in these elections. It's cost me over thousands of dollars . . . and I don't get it back because I don't [always] get over 4 per cent of the primary vote, especially when I've stood for the upper house. I keep running on principle. Standing as a candidate in politics is not a money-making process. I run for each election just like any other Australian that stands, whether it be Howard, Turnbull, Hockey, Xenophon, you name it.'

She gives me one of those laser-sharp stares, burning indignation laced with utter conviction, and I believe her. That's the thing with Hanson: she says what she's thinking. There is no mediation between the formulation of a thought and its delivery. It is one of the reasons she is so magnetic on screen, and why her supporters love her. I ask Hanson if she is tilting at windmills, to be campaigning again and again, only to fall short each election day.

'I don't consider myself a serial candidate because of Abraham Lincoln. He was a very determined person himself,' Hanson replies, without a flicker of embarrassment. 'I've had it tougher because the major parties see me as a threat.'

Hanson's determination springs from deep inner belief, an almost cosmic certainty that she's always been destined for greater things. It began with a vision. Slaving over the oil vats in her Ipswich fish shop in 1990, she saw a flash of herself at the head of a boardroom table, addressing a group of suited men in a big white room. That vision has sustained her for two decades.

Now, nineteen years since Ipswich's blue-collar voters first delivered the 41-year-old single mother to Canberra in a landslide, Hanson, at sixty-one, is making her tenth tilt at power: flying around her old heartland in a bespoke Jabiru two-seater, to reach the 'forgotten people' of rural and regional Queensland. The Australian-made plane's dinky doors are branded with the image Hanson hopes will secure her a Senate seat in the 2016 federal election. 'Fed Up', the cartoon thought bubble says, ballooning out of Hanson's oversized head as she waves an Aussie flag.

Hanson will not tell us who bankrolled the plane, only revealing, coyly, that 'he is a member of the Liberal Party and he said, "You're the only one standing up for us," and so he got behind me. Someone coming out with this support, I just feel so excited by it.'

We were there on the tarmac when Hanson and her new pilot-cum–spin doctor, James Ashby, landed the Jabiru in Rockhampton five months ago to unveil the 'Pauline Hanson's Fed Up Tour' to the nation.

On that now fateful July morning in 2015, Hanson was flying, literally and figuratively, under the radar: a handful of local journalists too young to remember her explosive arrival in 1996 poked iPhones through the fence for a sound bite. The national media hadn't bothered to show. No-one thought Hanson had a chance.

As the only documentary crew in attendance, we had privileged access to the runway. We set up our tripod next to a colony of sun-baking cane toads, to catch Hanson's triumphant emergence from the clouds, *à la* Leni Riefenstahl's heaven-sent Führer in *Triumph of the Will*.

The toylike Jabiru didn't glide from the sky so much as plummet, bouncing along the runway like a yoyo. Hanson climbed daintily out of the cockpit in a homemade blue knit, her voice hoarse from hours chatting with Ashby up in the air.

'I told my sister it's the "Fed Up tour" and she said, "Please explain?"' she said with a grin, nodding at her cartoon self on the side of the plane.

The delivery was vintage Hanson: self-deprecating but oddly astute, and lined with steel. She's trotted out the same phrase to the delight of her rusted-on followers ever since she immortalised it on *60 Minutes* in 1996, when journalist Tracey Curro asked the rookie member for Oxley if she was xenophobic. Hanson's reply, 'Please explain?' – complete with reedy upward inflection – is now part of the Aussie vernacular, along with another Hansonism, 'I don't like it.'

But the press pack covering Hanson at Rockhampton was dancing to The Wiggles when Curro demolished her on the national airwaves. They did not live through the violence and the bloodshed, the near civil-war-scale protests Hanson incited when she ripped through 1990s multicultural Australia like a hand grenade, denouncing Aboriginal welfare, foreign aid and Asian immigration.

'How's my hair? Does it need a lift?' Hanson whispered to her social media manager, Saraya Beric, as she strode into the hangar to front the waiting journalists. Beric, a talented violinist, shelved her career on the country and hip hop music circuit to do marketing and administration for One Nation and Hanson for $800 a week. Beric quietly reassured Hanson that her bright red pixie cut had survived the flight. The politician coolly sized up the press pack and planted herself in front of the 'Pauline Hanson's Fed Up' tour banner, which Saraya had carefully blu-tacked next to the aviation safety rules on the wall.

'Australians are feeling they've been forgotten. We're losing our prime agricultural land to foreign interests and in time we won't be able to feed ourselves,' Hanson began shakily, launching into the stump speech she'd been giving all year in pubs, clubs and church halls across Queensland.

'I don't see many cattle flying up here, I don't see them thriving. Farmers on average of four are suiciding a week, banks are buying up their properties, there's a big foreign takeover of our land and that's what my "Fed Up" tour is about. People want it stopped. When you have foreign companies buying up land like the Chinese, it's forcing Australians from having farms themselves. We've gotta take control of it here. I don't believe either side has vision in politics. They've opened up the flood gates for foreign takeover and we've lost our industries, so there's a lot of areas . . .'

Hanson petered out, her mind apparently blank. The journalists dutifully left their fingers on record.

'I am also concerned about halal certification,' she said suddenly, her wide-set eyes flashing with anger.

'It's a tax on transport, conveyer belts, everything. Australians are fed up with Christmas carols not being sung in schools. A fellow texted me and said he pulled his daughter from school because they had an imam there preaching about Allah. That's not what we're about. I will fight against the Islamicisation of Australia. I will oppose any sharia law in Australia. I can see our country changing and I am opposing it. We have 176 different nationalities that have come here. There's a difference between multicultural and multiracial. John Howard came out last year and said multiculturalism hasn't worked. That's what I was saying eighteen years ago – multiculturalism is about dividing everyone into different cultures and different laws and we can't have that in a strong society.'

Hanson stopped, satisfied. The distinction between 'multicultural' and 'multiracial' was a deft addition to her recycled 1990s rhetoric – a semantic buffer between her and the 'racist' tag she's been stuck with throughout her career. It appeared to be working: the Rockhampton journalists nodded pleasantly.

'Will you be running for the seat of Capricornia?' a 22-year-old in the front row wanted to know. No challenges, then, to Hanson's anecdotal evidence presented as fact, her economic simplifications or her blatant Islamophobia, from Queensland's newest members of the fourth estate.

Hanson relaxed visibly, chuckling at the smooth young faces in front of her.

'No, I'll be running for the Senate. Look, I'm a good way through my life. It's you guys, you're the younger generation and you need to start taking a real interest and listen to the older generation what this country was once like, because you don't have the same opportunities and freedoms we had. You may have all the gadgets and knowledge but you've lost so much, to what it used to be. Once you travel the world and look at other countries, they thought they were once great countries, but they've lost a lot of their freedoms. And I've seen that, and that's why I've not given up because what's happened to their countries I don't want to happen here.'

Hanson's travel-induced epiphanies about the problems of the outside world include a brief 1980 honeymoon in Asia, where she refused to pay $8 for a Coke until her waiter laced it with Scotch; a 1996 holiday in Washington, DC, with her then boyfriend (and President Clinton's bodyguard) Steve; and an ill-fated attempt to migrate to Britain in 2010.

After losing her seventh election in 2009, Hanson famously announced that she was quitting politics to live in the UK. Her campaign for the Queensland seat of Beaudesert had been derailed at the eleventh hour by media hysteria over nude photos of a teenaged Hanson spread-eagled on a bed in bondage gear. An ex-army guy called Jack Johnson claimed he'd taken the saucy snaps with Hanson at the Pelican Bay Resort in Coffs Harbour in 1975. Hanson shot back that in 1975 she was married on the Gold Coast with two children, the Pelican Bay had yet to be built, and she had an 'innie' belly button, while the woman in the photos had an 'outie'. By the time the *Sunday Telegraph* conceded Hanson was probably right, the damage to her political credibility had been done.

'I'm going away indefinitely. It's pretty much goodbye forever,' the humiliated Hanson told *Woman's Day*, attracting the ire of the Queensland Anti-Discrimination Commission when she refused to sell her 40-hectare Queensland farm to any Muslims. 'I don't believe that they are compatible with our way of life,' she'd told Channel 7's *Sunrise* flatly, and fled Australia to tour through the Czech Republic, Germany, Lithuania and France, before settling in the UK.

Less than two months later, Hanson was back, disgusted by what she'd seen. 'I love England but so many people want to leave there because it's overrun with immigrants and refugees,' she complained to the *Courier-Mail*, sounding like an early Brexit convert. '[The] English are losing their way of life because they're controlled by foreigners in the European Union.'

Hanson returned to Queensland to fight two more elections in 2011 and 2015, determined to save Australia from the multicultural scourge she was now convinced had polluted the once-proud British Empire.

The Rockhampton journalists covering her tenth campaign were in high school when Hanson's brief adventure as a refugee ended in failure – but, thankfully, one of them had done some research.

'Reclaim Australia is whipping up division at a time when we should be fighting for social inclusion,' the young woman piped up bravely, referring to the fact that Hanson was due to speak, as guest of honour, at Rockhampton's Reclaim Australia rally in two days' time. The rally was one of several ultra-nationalist protests the Reclaim movement was staging across Australia that 18–19 July weekend. In Melbourne, riot squads were already preparing for violence.

'What's your thoughts on that, Pauline?' the young woman prodded.

Hanson's friendly demeanour shifted to ice. 'No, that's wrong, there's been many rallies by Islam and Muslims around the country. Belgium is one that's about to be taken over by Islam, you've got Holland, England is in a hell of a mess and in France you've got 740 no-go zones by police because of Muslims, see there's a lot of riots that have happened. That's why they're now starting to say in Tunisia and Spain no more burqas, because they believe in assimilation. So you need to do research into those countries.'

Hanson glared at the young woman. Discussion over. Then she flashed one of her high-wattage smiles.

'But I welcome anyone who wants to be an Australian, no problems,' she said, shaking the rattled journalist's hand. Dismissing the press pack, Hanson, disoriented, wandered over to Saraya Beric in search of tea.

'My head's spinning. I just had a flight up and I'm not with it,' she grumbled, as a bearded octogenarian in a 1997 'Pauline for PM' T-shirt snapped a selfie with Hanson in front of the 'Fed Up' banner. Beric smoothly caught the moment and posted the snap to the 'Pauline Hanson's Please Explain' Facebook page, which she had been administering with savvy efficiency since 2013.

Hanson's Facebook 'likes' were climbing, thanks to Beric's and Ashby's punchy updates from the front line of the 'Fed Up' campaign. Followers had shot up to 55 000 in less than a year. A recent post condemning Australian Muslims fighting in Syria had reached over 4.2 million people, generating 4000 comments and 75 000 shares. Hanson's three most popular issues – farming, foreign investment and Islam – were regularly attracting more than 1.2 million clicks.

Which is why, on that brisk July morning in Rockhampton in 2015, twelve months out from the federal election, and with enough in the coffers to fly herself to every neglected backwater in Queensland, Hanson was blissfully unfazed by the fact that pundits across the board had set her re-election prospects at zero.

'These issues I am talking about get a huge response from the public – so I believe I am in touch with ordinary Australians and how they think,' Hanson divulged later. Balson's clunky 1990s website was Hanson's first taste of how the internet could be used to bypass the 'elitist' media, reaching One Nation supporters directly. Facebook, with its interactive interface, audio-visual streaming and global reach, was the same phenomenon on steroids.

'In my early days in politics there was never anything like Facebook. It's having a direct connection to the public so they can hear direct from me and not have any spin from media, so it's a great tool,' Hanson enthused. 'You still have the ones who think I am racist, and you've got these people called trolls and they could be from the other parties. And I don't respond to them because the supporters of my Facebook page, they defend me – they tell them to bugger off.'

'Do you ever buy your "likes"?' I asked, remembering the 7000 "likes" that suddenly appeared on the then prime minister's Facebook page in November 2014, from a devoted new fan base of 18- to 24-year-olds in New Delhi.

Hanson stroked her turquoise iPhone with satisfaction. 'No. Mine are all organic. Some posts I've put up, and you can look at statistics and it shows that high-ranking politicians, and even David Cameron, I've outstripped the people he's reached.' Abraham Lincoln, and now the British prime minister. Hanson's sense of political destiny doesn't belong in mere council elections; it's the stuff of giants.

Hanson ended the launch of her 'Fed Up' campaign standing in a treeless paddock, being miked for a live cross to Channel 7's *Sunrise*. Ashby ran into shot, pulling the feather-light Jabiru into frame, then held the reflector board under Hanson's face for the one-person *Sunrise* crew.

'After a stint dancing with some stars, she's back with a new party, a new look, and there's even a party song,' began one 'Hanson's Fed Up' clip, later uploaded to YouTube. Hanson's branded Jabiru was shown skidding comically across the Rockhampton tarmac. It was clear that the commercial media, unlike their publicly funded colleagues on SBS and the ABC, had decided to position Hanson as ratings-friendly entertainment rather than news. She was an amusing sideshow, a clickbait distraction from the real battle being fought across the country by Labor leader Bill Shorten and Prime Minister Abbott, as they posed in high-vis vests with burly workers in factories and at mine sites to spruik their pro-'working family' credentials to the jaded public.

'You've failed in previous bids to get into parliament – what makes this one any different?' *Sunrise*'s Deb Knight smirked at Hanson in the paddock. Hanson adjusted her earphone, placed her hands on her hips, and bridled.

'Deb, I'm sorry, I did not fail in the last election. I lost by 114 votes, and the way they counted them was not under full preferential vote,' she snapped, working herself up to one of those freewheeling, uncensored, white-hot rants that have made Hanson the darling of the populist right and the butt of the establishment media for decades. As an anti-politician politician, Hanson in full flight is riveting to watch, like a derailing train in slo-mo. Her bloody-minded refusal to be fettered by either accuracy or spin is as breathtaking as it is eerily absolute.

'Australians haven't given up on me and people come up and say, "Pauline, you've got the guts to say what we're thinking,"' Hanson declared, her voice trembling with indignation.

'People want the truth. They're sick of two-faced politicians backed by multinationals selling our country out. And I am so passionate about this, I love my country, I feel for my people, but they're not being listened to. It's amazing the number of people I spoke to over the years and they say, "We're fed up with high taxation, we're one of the highest taxing countries in the world, get the multinationals to pay their tax here." There are so many issues. The youth. No future. I was talking to a plumber, and they have to pay $12 000 more to get a licence. The whole system is over-regulated with red and green tape! We've got to get smart, Deb, and this is why the "Fed Up" tour, and this is what I'm saying to Australians – write to me at my Facebook page and tell me if you want me there. Work with the people and we can once again become the great country.'

Sunrise obligingly ran Hanson's Facebook address across the screen, and Deb Knight signed off. Hanson plucked out her earphone and strode triumphantly over to a waiting Mercedes. Another 340 000 viewers successfully in the bag. She wanted to prepare her Reclaim Australia rally speech with Ashby over a quiet meal. She'd forgotten to turn off our radio mic.

'Gawd, they're still filming! Don't they bloody ever let up?' she kvetched to Ashby in the back seat of the Merc. 'Don't forget my knitting!' she called out to us as the car pulled away. We jumped in our rental van and careened after her, the plastic bag of blue angora that Hanson had been working into a baby jumper for her grandson rolling around with our lighting gel tubes in the back.

We needed to get Hanson's knitting to her by 6 p.m. so she could sit down with it, as she likes to do, in front of the news – where she'd bitch with Ashby about the extent to which her campaign was being ignored. But, in reality, we'd become addicted to the surreal banality of Hanson's 'Fed Up' tour. We wanted to grab every frame of it as it hurtled – as it surely must – off the rails. In those relatively gentle days in mid-2015, Brexit and the US election were smudges on the horizon. The status quo was imperfect, but intact. Western democracy's moral compass had yet to implode. Like almost everyone else in the media, we thought Hanson was crazy for trying. Like almost everyone else, we were wrong.

In the USA, another far-right populist with colourful hair was facing similar derision. Since announcing his candidacy for president in June, Donald Trump had declared he'd 'build a wall' on the Mexico–US border, denied John McCain was a war hero, accused African American youths of having 'no spirit', denounced same-sex marriage, and labelled Mexican immigrants 'criminals' and 'rapists'. CNN set his odds of winning the Republican primary at 1 per cent. *The Guardian* conceded that while Trump might have an outside chance, the 'smart money' was against him – with political data wonks predicting his prospect of becoming GOP leader ranged from 2 per cent to a lowly minus -10 per cent.

If Hanson was the grumpy aunt at the wedding, Trump was the world's drunk uncle. The prospect of the bombastic US *Apprentice* star becoming president of the United States was as ridiculous as the prospect of Pauline, ex-semifinalist on *Dancing with the Stars*, getting into the Australian Senate. They were the unthinkable pursuing the impossible. There was no way these two fluoro-headed celebrity aliens would be allowed to gatecrash the citadel. At least, that's what I was telling myself midway through our 2015 shoot.

But now, cruising around Canberra's roundabouts towards Parliament House on our last day with Hanson in December 2015, I'm no longer sure.

The political media has continued to give One Nation a wide berth, focusing instead on the independent party du jour, the Nick Xenophon Team. Hanson's serial candidacy is no longer sexy news. But I have a year of footage in the can showing voters of all ages and from surprisingly diverse cultural backgrounds approaching Hanson in the street, unprompted and oblivious of our camera, to declare their undying devotion and love. Some have cried. Some have kissed her. Some have grabbed her in a full-body hug, refusing to let go. All have been genuine. Not since the true believers handed Gough Whitlam their unconditional loyalty on a platter have I seen an Australian politician display such visceral, godlike appeal.

Absent from our rushes are the furious leftists, the passionate multiculturalists, the proud Indigenous and Asian Australians who fought Hanson the first time round, dogging her every public appearance with ingenuity and rage.

Something has shifted.

'If Donald Trump's got a chance, Pauline's got a chance,' conservative shock jock Alan Jones shrugged when I asked if Hanson could achieve the impossible, as if it was obvious. One of the wiliest performers on air, Jones has been tuned in to the grievances and fears of Australia's 'forgotten' battlers, beleaguered Anglo-Australian farmers and the suburban blue-rinse set ever since Hanson first galvanised them in 1996 with her infamous maiden speech.

'They're the pub people and they love Pauline. I mean, she just spoke her mind. You've only got to look into America. Why has this Donald Trump, everyone thought he was a bit of a laugh, why is

Trump soaring ahead at the polls? He's saying things that the public out there are frightened to say, but they agree with him.'

Hanson, an ardent fan of Jones, agrees. We glide up Canberra Avenue, and the gleaming spire of Parliament House soars into view. Hanson grins fondly at the huge flag as if it's an old mate. She hasn't been back here for seventeen years.

'The last time I was here was 1998. And I gave one of my last speeches . . . and I said, "I'll be back!" and they called back, "No you won't!"' she chuckles. 'My God, they were so determined to get rid of me.'

Hanson folds her nuggety hands in her lap, twisting the sapphire ring she's put on especially for the occasion. The Nolanesque cut-outs in Parliament House's stark white walls sweep past, framing the blue sky like Ned Kelly's mask. Hanson studies them, uncharacteristically reflective.

'It would be nice to go back to that House, walk in that door and say, "I'm back,"' she says quietly, more to herself than to the camera. 'And I have six years up my sleeve, to make a difference.'

We head for the media car park, where our press gallery contact is waiting. Getting Pauline Hanson back into Parliament House in 2015 has been no easy task: we've been filling in forms for months. The serjeant-at-arms, with whom the grave responsibility of preserving the dignity and good name of Australia's highest parliament resides, has granted us permission to film Hanson in the media wing, on the forecourt and in the cafe, but not in the House of Representatives chamber. Permission to shoot Hanson in her old ministerial office, reminiscing about her heady days as the member for Oxley, has been abruptly withdrawn at the last minute. The independent MP who now occupies it, the Hon. Cathy McGowan AO, was being extremely cooperative – until the serjeant-at-arms intervened.

SHE'S FED UP, AND SHE'S BACK

'Parliament is not a movie set,' the serjeant-at-arms told me huffily as I boarded my Canberra flight last night. Oddly, Foxtel's *Secret City*, Channel 10's *Hawke* and the ABC's *The Killing Season* all shot around Parliament House without issue. Hanson may be a mere citizen these days, but she clearly casts a long shadow.

I ask Phil to stop the van before we get to the car-park ramp, so Luke can film Hanson with Parliament House's flagpole behind her. This is one thing we don't have a permit to shoot. Hanson, enjoying the subterfuge, scolds the boys happily.

'Behave yourselves. You carry on, they won't be looking at you, they'll be looking at me. See, the cameras are there, they monitor all this, and as soon as anyone stops, they send the car around,' she giggles, and suddenly she's one of us – a naughty kid at the back of the class, defying a pompous teacher.

Hanson's no fan of bureaucracy. She has flouted the rules here before. In March 1998, in the third year of her federal term, she invited a group of striking Cobar miners camped on the Parliament House lawns to use her office shower.

'I danced with the miners around their bonfire on the grass,' Hanson remembers. 'There was music and lots of dancing. Then the sprinklers came on. That's why I gave them showers.' A line of men, women and children, wrapped in towels and clutching toiletry bags, tramped up and down the House of Representatives corridor into Hanson's suite, leaving wet footprints on the pristine green carpet. The serjeant-at-arms was not impressed.

Determined not to get Hanson in trouble again, we put on our lanyards, unload our gear and place it carefully on the forecourt. I show her the 50-metre line she needs to follow through the centre of frame so we can capture her historic walk back through parliament's huge glass doors. Hanson obliges, sticking to the line with the accuracy of a movie star.

Then she sees the Kevlar-vested cops lounging beside the entrance and stops, wrecking the shot.

'God, you look dangerous. Wow, they've really beefed up security since I was here,' Hanson coos, admiring the SR-16 machine guns slung on the cops' shoulders.

'How are you?' the bigger cop asks pleasantly.

'Oh, okay, apart from having a bunged-up leg and being over this filming they're doing,' Hanson sighs, glancing back at us. I'm gesturing frantically for her to hobble back for a retake.

'Anyway, I hope you're not confronted with any . . . *incidents*,' Hanson confides to the cops with worried gravity. It's the tone she always uses for anything terrorism-related.

We shoot another take of Hanson walking purposefully over the forecourt, past three Dominican nuns snapping selfies and a gaggle of Taiwanese tourists. No-one knows who she is. A young Colombian spots the camera and gives Hanson a friendly smile. 'Australia is very beautiful,' he says.

'Yeah. I want to keep it that way,' she snaps, without breaking her stride. When she enters the security check, the guards scanning her handbag recognise her.

We regroup in the marble foyer, and Hanson draws Luke aside. She's ecstatic.

'They asked me, "Are you coming back here?" and I said, "To the cafe?" and they said, "No, to parliament!" and I said, "I hope so," and they said, "Good!"' she whispers, as if being overheard will damage her chances.

Our SBS liaison beeps us in to the Senate wing, and we enter the long corridor of the Canberra press gallery. Its bustling camera crews and sprinting journalists have been the backdrop to every leadership spill, legislative upset and act of political bastardry since Bob Hawke was prime minister.

But today, the corridor is whisper-quiet. The parliar
sitting calendar ended a week ago, and most politicians have
returned home for Christmas.

Hanson, poised and confident, strides up and down the empty corridor, replicating the triumphant walk she made long ago in June 1998, when One Nation gazumped the Liberals in the Queensland state election, transforming Hanson from an independent maverick into a national political force.

One by one, journalists emerge from their offices, staring at Hanson in a daze. Several do a double-take. Some look vaguely alarmed. How did this '90s apparition, this political anachronism, get back inside the corridors of power?

'Do you have a Twitter account?' a *Sydney Morning Herald* reporter asks Hanson as she strides past.

Hanson, pleased, calls Saraya Beric to get the handle right.

'It's PaulineHansonOz, capital *Z*. This is the official Twitter,' Hanson tells the reporter. But she's more interested in the photographers, who are starting to cluster around her like honey bees.

'I've got more to do with my time than fiddle around on Twitter,' Hanson announces to the cameras with a glorious smile.

A Eurasian photographer politely positions her under a Kino Flo light he's quickly rigged up by the wall.

'Are you a good photographer?' Hanson asks him cheekily.

'I hope so,' he replies, and Hanson laughs and poses, basking in the flashes and whirrs of ten clicking cameras. She is in her element, the flat planes of her face glowing in the soft white light. It's hard not to read the moment as proof of a deep inner hunger – not just for power, but for attention.

'They love you,' I say to Hanson.

She shoots me a knowing grin. 'Because there's no-one else around.'

The ABC's Chris Uhlmann steps into the melee, asking whether Hanson, since she happens to be in Canberra, would like to do an interview.

ABC News 24 may not rate as strongly as the commercial breakfast slots that Hanson's been doing all year, but it has serious political credibility. Unexpectedly loyal, Hanson tells Uhlmann he'll need my permission first. I give it, on the condition that Luke and I can film the interview from inside the studio. It really is a slow news week: Uhlmann immediately agrees.

We wait for ABC News 24 anchor Greg Jennett to prep for the interview, and Hanson studies a picture on the wall: Prime Minister Abbott posing with Chinese ministers during an April 2014 trip to Beijing. I ask her if she'd ever go to China.

'It's not a place I want to go. I'd rather go to Japan. Definitely, Japan is on my list, and Canada and the Rockies and up to Norway, that's another place I'd love to see.'

'Have you ever been to the Middle East?' I press, certain that if Hanson saw the relaxed crowds of Qatar's elegant souks, the laughing families dining al fresco in the downtown streets of Amman and Beirut and Muscat, she'd be less inclined to depict Muslims, en masse, as evil – as the malevolent 'other' to our 'us'.

'No, been there, done that,' Hanson snaps. 'Been to Kuala Lumpur, Thailand and the Philippines. Did all that in the 1980s.'

I'm not sure if she's misheard me or if she's geographically challenged.

'Would you go to the Middle East?' I try again, and Hanson's irritated now.

'It doesn't interest me, not at all. I wouldn't even go to Dubai. I just don't like it. I don't *like* it!' she says, and with her famous catchphrase hanging in the air like a slap in the face, Hanson strides into the ABC studio.

Greg Jennett welcomes her graciously as the live-to-air countdown begins.

'Pauline Hanson, a chance encounter with you here today. Most MPs have left Canberra, but you, as a former, have come back. For what purpose?' he asks.

'SBS is making a documentary about me on the twentieth anniversary of my maiden speech,' says Hanson, not without pride.

'And how much of the maiden speech still resonates today in Australia?'

'The whole lot of it,' Hanson replies bluntly, switching to the unblinking absolutism that is her default setting whenever she is challenged. 'A lot of points have been taken up as policy by the major parties. To abolish ATSIC [the Aboriginal and Torres Strait Islander Commission], build a railway to Darwin, national service, and address multiculturalism, which is still affecting the world today.'

'Twenty years on, no regrets?' asks Jennett helpfully.

'About speaking my mind?' Hanson flashes. 'No regrets whatsoever. And I had the support of the Australian people, which is why we went on to win 9 per cent of the vote! I was saying what people were thinking!'

Jennett blinks, checking his notes. The smooth political operatives who normally grace ABC News 24 are a little more circumspect, and a whole lot more nuanced, than the clearly pissed-off woman in front of him now.

He changes gear.

'Abbott, a former adversary, has said we need to look at radical Islam and the threat it poses to Western societies. Do you share his views on that?'

Since the Paris terrorist attacks three weeks back, clicks on Hanson's incendiary anti-Islamic Facebook posts have spiked dramatically. Hanson nods fiercely, drumming the table for emphasis.

'I do, and I've been saying all that before Abbott made his comments. We need a royal commission into Islam!'

Jennett does not remind Hanson that Islam, like Christianity and Judaism, happens to be a religion, and therefore falls outside the constitutional ambit of a royal commission. Instead, perhaps wisely, he decides to end the interview.

'Finally, Donald Trump has called for the shutters to be put up against Muslims in the US and to not let them in,' Jennett says. 'Do you make such claims for Australia?'

Hanson's jaw sets hard. 'I do. I'd like to see a moratorium on all Muslims coming into Australia.'

Jennett stares at Hanson and swallows, visibly shocked.

'How was that?' Hanson asks Luke, when we reassemble in the press gallery corridor. It's the highest-profile political interview she's done since launching the 'Fed Up' campaign. She seems unsure.

'What do you think?' Luke replies through his lens.

Hanson frowns and thinks, the interview playing back in her eyes. Then she straightens her back.

'I put my point across clearly. I was in control of it, and people want clear direction. And . . . there was definitely no political correctness there.'

With perfect comic timing, Hanson winks at the camera, turns her back on us and walks off down the corridor. Confident, calm and unbending.

As if she already knows she'll win.

Seven months later, on 2 July 2016, Hanson was back in federal parliament, with 9.2 per cent of the Queensland Senate vote. Four months after that, on 8 November, Trump won the American presidency, with a Republican majority in both houses of Congress. Both times, the mainstream media was blindsided.

In the US, Democrats and Republicans reeled in shock. No-one was celebrating; the mood, on both sides, was fractious. In the Yale University bar where I was watching the returns, female students raged tearfully into their Dirty Hillary cocktails; on a Los Angeles highway, anti-Trump protesters kept the traffic gridlocked for days; in New York, riot squads erected barricades outside Trump Tower to keep angry Clinton and Sanders supporters at bay; and at an anti-Trump rally in Portland, seventeen people were arrested and one protester was shot.

As half the country screamed and mourned, the other half exploded in righteous vindication. In Wellsville, New York, graffiti was spray-painted at a softball field with a swastika and the words 'Make America White Again'; Texas State University was flooded with flyers urging vigilante squads to 'arrest and torture those deviant university leaders spouting off all this diversity garbage'; and across the country, attacks on Muslims spiked, with 867 cases of intimidation and hateful harassment reported in the first ten days after Trump's election.

Spartacus star Kirk Douglas joined worried academics in the establishment media to draw ominous parallels with the rise of Hitler in the 1930s, while filmmaker Michael Moore – one of the few who'd predicted a Trump victory back in July – told his fellow citizens they had 'just elected the last president of the United States'.

I felt an odd affinity with Moore, as a leftist documentarian tracking my own far-right politician. In his 2016 film *Michael Moore in TrumpLand*, Moore's description of who would vote for Trump, and why, applied to several of the Hanson supporters I'd met on the

'Fed Up' campaign. Trump, observed Moore, was speaking to:

> people who are hurting. It's why every beaten-down, nameless, forgotten working stiff who used to be part of what was called the middle classes loves Trump. He is the human Molotov cocktail that they've been waiting for. The human hand grenade that they can legally throw into the system that stole their lives from them . . . They see that the elites who've ruined their lives hate Trump . . . The career politicians hate Trump. The media hates Trump. After they loved him and created him and now they hate him. Thank you, media. The enemy of my enemy is who I am voting for on November 8.

The Australian media was quick to link Trump with our own 'Molotov cocktail', the newly minted Senator Hanson. She too was anti-Muslim, ultra-nationalistic and against the 'bleeding-heart lefties' of the media and academe – whom she accused of favouring refugees, migrants and Indigenous Australians over 'ordinary Australians'. She too had ignited resentment against minorities and the elites, calling for a total overhaul of the major-party agenda – and, like Trump, the more the media had derided Hanson's outbursts, the more her supporters backed her.

Fed up with the erosion of local jobs and industry after two decades of globalisation, distrustful of the politicians who'd sold it to them, and denied a piece of the prosperity pie, which the trickle-down economics fanatics had promised them, Hanson voters backed her precisely because she was not part of the status quo. Just as Trumpers rejected Clinton's insider experience for the guy who'd 'drain the swamp' in Washington, Hansonites believed – rightly or wrongly – that, as an outsider, she was 'one of them'.

Only Hanson herself was unimpressed by the media's determination to compare her with the new 'most powerful leader of the Free World'. Speaking to the ABC's Barrie Cassidy on 23 November 2016, she said defensively, 'I see in Donald Trump a lot of me, I suppose, and people said I'm like Donald Trump. No, Donald Trump was a reflection of what I was saying twenty years ago and still do to this day.'

The statement was typical Hanson: grammatically blurry but politically focused. She did not acknowledge her comparative irrelevance, as an Australian independent politician who'd received less than 5 per cent of her home-state vote in 2016, against Trump's resounding national 46 per cent, or 62.9 million Americans. Had it not been for Hanson's vulnerable, reed-thin delivery, she'd have seemed as arrogant as The Donald himself.

Instead, Hanson's words rang true. She *had* done it all before, and her impact on Australia had been profound. In 1996, when the fifty-year-old Trump was reeling from a decade of bad business decisions and relying on court-appointed managers to cashflow his empire, the 41-year-old Hanson was a successful small-business owner in Ipswich. Three years later, thanks to her extraordinary pull with Australia's disenfranchised blue-collar battlers, she was the leader of the third most powerful political party in the country.

By the time Prime Minister John Howard had cleverly repackaged Hanson's reactionary message into the hardline anti-refugee policies that saw him cruise to a third-term victory in the 2001 '*Tampa*' election, Australia's welcome mat no longer said *Welcome*; it said *Go home*. That same election saw One Nation's support fall from 9 per cent to 5.5 per cent, with Hanson narrowly losing a Senate seat bid, despite winning 10 per cent of Queensland's primary vote. 'Howard sailed home on One Nation's policies,' Hanson declared angrily. And vowed that she'd be back.

On 2 July 2016, she was. The 'rude awakening' Hanson had promised Prime Minister Turnbull from the 'Fed Up' campaign trail in 2016, vowing to be a 'bloody thorn in his side' once she was in the Senate, had come to pass.

The establishment media went into a tailspin.

Hanson's unlikely victory, with three One Nation senators in tow, was variously blamed on the new Senate voting system, which had handed preference selection back to the voters; the demise of the Palmer United Party, which had driven anti-establishment voters Hanson's way; the rise in anti-migrant sentiment, following the successful passage of Brexit; voter backlash against Turnbull for ousting former prime minister Tony Abbott; and a yawning void in Australian politics for a radical right-wing party, which One Nation 2.0 had easily filled.

But three crucial things are missing from this picture of Hanson's momentous political return: Facebook, celebrity and the woman herself.

The year 2016 saw a fundamental shift in the way Western democracies function, with social media, and not political experts, determining for the first time how elections are covered and fought. As outgoing president Obama's political director David Simas observed:

> Had Donald Trump said the things he said during the campaign eight years ago – about banning Muslims, about the disabled, about women – his Republican opponents, faith leaders, academia would have denounced him and there would be no way around these voices. Now, through Facebook and Twitter, you can get around them. There is social permission for this kind of discourse. Plus, through the same social media, you can find people who agree with you . . . [There's] a sense of social

affirmation for what was once thought unthinkable. This is a foundational change.

Obama, in a melancholy postmortem with *The New Yorker*, twenty days after Trump's surprise win, summed up the challenge of campaigning in a 'post-truth' age, where fact and fakery are interchangeable, anyone with an opinion is an 'expert', and the truth of a story is less important than how well it sells:

> The lens through which people understand politics . . . is extraordinarily powerful. And Trump understands the new ecosystem, in which facts and truth don't matter. You attract attention, rouse emotions, and then move on. You can surf those emotions. I've said it before, but if I watched Fox, *I* wouldn't vote for me!

Hanson, to the political commentators and pollsters and election data crunchers, had been a consistently marginal prospect. But as a rolled-gold celebrity, she'd never been stronger. In the weeks leading up to her win, Hanson's social media following was so large she didn't need to send out media releases, posting instead to Facebook. Over eight months before the election, millions of Australians were already tuning in to Channel 7s *Sunrise* over their cornflakes, to watch 'Australia's biggest blowhards', Hanson and Derryn 'The Human Headline' Hinch, go head-to-head over refugees, Muslims and other trending topics.

Hanson's high-rating paid spots on *Sunrise* and Channel 9's *Today* was inflammatory populism repackaged as light entertainment: the more offensive she was, the more her clips were shared, and the bigger her social media footprint grew. In the news-as-vaudeville arena of 2016, it didn't matter if the people clicking on

Hanson were likers or haters; she was influencing opinion and 'surfing emotions' with the ease that Layne Beachley catches waves. Every download, emoticon and viral video expanded Hanson's reach.

From a commercial perspective, recasting Hanson the reality TV star as a political commentator made total sense. The majority of Australian voters *not* tuned in to the ABC and SBS had been watching Hanson's never-say-die, homespun charisma win ratings and 1800-hotline votes for years: from her endearingly wooden tangos on 2004's *Dancing with the Stars* to her sexy undie-clad car wash photo shoots on 2011's *Celebrity Apprentice*. Now, in her leopard-print blouses and RM Williams flannies, Hanson was playing the people's politician, discussing the 'serious issues of the day' with Kochie and Sam and Lisa and Karl.

The empathy and love she'd won as a celebrity stuck: Hanson the politician was as entertaining slamming Hinch over migrants and railing against big politics for destroying the Australian way of life as Hanson the TV contestant was scolding *Dancing with the Stars* judge Todd McKenney for failing her in the waltz. She was still a contender; it was just a new game. The viewers of channels 7 and 9, sensing the mother of all underdog battles, had logged on for the ride.

It's a powerful thing, the trust that reality TV stars earn for exposing themselves, warts and all, for our viewing pleasure. As a pleasant young Trump voter explained to me in New Jersey, the day after the American election, 'We know Trump lies, but everyone lies. People were sick of "time to change" under the Clintons and the Bushes and nothing happening. Trump is like a good boss: he ran *Celebrity Apprentice* for twelve years, so why can't he run the country? I voted Trump because even if there's a small chance things will change, I'm willing to take that chance. Trump winning is an inspirational dream come true. It's like a Hollywood movie, where your guy gets the ultimate prize – being president. Now we get to watch the epilogue: what's going to happen next?'

In the post-truth arena of self-curated newsfeeds and confirmation-bias bubbles and news-as-entertainment and entertainment-as-news, it is not surprising that Hanson and Trump, both huge TV celebrities, won the prize. They were, as Obama observed, experts at 'rousing emotions'. Their comfortingly human flaws gave them instant access to that raw, pyjama-clad intimacy that exists between net surfer and mouse. In this intensely private space, emotions, not social norms, dictate behaviour, and dark and destructive thoughts are free to flourish. As Michael Moore told voters who declared themselves 'shocked' by the US election result, 'years of being neglected by both parties, the anger and the need for revenge against the system only grew. Trump's victory is no surprise. He was never a joke. Treating him as one only strengthened him.'

Hanson, also, is no joke. And that's where her similarities with the world's most powerful far-right populist end. Hanson, for one, knows how to laugh at herself. Her blue-collar origins, unlike Trump's 'small one-million-dollar loan', which he cites as proof of his humble beginnings in Brooklyn, are genuine. The factors that helped Hanson evolve from Ipswich everywoman to political Frankenstein – or saviour of the great Australian dream, depending on how you vote – are unique.

Many far-right demagogues have risen and faded from view in Australian politics since World War II, from the anti-Semitic founder of the Australian League of Rights, Eric Butler, in the fifties; to the virulently Catholic, commie-baiting BA Santamaria in the 1960s and '70s; to the white nationalist leader of National Action, Dr Jim Saleam, in the '80s; and the anti-immigration, pro-gun leader of Australia First, Graeme Campbell, in the '90s. In

2009, even climate-change sceptic Nationals MP Barnaby Joyce was touted as a possible new champion of the far-right's 'large and powerful constituency' by Hanson's former adviser, John Pasquarelli, after Hanson lost her seventh election.

Each of these persuasive, charismatic men succeeded in stirring up strong anti-establishment, anti-minority sentiments. But somehow, none of them managed to retain the populist crown. None left an imprint on the national psyche quite as indelible as Hanson's.

What sets the senator apart? How did she convince enough Queensland voters to send her back to federal parliament a second time round, after two decades of failure, ignominy and pain? What qualities have enabled her to endure, and why is she different?

The answers lie in Hanson herself, and in the Australia she wants to protect.

Chapter 2
I don't like it!

I come here, not as a polished politician, but as a woman who has had her fair share of life's knocks.
—Pauline Hanson, maiden speech, 10 September 1996

If Hanson's mother, Hannorah, had obeyed her doctor, Pauline would not have been born. Hanson cherishes a childhood memory of her feisty Anglo-Irish mum pushing her on a swing and confessing she'd been warned not to get pregnant after the birth of Hanson's sister, Carolyn. Clearly glad she'd ignored the advice, Hannorah gave little Pauline an affectionate squeeze. As the fifth child of seven, Hanson treasures the moments when she had her hardworking mother to herself.

Pauline Lee Seccombe was born in the 1950s: the decade that spawned the Australian dream. It was, by her own account, an idyllic childhood — a loving, rambunctious but disciplined family of four girls and three boys, raised by the catholic Hannorah and protestant Jack in a flat above the family's cafe, in the inner-Brisbane suburb of Woolloongabba. From the age of twelve, Pauline worked behind the counter and waited tables when she got home from school. Her first sixteen years under Jack and

Hannorah's roof were severe but rewarding, based on an innate respect for the relationship between hard work and money, the value of independence, and the idea that no-one owes you a living.

The Anglo-Australian suburbia of Hanson's youth was a prosperous and orderly place: a neatly delineated land of white picket fences, freshly mown lawns, time-saving domestic appliances, permanent jobs, and thriving hetero-nuclear family units. Marriage was the moral bedrock of society, a sacred institution built on the Sunday roast, affordable housing, and an unwavering faith in Christianity and Empire. Wedlock was expected to last.

One of Hanson's warmest memories is of Hannorah belting out hits on the family piano, which held pride of place in the living room. Entertainment in the 1950s was analogue, not digital, and it united generations. The AGE wireless and Beale upright were household fixtures: Gwen Meredith's ABC serial *Blue Hills* and the 2GB comedy *Ada and Elsie* shared equal time with post-dinner family singalongs to 'Our Don Bradman', 'The Road to Gundagai' and other cherished Aussie ballads. Hannorah, who sent Pauline to singing and piano lessons for a couple of years, kept on tickling the ivories until arthritis turned her hands to knots.

In Pauline's first ten years, post-war American culture seeped onto Australian screens. Matinee idols James Dean, Marlon Brando and Marilyn Monroe were embraced by a new legion of Brylcreem-ed teens, as Peggy Lee and Doris Day crooned their way into their parents' hearts. But for every sexy torch-song singer and Kenmore mixer and Silex toaster and big-finned Cadillac imported from America, Australians – who had proved their ingenuity and mettle in the war – continued to punch above their weight in peace.

The 1950s saw Australia invent and export to the world the Victa lawnmower, the FJ Holden, the Jatz biscuit, the pneumatic broadacre agricultural seeder, steel dental braces, the black box recorder, solar hot-water systems and the SiroSet fabric-creasing p[rocess] which produced a global craze for permanently pleated sk[irts]. Bill Haley and His Comets rocked the charts, so did Bondi boy Johnny O'Keefe; Sydney diva Joan Sutherland wowed England's opera set at Covent Garden; and film adaptions of Australian novels *The Shiralee*, *A Town Like Alice* and *Summer of the Seventeenth Doll* held their own at the box office against Hollywood imports.

In this exuberantly nationalistic era, poets Dorothy Hewett and A D Hope captured the nation's imagination, while a Bendigo boilermaker conquered the nation's stomach with a canny reboot of the Chinese spring roll. Designed to be held in one hand so the other could hold a cold beer, Frank McEncroe's beef-and-vegie pastry was unveiled at the Wagga Wagga agricultural show in 1951. By the end of the decade, the humble Chiko Roll was as beloved as the pavlova and the meat pie.

The game-changing introduction of television in 1956, when Pauline was two years old, did nothing to shake Anglo-Australia's certainty about itself and its valued place in the world. At the 1956 Melbourne Olympics, an innovative ABC crew used outside-broadcast vans to transmit the gold-medal performances of Betty Cuthbert, Murray Rose and Dawn Fraser live; and irreverent home-grown celebrities Graham Kennedy and Dame Edna Everage quickly made the new medium their own.

Popular American TV shows did nothing to dampen Australia's loyalty to its British colonial roots. The one million non-Anglo-European migrants shipped in to work on huge post-war reconstruction projects, such as the Snowy Mountains Hydro-Electric Scheme, were in no doubt that their culture and customs must take second place to Anglo-Australian mores and values. Under the White Australia policy – which barred non-white migrants altogether – complete assimilation, not multiculturalism, was the official way to survive.

This is the 1950s Australia Senator Hanson loves, and this is the Australia she wants to resurrect.

Hanson's cherished 'Australian way of life' embraces a proudly monocultural world of tight-knit communities and church fetes, of gloves and hats at school and a fair day's work for a fair day's pay, punctured by Anzac dawn services and sunburnt Sundays at the beach. 'I have so much respect for the flag and the people who fought and died for my freedom and my way of life,' she tells me.

'It's respect as a whole and the sacrifices made. Yes, you have America and other countries, but I know when I travel to Asia and Germany, I can see the difference in the cultures. People say we don't have a culture; they're wrong. It's our mannerisms, our way of life, having a barbie, going down to the beach, our ruggedness, whether you want to live in the outback . . . how many other countries have the farmer who's the rough cockie, or whatever?'

'But what is it exactly that you are trying to protect?' I ask her.

'Our democracy, way of life, freedom of speech,' she replies. 'To be able to live in peace and harmony without oppression, to live whatever way of life. If you're a farmer, to be able to live it regardless of whether you make a dollar or a million. To respect our values and laws that define us as Australians. Our use of language, our way of having a laugh at ourselves, the larrikin within us. So many people think we're a great nation of people; they respect us. We're sportspeople, we like to win, to go and cheer them on and we're proud of them – it's part and parcel of who we are. We're generous and compassionate people as well.'

Hanson's vision of 1950s Australia is hopeful, not grim: a cheerful, outdoorsy, egalitarian place, run on down-to-earth family values and a simple faith in queen and country. Far from resembling Labor prime minister Keating's 'dark ages', the 1950s Hanson remembers were filled with future-focused underdogs and doers, suffused with a joyful optimism about what dinky-di Aussie ingenuity could achieve, under 'British to the bootstraps' prime minister Robert Menzies.

Another Australia exists alongside Hanson's sunny vision – an altogether darker place. The Anglo-Australian families of Hanson's childhood were wilfully ignorant of – and largely indifferent to – the suffering of Indigenous Australians, whose continuing repression had enabled them to thrive.

In 1954, the year Hanson was born, a young Queen Elizabeth, during her wildly popular first Commonwealth tour, met with Prime Minister Menzies in Canberra to sign the Aborigines Welfare Ordinance. The new law authorised the full-scale removal of the Indigenous people of the Australian Capital Territory to New South Wales. Despite the United Nations' 1948 convention on the crime of genocide being ratified in the Australian constitution in 1951, the systematic persecution of Australia's First People continued throughout the decade.

Under the Minister for Territories Paul Hasluck in 1951, the Native Welfare Conference consigned Indigenous Australians and their children to years of upheaval and oppression. Adopting the White Australia policy of assimilation, Hasluck decreed that all persons of Aboriginal or 'mixed blood' must, like non-Anglo migrants, blend in with mainstream society, living 'as do White Australians'. From 1956 on, British atomic tests at Maralinga in South Australia forced thousands of Indigenous people to leave their ancestral lands forever, while children of mixed parentage continued to be taken from Indigenous families and relocated to state- and church-run homes and schools across the country.

Any resistance to these punitive policies by Indigenous Australians, or those sympathetic to them, was given short shrift. On Queensland's Palm Island in 1957, seven Aboriginal men and their families were famously deported to the mainland in leg-irons after they dared to protest that the low wages and poor treatment they received were state-sanctioned apartheid.

The Australia Hanson wants to resurrect makes no room for these inconvenient truths, then or now. A staunch critic of the 'black armband' view of history, she sees no reason why she should 'pay and continue paying for something that happened over two hundred years ago', let alone in the 1950s, and regards herself as a 'native of this land' like any other Australian, 'black, white or brindle'. Along with her political mentor Paul Hasluck, Hanson believes all non-Anglo minorities should assimilate, and supports welfare handouts based on need, not race.

'If you feed a man a fish, you feed him for a day. If you teach him how to fish, you feed him for a lifetime,' she likes to say when challenged to explain her hardline stance. It's a quote she once heard on a World Vision ad while researching her maiden speech in 1996. Self-sufficiency underpins Hanson's core philosophy, in politics and in life. Standing over the hot cooktops beside her father Jack, a man who worked 106-hour weeks for twenty-five years, the young Pauline learnt the mantra that has driven her career: 'if you want anything in life, you have to work for it'.

Hanson has repeatedly claimed 'the majority of Aboriginals do not want handouts because they realise that welfare is killing them', citing concerned Indigenous voters who have approached her on the campaign trail over the years. She is adamant that the self-sufficient Indigenous agencies and initiatives set up by Labor prime minister Gough Whitlam in the 1970s, and developed by the Hawke and Keating governments in the 1980s and 1990s, led to a deterioration in, not an improvement of, Aboriginal living standards. For Hanson, the 1950s were – for all Australians – a better time to live. When a New York journalist accused her in

2016 of wanting to take Australia back sixty years, she laughed and replied, 'what's wrong with that?'

Hanson's love for 1950s Australia, her conviction that the nation has been going to hell in a handbasket ever since, and her deep anxiety about what we, as Australians, have lost, is genuine. It's as fundamental to her as religion is to others: a visceral certainty that leads to fanaticism and sleepless nights. Her passion springs from her formative years in the cultural epicentre of 1950s Anglo-Australia: the good old Aussie milk bar.

Jack's cafe was established by Hanson's parents in Woolloongabba in 1946, eight years before she was born. Drawing on their two-year stint running a deli in the Sydney suburb of Marrickville, Hannorah and Jack dedicated themselves to turning out delicious and affordable Australian meals from fresh, local produce. In the space of a few years, Jack's cafe had expanded to a staff of fifteen and a bustling, loyal clientele, funnelled in from the 42 000-seat Brisbane Cricket Ground, fondly known as the Gabba. Even today, older locals stop Hanson in the street to reminisce about their happy times at Jack's formica tables, devouring 'the best burgers in Woolloongabba'.

'He had the best sandwiches in the world, made the best pies and chips, he was the first to make the chicken rolls later known as Chiko Rolls, and he was making dim sims in the 1960s,' declares Hanson as we drive along Brisbane's Fiveways intersection in November 2015, past the bank near the Gabba where Jack used to send the kids to deposit his weekly take. Hanson, always up for a scrap when an Aussie icon is at stake, is not the only politician to dispute the origins of the Chiko Roll. Labor's member for Bendigo, Lisa Chesters, endorses the official story, which has Bendigo's Frank McEncroe inventing the snack. But New South Wales Nationals MP Andrew Gee claims the Chiko Roll was born in Bathurst in central western New South Wales, along with Nutella and Tim Tams.

Hanson, who has named Jack her 'biggest political inspiration', is adamant her industrious father conceived the iconic roll, out of rice, carrot and minced chicken on his Woolloongabba counter. She should know: she spent hours after school helping Jack hand-grind the meat for his rissoles and snags. Jack's culinary legacy is a thing she's determined to enshrine, in the face of multiculturalism's continued onslaught. Near where Jack's cafe once stood at Fiveways is the Woolloongabba outlet of the Ribs & Burgers chain. Ribs & Burgers boasts several halal options on its menu, for Muslim Australian patrons.

Halal tops the list of the 'un-Australian' developments Hanson wants banned, in her dogged quest to resurrect 1950s Australia. She has frequently – and erroneously – claimed that halal certification is a Muslim-backed conspiracy to rort Australian farmers and consumers out of their hard-earned dollars, channelling the proceeds to Islamist terrorist cells around the world.

Today, as we cruise round the Gabba past the little walk-up that was once Hanson's childhood home, I decide not to push her on halal. *Woolloongabba* means 'fighting place' in the language of the Indigenous Turrbal people, who were here long before Jack and Hannorah Seccombe set up shop. I'm not keen to test if the name is more than a linguistic coincidence. Hanson's smiling out the window, lost in her memories. She's less combative when she's happy.

'I went to Buranda Girls, ten minutes down the road. We had a tram – that's when Brisbane had trams. It cost five cents to catch a tram in those days, and we'd catch it to school. Then sometimes I'd walk back the five kilometres from school to save my five cents, and I'd buy a bag of lollies and eat them on the way. No way in the wide world parents would let their kids do that now,' Hanson muses.

'Did you ever steal lollies from the cafe?' Luke asks.

'No, we didn't, and they trusted us. We weren't allowed to eat any crap out of the shop. They made us eat good food and veg. But we were allowed one soft drink and one chocolate on a Saturday night. At any one time, you'd have four of us there – two waitresses in the milk bar and two in the takeaway cooking the meals. It was a different lifestyle for kids at that time. We had our chores to do, we got some pocket money, and we couldn't sit around and do nothing. And I think that's great for kids. And they need to do it today. They're sitting around in front of computers all day, they're lazy, irresponsible, not helping their parents and they take it all for granted. And when they get out into the real world, it's a shock to them and they don't know how to handle it. So that's why we're all the same, my brothers and sisters. We have such a strong work ethic and commitment. My kids say, "You Seccombes, you're all tarred with the same brush!"'

'What car did you have?' I ask Hanson, who loves driving, and fast.

'A Morris 1100, that was our first car, then a Kingsford station wagon, then a Vauxhall Gazelle, and it had all the timber panelling. Dad had a big Chevvy or a Pontiac. I used to polish it to blazes.'

'A classic,' Luke says with a grin.

Hanson won't be teased. 'How old are you?' she asks.

'Thirty,' Luke replies.

'My youngest is older than you, so don't give me cheek. I'm old enough to be your mother,' she lectures Luke cheerfully. 'Don't you worry – my sons try me. They push the buttons too . . .'

If Jack's cafe was the beating heart of young Pauline's week, the family car took the precious role on weekends. Every Sunday without fail, Jack, after working all night, would wake the seven little Seccombes at 3 a.m. and drive them to the Gold Coast. They'd play all day in the surf with Hannorah as Jack slept in the car. In the sibling turf wars that are waged in the back seat of any family road trip, Hanson, fifth in the pecking order, wasn't allowed a seat. She had to curl up under the windscreen in the rear. She loved it.

Hanson sees herself as an introvert, 'the quiet one of the family'. She likes to joke that 'John Howard would have had his hands full with my other siblings.'

'I'm basically a shy person. I never had much trouble with Mum and Dad,' she says, describing the bed she slept in underneath the window in the little room she shared with her sisters. 'I used to snuggle under the blankets. I loved looking up at the stars at night; it was just lovely,' she says with a smile. 'Even in winter I kept the window open. I just loved the freshness of the air, and to this day I don't have aircon and I like plenty of fresh air. It's no different to when I was a small child.'

It can't have been easy for Pauline, vying with her rowdy siblings for her parents' attention. Hannorah was known to punish misbehaviour with 'taps' and well-aimed tomato crates, and Jack was permanently chained to his stove. 'If you started whingeing, you were out in the backyard. We weren't mollycoddled, we had plenty of love – but we had to be strong, otherwise I'd have my brothers bossing me around and giving me a hard time,' Hanson says.

'Pauline' is derived from the Latin *Paulus*, which means 'little one'. As the littlest and 'shyest' daughter, Pauline was no match for her extroverted brothers and sisters. But what she lacked in stature, she made up for in personality. 'I was the best-behaved. I was the only kid who cooked Dad breakfast and washed the car,' Hanson says with satisfaction.

A school photo of Pauline at six, her mouse-brown hair cut in a no-nonsense bob, clutching a netball with proprietorial pride, reveals a determined little girl with inner strength to burn. Hanson insists that Jack 'right up to his death... had no favourites over anyone else. Every night, after eighteen-hour days, he'd still come and tuck everyone in at night.' But from an early age, Pauline would rise at dawn before her siblings to prepare Jack his favourite meal of pikelets.

It's also clear, from family snaps of Pauline and her sisters, that the Seccombes' youngest daughter was 'the pretty one', born with an unusually telegenic bone structure. As a freckle-faced child with a pixie chin and wide-set eyes, young Pauline was already exhibiting that in-built chiaroscuro lighting that appears to make her glow under the lens. Like the flame-headed 1950s celluloid star Maureen O'Hara, Hanson has no 'bad' angle: whether she's furious or delighted, she's magnetic to watch – a gift to any camera.

'I don't like being filmed. I don't need to see my face on TV and I don't need to hear my voice on the radio. I only do it because I have to do it. There's times I really don't want to do this, and I push myself because I believe in what I am doing, and the people need to hear me if they want a representative on the floor of parliament,' Hanson tells the camera tetchily, back at her farm.

Her sprawling 147-acre property, with its lush gardens, cow-studded paddocks, salt-water swimming pool and fish-stocked dams, is worlds apart from the poky Woolloongabba flat of Hanson's childhood. Hanson attributes her 'love of the land' to her maternal grandmother, Alice McKee, whose well-to-do farming family ran a successful stud of Clydesdale horses.

Hanson bought her land, nestled in a sleepy pocket of south-east Queensland, in the early 1990s, scrimping together her fish and chip shop savings to stump up the deposit. In 1993, she hired a local architect to design an airy, five-bedroom, brick and timber pile at the top of the hill, with 360-degree views to Mt Taylor and the fertile valleys of the Scenic Rim.

In August 1996, one month before Hanson delivered her notorious maiden speech, she moved her children out of their Ipswich cottage near the fish and chip shop and took up residence on the farm. She named the property Serendipity. It has been her sanctuary ever since.

An early episode of *Burke's Backyard* shows the rookie member for Oxley, in double denim, proudly showing Burke round her new home. The just-completed house juts over the barren hill like a shag on a rock. The paddocks are brown and treeless. Burke, surveying Hanson's rubble-strewn land, cheekily suggests she plant 'a good multicultural mix' of orientals, Chinese jade and 'a few blackboys'.

'No problem, as long as they blend in and complement each other,' the young Hanson retorts, accepting Burke's dig with a good-natured smile.

'It was nothing, it was just a building on a hill, with one mango tree about fifty years old,' Hanson says now, sipping tea on her beautifully polished deck. 'It was just: get out the crowbar, dig a hole, plant a tree and move on to the next. It's changed dramatically. I've made my house a home and I love it. I love my gardening, I love being here, I love the tranquillity.'

Hanson looks out over the blooming flowerbeds, rosella-filled thickets and tree-lined dams that she coaxed to life from scratch. The self-sufficiency she learnt at Jack's cooktops is on full display in this thriving haven. As is Hanson's thriftiness and economic acuity: with her cash-strapped days as a single mother long behind her, she still refuses to buy a washing machine or an air conditioner, avoids designer brands, grows her own vegies, and cuts and dyes her own hair.

But the formal living room of Serendipity reveals a more

extravagant side to Hanson's nature: an opulent Victorian armoire, full of gleaming crystalware, dominates an entire wall. An elaborately carved ten-seat mahogany dining suite, with crenulated tapestry-backed chairs, flanks a huge double-brick mantelpiece bristling with silver-framed family photos. Hanson's piano, which she is determined to take up again one day, sits under a dust sheet next to a thickly cushioned window seat. Generously stuffed cream couches and a luxurious kilim set off a heavy glass coffee table, on which a white porcelain Lladró sculpture of galloping horses has been set on a delicate lace doily.

Hanson's hallway, TV room, home office and guest wing are more eclectic and relaxed, with comfortable cane chairs and dark velvet sofas thoughtfully placed around the gifts and artworks she has received over the decades.

There's a handmade wooden clock shaped like Australia, ticking on a wall. A 1950s Australiana ashtray nestled on a shelf. Original Pro Hart bush landscapes, given by the patriotic artist himself. Shelves of books by Hanson's friends and foes, from nationalist demagogue BA Santamaria and pro-assimilation politicians Arthur Calwell and Paul Hasluck to a glossy picture book celebrating the history of Ipswich and *Not Happy, John*, the virulently anti-Howard critique by Hanson's chief 1990s media antagonist, ex-Fairfax journalist Margo Kingston.

In the folksy, welcoming kitchen, a honey-stained dining table and the Caesarstone benchtop reflect the golden tones of a circular stained-glass window, cut to resemble a mid-century rose.

Throughout the house, Hanson the politician and Hanson the TV celebrity smile down at the visitor from huge canvases and brightly lit photographs on spotless cream walls. In one painting, Hanson is depicted as an Australian Joan of Arc, beaming above a harmonious collage of urban and rural streetscapes and the

Aboriginal flag, all apparently united under her steady, blue-eyed gaze. In a massive photograph hung above the wine racks in the hallway, the slender fifty-year-old Hanson poses with her arms akimbo in ballroom heels and a sexy sheath, the beloved *Dancing with the Stars* underdog who held her own against starlets half her age.

Hanson, at sixty-one, has maintained her fashionably toned figure. It is not an expensive gym investment, but the product of her daily routine. Every day, she rises at sunrise to feed the cattle, mow the lawns, weed the garden and do maintenance around the house. She can repair a gutter, tile a roof, stain a deck, paint a room and mend a leak. She knows more than the average Jane about toilets and pipes, having helped her second husband, Mark Hanson, run a successful Ipswich plumbing business in the 1980s.

When she's not in election-battle mode, Hanson likes to stay busy. Downtime at the farm will find her knitting a woollen sweater for her new friend, Sydney shock jock Kyle Sandilands, scouting cheap suppliers of redclaw crayfish to stock her lower dam, riding the horses she agists for a mate, potting balls on the pool table in her office, or furnishing her freshly built guest cottage down by the front gate. When she's not 'pottering around' with these pleasant diversions, Hanson does power walks up and down the valley, flies around the state to canvass rural voters, meets with potential investors and candidates, updates her Facebook page with her campaign adviser James Ashby, and gets up before dawn once a week to do a live cross to commercial breakfast TV.

On those mornings, Serendipity's birdsong-filled bucolic landscape is interrupted by the odd sight of a digital satellite camera pointed at the fully made-up Hanson, ranting and raging about Islam and refugees at the top of her lungs, apparently at no-one. Kochie and Karl and Derryn Hinch argue back in her earpiece as the cameraman keeps Hanson in focus, with Mt Taylor in the background.

I DON'T LIKE IT!

Hanson, who has received several violent death threats over the years, is fiercely protective of her privacy. She insists that her house is never shown on the screen and her address is never broadcast. Most interstate viewers of *Sunrise* and *Today* think Hanson spends most of her time standing around in a Queensland paddock, in a place known vaguely as Scenic Rim.

Of course, when Hanson announced she was migrating to Britain in 2009 and refused to sell her farm to any Muslims, her address, complete with Google coordinates, was broadcast all over the web. This is a fact she chooses to ignore. Luke and I want to film a drone shot flying over Hanson's roof towards her pool – but she's having none of it. We are on no account to fly our camera up her driveway, over her house or anywhere near the goddamn pool. Ashby quietly concedes that the real estate photos of Hanson's farm, posted by a Queensland realtor in 2009 with expectations of $1 million-plus, can still be found in a few clicks. But Hanson's furious I've even asked.

We have a day's filming ahead of us, and I decide not to argue. Instead, I follow Ashby's advice to let Hanson cool off, and wander down to the guest cottage with the boys, to fly the drone over Hanson's well-fed Brangus cows.

When we return to the farm, Hanson, showered and refreshed, emerges from her bedroom with an armful of neatly pressed clothes in thin plastic wrappers. These are the suits and gowns she's preserved from her volatile early years in the spotlight, from 1996 to 2004. 'This is my first outfit I bought for parliament; this is the outfit I got sworn in in,' she tells our camera, unwrapping a bright tartan jacket with bold shoulders and chunky trim. The jacket's uber-feminine cut and cheap, eye-catching fabric encapsulates the sartorial style that would see Hanson's wardrobe dissected almost as widely as her policies during her first federal term.

As one of only eighteen women in the 176-member House

of Representatives in 1996, the brightly clad member for Oxley popped in the grey-suited chamber like a pavlova at a boot camp. On slow news days, the Canberra press gallery would run straw polls on who was 'best dressed in parliament'. With the more conservatively inclined Bronwyn Bishop, Carmen Lawrence and Jenny Macklin as her nearest competitors, Hanson invariably won.

'Their style wasn't my style, put it that way,' says Hanson with a little tilt of her chin, as she peels cellophane off a shimmering scarlet gown. 'That's the one I wore when I launched One Nation. I don't think I'll wear it again. I don't like it very much.'

Footage of an agitated Hanson in the form-fitting red gown being shouldered by her bodyguards through screaming protesters into the Ipswich Civic Centre in 1997 made news bulletins from Taiwan to Tokyo. Back then, Hanson's new anti-immigrant, ultra-nationalist party was seen as a shocking aberration, a horrifying exception to the multicultural norm. Songwriter Yip Harburg's quip that 'all the heroes of tomorrow are the heretics of today' characterises Hanson's trajectory perfectly. Her One Nation launch speech, which once incited hundreds of thousands of Australians to take to the streets in anger, would barely raise an eyebrow today. It reads as no more incendiary than a 2017 press release from the hard-right faction of the Turnbull government.

Hanson pulls out a second gown in purple viscose with crystal embellishments. This one she strokes with pleasure. 'This is another I wore. I think it was state parliament when we won three seats in the Queensland election in 2001. I wore it on election night in Brisbane.' In the 2001 Queensland state election, One Nation, despite suffering a 13.98 per cent swing against it, retained three seats and split the conservative vote, helping drive the Coalition's thumping seventeen-seat loss and securing a fifth term for Labor. The result was proof that Hanson, who had lost political office in

1998, was still a headache for Liberal prime minister John Howard.

News reports from the tally room that night show Hanson, looking a million bucks in her purple gown, gliding triumphantly through the Queensland press pack like a movie star. The awestruck journalists clustered around her with notebooks could be autograph hunters on the red carpet at Cannes.

'I always took pride in my dress and my appearance, even as a young mother dragging five kids around shopping. It was something I grew up with, with my mother. I think it's important,' Hanson says firmly. The teenage Pauline topped her sewing class at Coorparoo State High School, and she can still knock up a ball gown without a pattern. Achieving the highest mark in a class of forty in Year Nine, Hanson was described by her principal as 'well-behaved and reasonably industrious. Most reliable, sociable and cooperative.'

Coorparoo State girls recited the Lord's Prayer and sang the national anthem every morning. They wore hats and gloves, with their hair pinned back, and had to ensure their hemlines, when kneeling, hung no more than five centimetres above the ground. 'I have no complaints. It instilled in me a sense of pride in myself, my school and my appearance,' says Hanson. Hannorah ironed her daughters' uniforms, but they made their own school lunches and polished their shoes. Hanson excelled at typing, geography and citizenship at Coorparoo, but when she was encouraged to go into the Year Eleven and Twelve academic stream, she opted to stay in the commercial stream with her girlfriends, and left school after Year Ten.

It was a fateful move: at fifteen, fresh out of high school and using her meagre pay as a typist at the Drug Houses of Australia to cover her board above Jack and Hannorah's cafe, Hanson met the dashing Walter Zagorski. Walter's mother, Lydia, was the Jewish survivor of a World War II concentration camp. Hanson adored them both. 'I was madly in love with my first husband. Very much so. He was Polish. Came out at six with his mother. They came to Australia for a new way of life and they embraced the Australian culture and learnt the language and she was a lovely woman. I had a lot of time for my first mother-in-law.'

Pauline was pregnant by sixteen. In the optimistic flush of first love, she sewed the bridesmaids' dresses for her hasty wedding to Walter in 1971, and sang her father's favourite song, 'Edelweiss', at the wedding dinner. Jack cried. 'I was first married at sixteen, had my first child by the time I was seventeen and my second child when I was twenty, and that split up when my second child was only six months old,' Hanson now states flatly. The charming Walter proved an incorrigible womaniser. Hanson, while cleaning their little unit one day, discovered Walter's voice mistakenly recorded on a cassette tape, asking another woman if she loved him.

Isolated and heartbroken, Hanson moved with her sons back to Jack and Hannorah's in Brisbane, alternating between her parents' house and a succession of poky rentals throughout the 1970s, as she and Walter struggled to repair their marriage. The pre-cut potato chip business that Hanson's parents had helped her and Walter establish failed, as did a snooker and pinball hall they ran briefly on the ground floor of one of their units. Forced to take on a string of waitressing jobs to support her two sons during Walter's increasingly frequent absences, Hanson, never one to give in, put her schooling to good use and sewed her own work outfits.

Hanson has always followed her mother's advice assiduously – perhaps to her own detriment, she likes to joke, when it comes to sex. The only contraception tip she received from Hannorah was to '"never let a man sit you in a corner and put his hand on your knee". Great advice, Mum, thanks!' Hanson laughs now. But Hannorah's instruction to be dignified and ladylike, to always 'keep yourself nice', has reaped dividends for Hanson throughout her working life. While pulling beers behind the bar of the Grand Central Hotel on the Gold Coast in the late 1970s, Hanson was asked, along with her female colleagues, to wear a bikini.

'I said to the manager, "I won't do it; I am not wearing a bikini." He said, "Okay, you can be restaurant manageress." So instead of bikinis, I wore the long gowns, which I made myself,' Hanson remembers with pride.

The 22-year-old Hanson, in her hand-sewn gowns, turned heads as the new dining-room hostess at the Grand Central Hotel. Her glamorous clientele included English comedian Reg Varney and American TV host Tommy Hanlon, Melbourne rock band The Mixtures, and pop legends Roy Orbison and Col Joye.

The restaurant, with its rotating roster of travelling male stars, must have been quite the training ground for the shy but defiantly feminine Hanson. Perhaps this is where she developed her taste for public attention, ensnaring her first male fans with her intoxicating mix of vulnerability and steel. Hanson has used her seductive talents to devastating effect as a politician over the years, winning over many male voters, interviewers, advisers, bodyguards, celebrities and investors. In the late 1990s, her legendary appeal with older Anglo-Australian men even conquered a political adversary: Labor opposition leader Kim Beazley was rumoured to keep a picture of the Member for Oxley hanging in his office toilet.

'Apparently, the security guards told me he had a shirt of me on the wall. Maybe he did it because he was looking for guidance. Who knows,' Hanson shrugs in the kitchen at her farm as she unwraps a black blouse with multicoloured panels.

The blouse featured in many rowdy pressers Hanson conducted in shopping malls on the Gold Coast in 1998, to attack the proliferation of Japanese signs in the streets. In the late 1990s, Queensland's tourism industry was enjoying a booming trade with Japan. Cashed-up Japanese newlyweds, keen for a taste of the laid-back Aussie lifestyle, were snapping up 'Hello Aussie'-style honeymoon package tours in the thousands. Hanson was determined to spoil the party, disgusted that the alien hieroglyphics of kanji and hiragana should have been allowed to pollute the pristine 1950s Anglo shopfronts she remembered from her girlhood Sundays down on the Gold Coast sand.

The Japanese producers of TV-Asahi were as fascinated by Hanson's redneck novelty as the Australian media were in the pro-multicultural '90s. TV-Asahi dispatched a young reporter from Tokyo to find out what made the One Nation leader, sworn enemy of the invading Asian hordes, tick. In impeccable English, the reporter asked Hanson if she was racist, to which Hanson shot back, 'What about Japan? Go home and look at your own racism. You Japanese hate foreigners, it's well-known.' Then, genuinely intrigued, the young woman asked Hanson if the black blouse she was wearing was silk. Hanson reeled back, as if the reporter had insulted her intelligence. 'Oh no, not *silk*,' she said vehemently, shaking her head. Hanson, ever her mother's daughter, prides herself on being able to bag a bargain, and shops with eagle-eyed efficiency at no-name budget outlets and high-street boutiques.

'I'm not a brand-name person. I buy what I like if it suits me. If it's Target, if it's Kmart, it doesn't worry me,' Hanson says now, draping the black nylon blouse back on its hanger. Fabric 'doesn't matter. It depends on the outfit whether I like it or not.' I ask about the sombre, militaristic dress she wore for her 1996 maiden speech, and the sequined sheath with the thigh-high split in which she tangoed into the semifinals of *Dancing with the Stars*. These outfits are almost as iconic as Hanson herself, captured on prime time years ago but recycled in viral tributes, Vines and memes today. One

YouTube wit, Michael Tan, has inserted a three-piece a
into footage of Hanson delivering her maiden speech,
her divisive words with low-key improvisational jazz.

Hanson admits she still has her maiden speech dress somewhere but refuses to get it out. My relentless questions about which outfit she wore, on what date, have begun to grate. 'If you're going to determine where and which day, it's not going to happen,' she snaps, and starts shoving her clothes back into their bags. Her bold yellow and black striped suit, which the 1990s press pack irreverently dubbed 'the Bumblebee', is missing, as are several other famous outfits featured in protests and news reports throughout the 1990s.

Some of these clothes were bought for our feature film, when it looked like it was going ahead. But in the intervening years, Hanson's gowns somehow made it out of storage and onto the backs of a bunch of Brisbane drag queens, who wore them out for a sardonic night on the town. The taffeta ball gown that a tearful Hanson wore on the night of her 1998 defeat, and the floral pastel blouse in which she famously told the nation 'if you are seeing me now, I have been murdered', are probably lying in beer-stained shreds behind Brisbane's gay Beat Megaclub, in the Brunswick Street Mall. Hanson, understandably, is cross that her iconic outfits have gone.

'What would you have liked to be, if you hadn't become a politician?' I ask her gently, trying to switch to something more pleasant.

Hanson stops frowning and thinks. 'There were some professions I'd have liked – a police officer, or a singer,' she says, and smiles. Like a five-year-old child's, Hanson's moods can swing on a dime.

'Actually, I think it would be wonderful to be able to entertain,' she says, warming to her theme. 'I love my music, especially Whitney Houston. I would have loved to be a star on the stage. That would've been a fantastic profession. I just admire those people and the talent they have. And they just bring so much joy to people's lives because of their talent, and I think music is beautiful. And that's why I did the show with Todd McKenney. We toured all over Queensland.'

I remember Hanson's stilted 2005 rendition of Peggy Lee's 'Fever' with the exuberantly camp McKenney, which she sang on a bar stool for the enamoured audience of *This Is Your Life*. Hanson's trademark reedy voice was thin and out of tune. She won over the crowd with the sheer force of her personality. After her short-lived career as a cabaret star with McKenney, Hanson, reluctantly, had to accept she'd never make it as a singer. 'It's hard – my voice gives way on me too much,' she says wistfully. 'It was exciting, and I had a go, but I'll stick to politics, I think . . . Although lots say I shouldn't!' She shoots me a look and giggles.

Hanson's wish-list professions – the police officer and the performer – have flourished in lateral ways throughout her political career. As a politician, she is visibly impeccable and emotionally true, no matter how mangled her grammar. And despite her claim to dislike the camera, the camera likes her. She's a natural, even if she does have to force herself to deliver. Australians have seen Hanson cry and rage and laugh without self-consciousness or hesitation – and while detractors accuse her of 'performing' like any other politician, I can confirm, having filmed her in all kinds of moods and situations, that Hanson never 'acts' for the camera. She says what she means, and it shows.

The reason Hanson 'works' for her rusted-on political supporters is the same reason she failed as a performer with McKenney: she is terrible at artifice. Hanson the campaigner is utterly genuine, while Hanson the performer can be awkward and strained. 'I think they're two different things,' she says of performing and politics. 'One, you're acting the part to be the part, and I think with politics it should come from the heart, what you truly believe in. And

I don't believe in being hypocritical – what people see is how you should be all the time.'

The cop inside Hanson has also flourished in her politics. Her respect for old-fashioned, patrician authority can be seen in her hardline stance on the punishment of first-time offenders and minors, her endorsement of Australia's cruel and illegal incarceration of asylum seekers and their children, and her repeated calls for mandatory military service and a bigger, tougher police force. Hanson is the kind of driver who will not hesitate to write down the plate of a speeding car on the highway, then phone it in to the police. She likes to shoot a gun and stick to a strict routine, and she has a taste for discipline, order and militarily fetishistic outfits. This year, the senator called for Queensland's police service to be given more power, and to be renamed the Queensland Police Force.

Hanson, since her early childhood, has had no difficulty following patriarchal rules or enforcing them: as long as she thinks that they're right. Her infatuation with male authority figures was no doubt forged during her precious dawn breakfasts with her beloved father, Jack. Hanson has courted the approval of many older, powerful men throughout her political career, from entrepreneurs R M Williams and Dick Smith to radio announcers Alan Jones and John 'Golden Tonsils' Laws. She's frequently sung the praises of nationalist political strongmen, from Arthur Calwell and Paul Hasluck to Abraham Lincoln, Vladimir Putin and Donald Trump. Her bonds with the police officers and secret service agents who've shielded her from protesters and stalkers over the years have always been close. Like the male rule-makers she admires, Hanson sees herself as a 'protector', shielding the weak from harm.

'I am very protective of people and my family and Australia in general, and I can't stand threats and bullying and I think we just don't need thugs like that in society,' Hanson says now in her opulent living room, surrounded by her gleaming crystalware and Lladró sculptures.

'There are people who can't stand up and fight for themselves on an issue, and I think that it's important as a member of parliament to fight for these people. Everyone's entitled to a fair go. Just be fair, just be honest, and that's who I am,' she says with quiet finality.

Hanson's two sides – the righteous protector and the reluctant performer – were seeded in her first twelve years, as Jack's attention-hungry youngest daughter. Two episodes left an indelible mark on the young Pauline, revealing her extraordinary determination and the steely conviction of the politician she would become.

'It's amazing that you're interested in telling my story to the Australian people. I am not that different to many people ... I don't see myself as anyone special,' Hanson insists. But Pauline's actions at Buranda Girls State School when she was eight years old tell a different story. She was, in fact, one of those very rare things: a born rebel *and* a natural leader.

'In primary school ... even at an early age ... I could be strong-minded and a bit rebellious,' Hanson admits. 'We had a third of a pint of milk delivered to us at school, and in Queensland it gets hot and the milk would sit in the sun. And it was warm, and it was vile, and I couldn't drink it. If I couldn't give it to the other kids, I'd pour it down the drain. And when they asked who hadn't drunk the milk, I'd stand up in class and the teacher would say, "Pauline, you have to." And I said, "I won't! I don't like it!"'

In 1962, corporal punishment was an acceptable educational tool, and teachers were godlike figures, never to be answered back. Had Pauline been an ordinary child, she might have sat mute with her classmates when confronted by her teacher. It would have taken huge courage to stand and out herself as the culprit, in front of the whole class. But Pauline was no ordinary child.

The way Hanson remembers it, it was a simple matter of right and wrong. The malted milks she and her siblings were allowed to drink at Jack's cafe were cold and delicious. But the wax-sealed government milk bottles, baking in the schoolyard of Buranda Girls every morning, were hot and revolting. Pauline's classmates hated the milk as much as she did. It wasn't fair. The rule was wrong. So why should she be afraid to call it out?

'I don't like it and I didn't, either! I was determined. I was not drinking that milk!' Hanson laughs. 'My parents had that problem with me ever since I could talk. Look, we were taught to have an opinion and be independent. We had to be, you know, with seven kids.' Rather than admonishing Pauline for repeatedly disobeying her teachers, Hannorah and Jack let their headstrong girl have her way.

Four years later, at age twelve, Pauline experienced her first taste of celebrity. The Seccombes may not have played favourites with their seven children, but something about their youngest daughter was powerful enough to compel Hannorah to scrimp together some fabric to knock up a formal frock and persuade Jack to leave his precious cooktops and drive Pauline all the way to Brisbane to appear on Channel 7's 1960s children's talent show *Jill and Beanpole Present*.

'I was learning singing at the time, and I can't remember how it came about, but Dad took me up to it, and when I went on the show I actually sang "Feed the Birds" from *Mary Poppins*. And, um, I didn't win it, but it was an interesting experience,' Hanson reflects. 'I'm basically a shy person, and getting over that was the same as politics. You have to force yourself to do it.'

Pauline may not have won the contest, but Jack's reaction, when she walked out of the glare of the studio lights and joined him by the curtains, is seared in her memory.

'Dad was very proud. He said I had done an excellent job and hugged me,' Hanson beams. 'I think it was someone who played the piano who actually won, and I remember thinking she's very good. But you know, you can't always be a winner. That doesn't stop you from getting up and having another go.'

It's a testament to the close-knit Seccombe siblings that little Pauline, the 'pretty one', and now a bona fide TV star, was not picked on by her brothers and sisters when she got home. Or if she was, she's not telling me.

I look again at the school photo of the bob-cut Pauline, clutching her netball with solemn pride. The fourth and quietest daughter, who yearned for her father's approval and earned it by working hard, obeying his rules and 'having a go'. The instinctive, wilful rebel, who knew when something wasn't fair, and learnt that she could change it by speaking out. The introverted performer, who grew up to become Australia's most controversial celebrity politician, a defiantly feminine woman who idolises hardworking men like her father, believes it's her duty to fight for others, and never gives up.

At sixty-three, Hanson still says 'I don't like it' without fear or hesitation, and has got what she wanted – by being herself.

The tragedy of Hanson's conviction that 'everyone's entitled to a fair go' is that Hanson's 'everyone' are the people of her tribe. The Pauline who sang 'Feed the Birds' at age twelve is as genuine today. She is still exhorting her townspeople, like the old lady in the song, to feed the 'young ones' and line their 'bare nests' with compassion and care.

But the 'little birds' Hanson wants to feed live inside her rosy 1950s vision of Australia. They are patriotic, fully assimilated Australians who believe in her notion of the Australian 'way of life'. They are not the war refugees and crying babies languishing in cages on Manus and Nauru. They are not the stolen generations, who relive the pain of dispossession and genocide every Australia Day.

They are not the Asian, African and Arab migrants who continue to be abused for joblessness and social disunity, as Hanson's beloved Trump and the one-percenters continue to pillage and thrive.

Hanson's little birds are not 'all Australians', for whom she claims to speak. They are, and always have been, people like her.

Chapter 3
The fish and chip shop

My view on issues is based on common sense, and my experience as a mother of four children, as a sole parent, and as a businesswoman running a fish and chip shop.
—Pauline Hanson, maiden speech, 10 September 1996

In one of those delicious ironies life sometimes throws up, Hanson's old fish and chip shop is now owned by a Vietnamese refugee. Thanh Huong Huynh, who runs the business with the help of her husband and their twelve-year-old son, Thomas, fled Vietnam by boat in 1990, migrating to Australia from a processing centre in Malaysia.

Thanh's glass display counter contains homemade dim sims and spring rolls, stacked neatly beside the usual takeaway staples of chips and battered flake. On the countertop, three gilt Japanese toy cats, or *maneki neko*, wave their paws, encouraging customers to enter. The take-out menu, headed 'Australia's most Famous Fish & Chip Shop', is propped up in a plastic frame, next to a translation in Chinese. Pineapple fritters, chicken nuggets and dagwood dogs are available to order, along with family packs of '4 cods and chips'. Thanh, a shy woman with a warm smile, only recently discovered that Hanson began her historic quest to reshape Australian politics behind this very counter.

THE FISH AND CHIP SHOP

'I must say with Ipswich, they've always taken great care with their parks and their environment; they always did. It looks lovely,' says Hanson, peering out the van window. We're driving through central Ipswich towards Silkstone, the down-at-heel suburb where Hanson ran her fish and chip shop for a decade.

Ipswich's utilitarian 1980s office buildings, telegraph-pole-studded boulevards and gracious, bougainvillea-clad Queenslanders gradually give way to wood and fibro cottages as we enter Hanson's old stomping ground. There's the odd cracked window glinting through scrubby frangipani, a few rusted gutters among the palms, some faded utes chocked up on bricks in dilapidated yards. On a sagging porch, a large woman in a dressing gown wrenches her tearful daughter's hair into a pigtail for school, swearing at the girl to keep still. A massive Mack truck thunders past, rat-running the lights. Not much has changed around here since Hanson was last in residence.

'In town there's the big shopping centre, but everything else is just the same. I don't have a lot to do with Ipswich. I don't read the newspapers. I'm in another shire. Turn right at these lights,' Hanson instructs Phil, and we enter the sleepy street in which she spent ten years as a single mother, from 1986 to 1996, working eighty-hour weeks to support her four children. Hanson's old cream bungalow in Doyle Street squats behind an overgrown hedge, its lopsided carport tacked over the front door, above an oil-spattered slab. Hanson bought the cottage for $49 000. She liked the big backyard and the wood-floored sunroom. The house is a five-minute walk from her shop.

'Gawd, it's all gone to wrack and ruin,' Hanson tuts, surveying the weed-strewn driveway. She hasn't been back here since 1996, when she moved out to her new farm as the member for Oxley, no longer a struggling small-business owner but a rising political star.

Today, Hanson's wearing a *Mad Men*–style lilac floral frock with d-in waist and a petticoat. It is not a good-mood day: her ee has just given out, and each step she takes in her matching pumps is agony. I am feeling guilty for making Hanson revisit her old haunts on Struggle Street, but I'm hopeful they will jolt her out of her generalised recollections and trigger something spontaneous. Hanson, through gritted teeth, is cooperating. She's given me her word, and her word is her bond.

Hanson's stoicism is impressive and deeply ingrained. It helped her endure, then leave, two abusive marriages, without complaint or a backwards glance. When she split from the unfaithful Walter in 1977, Hanson was supporting their two sons, Tony and Steve, on modest state handouts and her earnings at the Grand Hotel on the Gold Coast.

'There was no income, no child support, nothing. The few dollars I was making barely paid the rent. My parents helped me a bit, but it was a struggle and I made sure the kids were always fed, but sometimes I went without a meal so they were fed. And this is what some politicians don't understand, and why I understand people. Welfare is a helping hand – it's not the government, it's taxpayers – to help people in times of hardship.'

Determined to get off welfare, Hanson took on a better-paid job at the Penthouse nightclub in Surfers Paradise, where she served cocktails to well-heeled locals and touring celebrities, including '70s pop star Renée Geyer. It was here, over the bar one night, that Hanson fell into deep conversation with the affable man who'd become her second husband, Mark Hanson.

'He always wanted to start up his own business but he just needed that support, which I gave him. We started our own plumbing business, and I gotta say, he was a great plumber. He was a hardworking man but it was a shame the way our marriage headed,' she reflects now.

In 1978, Hanson and her sons moved in to Mark's home in Ipswich, which he shared with a daughter from a previous marriage. Together, they established Hanson's Plumbing Service, with Hanson doing the admin and odd jobs as Mark attended to clients. Both the business and the family thrived: in 1980, Hanson was pregnant with her third son, Adam, and the loved-up couple honeymooned in Asia. By the time her daughter, Lee, was born in 1983, Hanson was building a new extension under the house, helping Mark run the business, and managing an expanding portfolio of investment properties.

'I had five kids with me a lot of the time, so running the plumbing business and keeping up the yard and [the tenants] and the kids, I was kept busy, but who isn't?' she laughs. But Hanson's happiness was short-lived. Around the pool table in their new den, Mark indulged in increasingly alcoholic benders, wiping out whole weekends with his footloose mates. He began to terrorise his stepsons Tony and Steve behind Hanson's back: forcing them out of their beds in the middle of the night to watch him play guitar, and abusing them physically and verbally.

Then Mark moved on to Hanson. He banned her from applying for a part-time job, punched holes in the walls, threatened to kill himself and became increasingly sadistic. He'd fling the dinners Hanson made for him in the rubbish, and strip the sheets from her bed while she slept, returning to her room throughout the night to flick on the lights. As Mark's alcoholism intensified, so did his unpredictability and rage. When Hanson discovered the terrified Tony standing on his windowsill ready to jump as Mark bashed in his door, she realised she had to act.

'Men can survive without women and vice versa, people don't realise how strong they are. But sometimes people in a marriage expect the other to do everything for them and you become too dependent and you lose your self-confidence,' Hanson says. 'And it was all because of drinking and abuse, and I couldn't allow that to continue. And my eldest I had to send to live with his grandmother, because of abuse from my second husband.'

Hanson left Mark six years into their marriage in 1986, buying him out of their four investment properties and leaving him the plumbing business. Taking up a part-time job at the Booval Bowls Club, she sold the rental properties to buy the Doyle Street cottage in Silkstone, and moved in with eleven-year-old Steve, six-year-old Adam and three-year-old Lee. Hanson left Tony with his grandmother.

In her 2007 autobiography, *Untamed and Unashamed,* Hanson admits to wishing she'd left Mark much earlier, and describes the pain she still feels over his treatment of Tony and Steve. She refuses to discuss in any more detail the abuse she and her children suffered. Nor will she identify as a domestic violence survivor. 'I'm not a person to worry about things. I only worry about something when it happens. I deal with a problem at the time,' she says to me now.

I'm struck by Hanson's refusal to empathise with other women who've been abused. As a politician, she has railed against domestic violence survivors, accusing them of making 'frivolous' claims to rort the system. Despite the fact that one Australian woman, on average, is killed every week by a close relative or partner, Hanson insists that men are the real victims of the epidemic: 'Men have nowhere to go – [domestic violence against males] is very widely spread. I want to . . . give them a voice, because they feel like they're not being heard.' One of Hanson's first moves as a senator was to support pension cuts for single parents, the overwhelming majority of whom are women.

When I suggest that this doesn't tally with Hanson's notion

of the 'fair go', given she herself was an abused single mother who relied on welfare for a time, she's furious.

'It's no-one's fault but mine that I ended up alone with four kids. No-one owes me a damn thing. Everyone feels sorry for themselves. Just get on with life and start working. I stood up as an individual. But Australians won't work. Why would we work? The government is looking after us. We've got to lose that mentality and get back to work. It's not right. I'm so sick of it. Seeing these ones sitting around all day, third and fourth generations on welfare, and it's become a way of life – like it's their right. It's not your right. It's not your right that taxpayers pick up the bill. Stand on your own two feet: you're responsible for yourself. There's people been on welfare for thirty, forty years. That's not good enough. The government has to say there's a cut-off point!'

I remember industrious little Pauline, competing against her three older sisters for her father's approval. The self-sufficient teenager, who did five-hour shifts in Jack's cafe when she got home from work, then climbed the stairs to her room, handing the $5 her father gave her straight to Hannorah for board. If Hanson, through hard work and endurance, could survive, why can't other women? Her father and brothers were loving and kind, so why should all Australian men be labelled monsters? It's clear Hanson sees her abusive husbands as the exception to the dignified Aussie masculinity she cherishes, and not the rule.

Hanson's determination to play the lone feminine crusader in a man's world, rather than sister to those it oppresses, has won her a loyal army of older Anglo-Australian men. One of them is Jonathan, who has rented Hanson's old Silkstone cottage for six years. He lost his house, car and 25-year business when he fell foul of the tax department, and is now mostly supported by his wife. Jonathan stands in thongs under the carport, fag in hand, as

Hanson, instantly in campaign mode, glides towards him in her lilac frock.

'I'm a bit like you. I got very strong views on things,' says Jonathan approvingly.

Hanson flashes him a brilliant smile. 'You must be a fair dinkum Aussie.'

'Yep. I know what I think and I say it. I get really annoyed with our so-called immigration policy. People that come here, as far as I'm concerned, abide by our rules, and if they don't, send them back. Don't even blanket it.'

'I think Australians do feel that; it has changed dramatically.' Hanson nods supportively.

'Like blackfellas and Abos – if you call them "Abo" now, you can get in trouble.' Jonathan gives her a conspiratorial look.

'Well, I'm laughing because I just did a Reclaim Australia rally,' Hanson chuckles, catching his drift.

'The problem with politics now is there are too many fancy-pants,' Jonathan states.

'Bleeding hearts, do-gooders?' prompts Hanson.

'Yes, they beat around the bush. Don't do what they say. Anyone that knows me, if I say I'm going to do something, that's it. Anyway, I believe in what you stand for,' Jonathan says solemnly, and holds out his hand.

'Thank you,' says Hanson, shaking it with equal solemnity. 'It means a lot that people still believe in me, and it's all been worth it then. And I have to keep going and I have to change the system, because it's corrupt.'

'It is, and I don't like it,' says Jonathan, using Hanson's catchphrase without irony.

The two of them fall into a comradely discussion about fly-fishing for yellowbelly, and what kind of fish Hanson should put in

THE FISH AND CHIP SHOP

her billabong, as we film inside her old home.

The unrenovated two-bedroom bungalow has beautiful bones, with thick sills and doorways, wide-planked floors and gracious ceilings. The little kitchen, where Hanson scrimped on her meals so her children could eat, looks out over a rambling yard, dotted with Hills Hoists and sheds.

'There's a new deck out the back. But the kitchen's all the same,' says Hanson cheerfully, joining us by the window over the sink.

'Out there is the laundry. And I had a calf out there – I paid a lot of money for a stud bull, and I had a newborn calf, and the cow died on me. And the kids met me after the shop and my daughter thought it was a kitten, they thought it was wonderful. And my son had a vegie garden, and the calf ate everything. Anyway, the calf grew, and then I put it on the property and it disappeared. There was none of this swing up the back, and none of the sheds there. I had a vegie garden where the clothesline is, and big magnolia trees. It was a nice quiet area, the school was just down the road, and the kids could go to the shop to see me.'

In 1987, with no child support and three kids under twelve, Hanson knew she was on a dead-end streak, tending the bar at the Booval Bowls.

'I was doing eighteen hours a week,' she says. 'It was not enough to support the family, there was no assistance from my ex-husband, and I saw the shop for sale at a reasonable price, and I bought it. It was called Marsden's Seafood, so I kept the name.'

The little takeaway shop was owned by an uncle of Morrie Marsden, a mild-mannered Ipswich realtor whom Hanson started dating after her split with Mark.

'The kids loved him; he was a great help,' remembers Hanson. 'He told me business was good, and that's when I made up my mind I would give it a go. Morrie was in love with me, he was a beautiful man, and we were good friends, but I didn't love [him] enough to marry him.' Her voice hardens. 'I did *not* want to be married again.' Hanson stares straight ahead, a battle-hardened survivor. I'm a single mother myself – it's a look I understand.

Hanson's decision to take on the fish and chip shop was met with fierce disapproval by the one man whose opinion she valued most. Jack told her it was 'no job for a woman' and was convinced that she'd fail.

'Dad was always concerned about me running it with young kids. He was old-school – you know, you need a husband or man around. But I was quite capable of doing it myself,' Hanson states. Determined to prove Jack wrong, she took on a part-time female boarder to help with the kids, and began the gruelling routine that would see her transform Marsden's from a run-of-the-mill takeaway to a local legend, as beloved in Silkstone as Jack's cafe was in Woolloongabba.

'I didn't eat seafood at all. I didn't like prawns, so I wasn't eating the profits, was I?' Hanson jokes. 'But I knew how to make a good steak sandwich and hamburger, and that was all coming from my father. You had to put the effort into making your shop different to the one that was only a couple of kilometres down the road. I worked six days a week by myself, and spent Mondays off to do the books and be with the kids.'

'You're quite the feminist, aren't you?' I tease her.

Her eyes flash with indignation. 'I'm not a feminist at all. I call myself a lady and I like to be treated like a lady, and there are some men out there who like to treat women as ladies, and there are some women out there who don't want the door opened for them and say "I'm equal" and all that, but it's not about that. It's having respect for each other. You're male, and you're female. I had a hot meal waiting on the table for my husbands every night they got home.

And I love being treated like a lady.'

Clearly, third-wave feminism – which made it quite okay for women to fight for equality while wearing heels and make-up and cooking for their men – never made it to Ipswich. The 'sexy' feminists of the 1990s flourished in urban Australia's intellectual bubble – a place that Hanson, with her belief in the 'school of hard knocks' and the 'university of life', tends to scorn. As a tertiary-educated, inner-city greenie, I belong in that bubble. I'm one of the 'fancypants do-gooders' that Hanson and her supporters deride; a 'bleeding-heart leftie' cocooned in my idealistic ivory tower, too 'out of touch' with the suffering of 'ordinary Australians' to make the 'tough' calls on climate change, welfare and refugees, which she is adamant are required.

But Hanson and I are two people who violently disagree with each other yet want to get on. We are searching for points of connection. As we drive from her old Doyle Street cottage to Marsden's fish and chip shop, we take playful pot shots at each other across our cultural divide, using the stark differences in our backgrounds and beliefs to have fun rather than fight. When I tell her I finally received the PhD I've been slaving over for ten years, she says, 'Congratulations – I reckon I'm a doctor of philosophy too. Streetwise philosophy.'

'There are lots of ways to learn,' I agree, and mean it.

'There are. Lots of ways to learn. Sometimes I think learning straight from life's experience and on the street is better, in a lot of ways, than memorising from a textbook,' Hanson declares.

'I still think you're crazy not to admit you're a feminist,' I counter. 'Besides, if you call yourself a Ms, you're telling men you might still be available. It's mysterious.'

I'm convinced that Hanson, if you overlook her shockingly misogynistic stance on domestic violence, is in fact a textbook feminist. A survivor of two abusive marriages, who turned her back on welfare and worked to support her kids, defying her father to set up a successful business in a male-dominated industry. A political campaigner who became the first female independent MP, battling the 'boys' club' to lead one of the most powerful independent parties in Australia. A fearless public performer, who has repeatedly fought back against sexist claims that she can't think for herself. A fit single woman who has continued to enjoy a healthy sex life long after her kids have left home, once advising a young female staffer 'men are only good for one thing: use them for their bodies, then move on'.

'I am definitely not a Mrs. I've been there, done that, and I definitely don't belong to anyone,' Hanson concedes. 'I'm probably a Ms or a Miss. I don't get offended by that. Right, then, what's happening?' She slides open the van door and steps onto the footpath, wincing at the pain in her knee.

On Hanson's instructions, we've parked the van in a side street next to Marsden's Seafood on Blackstone Road. A few of her old neighbours still live here, and they remember the yelling press packs and traffic-blocking OB vans she attracted in 1996, as the only fish-and-chip-shop-owning MP in Australia. Hanson's old neighbours like to complain.

Hanson sniffs dismissively in their direction and flicks her thumb at a spit-polished white weatherboard behind a privet hedge. 'This used to be the doctor's surgery where the kids went. So, Lee, she must have been four or five years of age, and she went by herself around the corner. I'm in the shop, and I'm straight on the phone to him, and he told me what's wrong. Too many kids are mollycoddled now. Our society has changed. I'd still let her do it today.'

We line Hanson up in front of Marsden's Seafood for a portrait. The little takeaway sits in a line of square-windowed, single-storey shopfronts, framed in nondescript blond brick. To the left is a ladies' hair salon. To the right, a denture clinic and Denman's Party

Hire, a fancy-dress outlet with apparently random opening hours. The suburban mise en scène seems frozen in time, as if the plastic chairs, the potted plants, the menu boards handwritten in chalk, haven't been touched since 1987, the year that Hanson set up shop.

Across the road, the faded neon of the Marco Polo Chinese Restaurant rises above its chipped facade. This is where Hanson used to go with Morrie Marsden on Friday night dates, taking a rare break from her fryers to enjoy the exotic taste of Bonfire Beef and Pineapple Chicken. Hanson squints into the sun for our camera, gripping her cream handbag. She's not happy. Cars thunder past her along the hot bitumen of Blackstone Road, headed for somewhere better.

'It never looked like that when I had it.' Hanson frowns, scrutinising her old shop window. A closer look reveals that twenty years of globalisation have in fact left their mark. Multinational energy drink stickers plaster the glass, and a newish Chinese air conditioner blasts the pavement with a dull mechanical roar.

'I think they're just making ends meet. It's not a thriving business,' Hanson continues, casting a proprietorial eye over the shopfront. 'It should be painted. And all those stickers over the doors – it needs a really good brighten up. Too much junk and everything over the place. You know, I'd give it a complete big clean-out. People think, "Oh God, if it looks like that on the outside, what's it going to be like on the inside?" That's the truth. It's had about five different owners since I had it. They only last two years; they can't handle it. I had it for ten!' she says with obvious pride.

'How much did you sell it for?' I ask.

'That's no-one's business,' she snaps.

Hanson still treasures this little business, which she coaxed up from scratch. She eventually sold it for the princely sum of $104 000 in 1997, in her second year in office. But her first days behind the

Marsden's counter had not gone well. A tradesman had bought a pack of prawns and chips to go, then returned to throw them in Hanson's face. 'I catch prawns – no way I'd eat shit like this,' he snarled. Mortified, Hanson dumped her frozen stock in the garbage skip and started to rise before dawn, driving fifty minutes north to the fish markets in Colmslie.

Her decision to only sell fresh produce paid off: by the early 1990s, Hanson's rebadged shop, Marsden's *Fresh* Seafood, was doing a roaring trade. In order to spend more time with her kids, Hanson employed two women full-time and several part-timers to turn out her signature pineapple fritters and prawn curries, along with the fresh fillets and hand-cut chips that had put Marsden's on the map.

'It wasn't easy, it was hard,' says Hanson of her early days in the shop. 'I was grateful the kids were in good health because I had no-one to look after them. Morrie and his family helped out, but yeah, it wasn't easy juggling everything. I'd get up at 4.30 a.m., go to the markets, then go to the shop, work all day in the shop, and I'd be home by about eight o'clock at night. And if I didn't have to go to the markets, it was doing housework, organising the kids, doing the washing. And then it was a matter of taking the kids to gymnastics, athletics or whatever they had to do, so it became easier when I grew the business and put on staff. But in the beginning, I averaged eighty to ninety hours a week.'

As the only regular female buyer, the flame-headed Hanson cut a striking figure in the hyper-masculine world of the Colmslie fish markets. News footage from the mid-'90s shows the forty-something Hanson in overalls and boots, standing on tiptoe at the back of a boisterous pack of Mediterranean men. Bidding for snapper, Hanson waves her hand with an exuberant grin. She's in her element.

'I love these male-dominated environments, don't I?' Hanson

looks cheekily at Luke. 'The auctions would start at 6 a.m. It was a hive of activity. Cod, shark, whiting, bream, tailor, barra, rainbow trout, mullet, sea perch, Nile perch . . .' she recites, listing her daily haul. 'There were trawlers – the crates came through and you just bid on the fish. The guys down there, they got my number-one vote, not the politicians! It was mainly Greeks, and some Aussies as well. I had a great friendship with the Greeks – they'd have a joke with me. They were the old-school, hardworking people. I have a lot of time for them. They tried to look after me when I first came here as a female. Then they saw I was quite capable of lifting 25-kilo bins of fish, and I did my own thing.'

Hanson's smile fades. 'Then the Vietnamese started to move into the fish and chip shop business and takeaways around. There was a real change then; you could see the difference between the cultures. They'd just buy anything. Totally different buyers. A lot of them didn't speak the English language at all, and they were very much to themselves. I didn't see that they went out of their way to mix.'

In the decade that Hanson ran Marsden's, Australia experienced a surge in immigration from South-East Asia, in particular, Vietnam. Malcolm Fraser's conservative government had been steadily resettling Vietnamese war refugees since the end of hostilities in 1975, effectively ending the White Australia policy. But in 1980, Vietnam's communist leadership nationalised the economy, and a new wave of 12 915 Vietnamese migrants arrived, many of them Catholics and ethnic Chinese, fearing persecution under the powerful regime in Hanoi. In 1982, Vietnam agreed to allow its citizens to emigrate with impunity, and the refugee resettlement program begun under Fraser expanded under his Labor successor, Bob Hawke.

Threatened regional voters, including Hanson's customers in Ipswich, complained that the new Vietnamese arrivals were, as former conservative immigration minister Ian McPhee had put it, 'illegal immigrants' and 'queue-jumpers', coming to 'seek a better way of life rather than to escape from some form of persecution'. Despite growing resistance among less-affluent Australians, 70 000 Vietnamese migrants had been resettled in the country by 1985. By 1991, the number of Vietnamese-born Australians had jumped to 124 800.

Thanh Huong Huynh, the current owner of Hanson's shop, was one of the last wave of Vietnamese immigrants to call Australia home. She's waiting for Hanson now, behind the cash register at the back of Marsden's. Her hair is freshly curled and set, and she's put on a neatly pressed floral apron. Hanson plasters on her brightest campaign smile, slides open the door and breezes into the shop. She's clearly determined to make her on-camera encounter with Thanh as uncontroversial as possible.

'Hello, been busy?' Hanson beams, and Thanh breaks into an embarrassed laugh.

'Yes, busy,' she replies in stilted English. Her twelve-year-old son, Thomas, hovers beside her, ready to translate.

'I've got to give you some advice,' Hanson begins, coolly surveying Thanh's Chinese takeaway pamphlets, her little pyramids of dim sims, her cluster of Japanese cats waving on the counter. 'When you have it this hot, then there's a storm, and everyone has blackouts. Then everyone comes here to eat and it's bedlam. You're flat out!'

'Oh,' says Thanh, nodding politely, taking care to show her famous visitor the respect that her age and status deserve.

'Your menu is still the same, but the board is a lot nicer. You've had it all done up,' Hanson notes, impressed by Thanh's brightly chalked board hanging in pride of place above the fryers.

'What is "Fence Co."?' asks Thanh, pointing at the blue sign above the board.

'Fence Co. was the guy down the road. He did some fencing, so

I put it on top of my board to help him with business. Just helping a friend and a neighbour,' Hanson replies.

'A customer say to me, "Oh, you do fencing." They trick me!' Thanh jokes nervously.

'How did you get here?' Hanson asks, inquisitive beneath her professional smile.

'We went to Malaysia and stay two years. With cousin there. I come by boat to Malaysia and then by plane,' Thanh answers carefully.

Hanson shoots the camera an approving look. 'She applied for refugee status and went through the right channels, so it's great,' she says.

Thanh nods, relieved. But the interrogation's not over.

'Do you go to the fish market?' Hanson asks.

Thanh looks blank, and turns to Thomas. 'No, we order,' he answers.

'Do you cut your own chips?' Hanson tries again.

Mother and son exchange a worried look. Thomas takes a deep breath. 'Chips we order from —'

'So you don't make your own chips,' Hanson interrupts, nodding as if that explains everything. She scans Thanh's Coca-Cola fridge, her trays of frozen hoki and flake, the Seafood Bites and Fisherman's Basket menu options drawn in pink chalk above the cooktops.

'I used to go and buy the fresh fish. And you don't have any of the prawns, like I did,' Hanson continues. 'I don't know your technique, but it worked for me. It was such a run-down business, it was nothing at first, and it was all what I learned from my father and listening to your customers. When I went to the markets, I had a product that the fellow down the road didn't have. So you've gotta have something that makes them want to pass his shop and come to yours.'

Thanh blushes, then covers her mouth with her hand. 'I'm shy,' she whispers, trying to wave the situation away with a self-deprecating giggle.

Hanson studies Thanh with empathy. It's a quality that strangers remember, when they meet Hanson on the street. No matter what vitriol is pouring from her mouth, Hanson in the flesh has the uncanny ability to make you feel like she cares.

'You make your own dim sims, don't you?' she says now, giving Thanh an encouraging smile.

Thanh nods brightly: 'Dim sims, spring roll, potato scallops . . .'

'Spring rolls and dim sims; they are the only Asian things we have,' Thomas adds quickly.

Hanson is pleased. 'I used to make 3000 potato scallops a week, and then sacks of potatoes, I'd go through stacks this high a week!' Hanson holds her hand up to Thanh's head, and Thanh lets out a belly laugh of recognition. The ice between them is broken.

'A lot of shops have frozen scallops; they're not as good. I used to sell them for twenty cents each. And I tell you what, drop the price,' Hanson confides warmly, as Thomas translates. 'Because everyone else is selling them more expensive, at eighty cents. You make it cheaper, then people will come in and maybe they'll also buy a drink. Do you understand what I'm saying?'

'Yep!' nods Thanh.

'Give them something they value for money, and if you do that, they'll come back. And I used to put a sign outside my shop, I'd put, "The Best Burgers and Best Steak Sandwich in Town!" Then people would pull up to try it. Advertise yourself. Say you're the best! Anyway, it's just my way – it's what I do. And I used to make my own scallops, and have a rumbler, and make my own chips and have a chipper,' Hanson continues, checking out the battered sausages in Thanh's display counter.

'You make the dagwood dogs. They're the ones I made, so everyone's carried on making dagwood dogs.' Hanson nods contentedly. 'Dad used to make the dim sims before they were even known in Australia, with the chicken and the rice. And after that, dim sims started coming out, but Dad was the first in Brisbane to make all that. I didn't have enough time to make my own chicken rolls and dim sims,' she says, striding behind the counter to inspect Thanh's deep steel fryers.

'And that's still the old cooker – that was here when you bought it, wasn't it?' Hanson says excitedly.

Thanh nods happily.

'I used Frytol, the dearest oil. I always believed you should use the best oil. There was a big machine that I had to filter the oil every night. What kind of batter do you use?'

Thanh gives Luke's camera a playful look. 'I'm saying this in front of Pauline Hanson,' she says, grinning. 'Cornflour and milk.'

'Yeah, well, don't tell them any more, don't give your secret away,' Hanson instructs Thanh, dead serious. 'The thickness of the batter is important. When you do potato scallops, the batter has got to be thinner than it is for the dagwood dogs. Do you notice that?'

'Can you assist me?' Thanh asks sweetly. 'Because you work long time!'

'I should come in and give you a hand!' Hanson agrees, delighted. 'How would you like it if I came here one night, and put up a sign and said I'm going to work here? You could show me a few things with your dim sims and spring rolls!'

'Okay, thank you!' Thanh holds Hanson's hand, and the two women hug. Phil seizes the moment, snapping off some shots of Hanson with Thomas and Thanh, a happily united trio beneath the fish shop menu.

'You know I ran my campaign here from the shop?' asks

Hanson, remembering her cash-strapped 1996 federal election campaign as the independent for Oxley. 'And the phone was ringing, and I had the press here, and I'm trying to make the chips and the potato scallops, and it was crazy!'

Hanson points at the Vietnamese calendar on the wall. 'This is where the phone was, and this is where I put an ad in the *Queensland Times* saying I want [to hire] a female. And they said, "You can't say that, that's discrimination!" and I said, "Well, you just say that I want someone with boobs!"'

'Oooh,' says Thanh, not understanding a thing. Thomas is too shy to translate.

'You're very busy, you're working for government,' Thanh observes.

'I am. I'm now running for the federal election for the Senate for Queensland. So I'm running all over the country, a political party,' Hanson concludes, and shakes Thanh's hand. 'Bye, Thomas. Look after your mum and work hard, okay?' she says firmly, and glides past the Japanese cats to the door.

As we shoot close-ups of Thanh's dim sims, Hanson rests her dicky knee on a plastic chair outside. She pulls out her phone and sends Phil's shots of her with Thanh and Thomas to Saraya Beric, to upload to the 'Pauline Hanson's Please Explain' Facebook page.

It's an astute political move. Hanson, standing arm in arm with the Vietnamese owners of her old fish shop, as 'one proud Aussie helping another proud Aussie', is the perfect visual antidote to the racism label that has continued to dog her 'Fed Up' campaign.

The forty-year-old fish and chip shop lady who once advertised that she made 'The Best Steak Sandwich in Town' has come a long way.

Chapter 4
The Member for Oxley

I may only be a fish and chip shop lady, but some of these economists need to get a job in the real world. I wouldn't even let one of them handle my grocery shopping.
—Pauline Hanson, maiden speech, 10 September 1996

'To be named as one of the stars of the twentieth century, although I see it as a great honour – it's more important to me to be on the floor of parliament and representing the people,' Hanson says, with genuine modesty.

She's showing us a glossy 1990s coffee-table book celebrating 'Australia's Most Influential People'. Beside the Great White Shark, Greg Norman, and the grinning media mogul Kerry Packer, Hanson graces a full-page spread in an androgynous '90s suit, her hair in a spiky red bob. 'It's a great honour, but I'm not too wrapped up in it. It's nice but it's over the top of my head. There's more important things in life I want to achieve than get my face in a magazine.'

Hanson's political awakening began in the early 1990s, behind the counter at Marsden's. Within six short years, the fish and chip shop lady would become Australia's most polarising politician: a woman so famous, many TV viewers in Singapore, Hong Kong and beyond thought she was the Australian prime minister.

'I would never have dreamt for this to happen to me. It has been an interesting life. But when I was thirty-six, I was in my shop, and I said I am not meant to be here. I knew my life was not meant to be in that shop,' Hanson says simply.

If the 1950s, for Hanson, represented Australia at its zenith, the early 1990s were its nadir. The anthemic beats of Midnight Oil's 'Beds Are Burning' and Yothu Yindi's 'Treaty' had captured the airwaves with their defiant call for Indigenous land rights and recognition, while inclusive identity politics, playful postmodern 'geek' culture and the humanistic philosophies of the New Age movement blossomed in the streets. The pro-reconciliation, pro-multicultural policies of the Labor government, enjoying its fourth term under the flamboyant prime ministership of the Zegna-clad, Swiss-clock-collecting Paul Keating, were at their peak.

In 1992, as Hanson slaved over her chip vats and fretted about local Aboriginal kids graffitiing the white walls of Silkstone, Keating gave his historic Redfern speech, becoming the first Australian prime minister to publicly acknowledge the damage and pain European settlement had inflicted on Australia's First People. 'We committed the murders. We took the children from their mothers. We practised discrimination and exclusion. It was our ignorance and our prejudice,' Keating told hundreds of Indigenous Australians sitting in the grass at the Block in Redfern. His audience, stunned, slowly began to clap.

That same year, the High Court of Australia issued its revolutionary Mabo decision, declaring that Aboriginal and Torres Strait Islander people had rights to the land that existed before the British invasion, and continued to exist in the present day. The myth of *terra nullius*, which had been used to justify the oppression and dispossession of Australia's First Peoples for over two centuries, was officially dead. In 1993, under the guidance of Keating and the minister for Aboriginal and Torres Strait Islander Affairs, Robert Tickner, the *Native Title Act* passed into law, protecting Indigenous claims to ancestral lands and allowing these claims to coexist with those of non-Indigenous land owners and farmers.

A sophisticated new mood was sweeping the country – one that was focused on acknowledging the brutal truth behind colonial Australia's airbrushed history, accepting responsibility for past wrongs, and facing the future in a fairer, more unified spirit. Shaking off its adolescent fixation with its Anglo-American mentors, Australia was boldly reinventing itself as a unique multicultural nation, one that embraced its diversity as its strength. In 1991, novelist Tom Keneally, cricketer Ian Chappell, film director Fred Schepisi and ambitious young investment banker Malcolm Turnbull launched the Australian Republican Movement, intent on cutting the nation's infantile attachment to Mother England's apron strings once and for all.

While Regurgitator and Pulp and REM filled their videos on *Rage* with variously sexed, ethnically diverse, ambiguously gendered Shiny Happy People, Keating refused to kowtow to the British and US alliances, forging new cultural and economic ties with Asia. An avid fan of the arts, the Mahler-loving Boy from Bankstown unveiled a multimillion-dollar suite of endowments for Australian writers, filmmakers and musicians, and expanded the budget and reach of the multicultural broadcaster SBS, in a glamorous new headquarters in Artarmon.

In the thriving, left-wing urban conclaves of the early 1990s, Anzac Day and military memorial services were viewed as the decaying traditions of a less spiritually evolved past. War was so twentieth century. The tech-focused future of the new millennium beckoned, and it promised prosperity and peace. World War III was nothing more than an escapist B-movie fantasy, sold on the discount shelves of the local video store. 'Love', as crooner John Paul Young told the bedazzled audience of Baz Luhrmann's global hit *Strictly Ballroom*, under the swirling mirror ball of the Paddington Academy Twin, was 'in the air'.

The Australia described by multicultural and Indigenous leaders of the early 1990s could have been a different planet. 'It was a relaxed society. It had accepted diversity with good grace and good humour. It was friendly, it was egalitarian,' remembers the former chair of the 1990s National Multicultural Advisory Council, Indian-born businessman Neville Roach AO.

There was 'a real conversation happening, about the relationship between Aboriginal and non-Aboriginal Australia, and the way in which we would be able to live, respecting each other', reflects Labor politician and Wiradjuri woman Linda Burney, from an opulent meeting room in Sydney's Parliament House, surrounded by the marble busts of dead white leaders.

Indigenous barrister Pat O'Shane QC, seated on a bench outside the World War I cenotaph in Sydney's Hyde Park, describes a nation in which community values, and not the needs of the individual, still influenced the national debate. Politicians were judged on their ideas and vision, rather than their standing in the latest polls. O'Shane's early 1990s Australia is a hopeful, idealistic place, untainted by the neo-con belief that progress is best measured by economic graphs, and not by the happiness and wellbeing of society's most vulnerable.

Watching archival footage of Keating discussing Indigenous land rights with ABC talkback callers in 1992, it is impossible to imagine an Australian prime minister speaking the same words today. Keating seems to inhabit a utopian parallel universe, in which *The West Wing*'s humanitarian president Jed Bartlet is the real leader of the Free World, and Donald Trump and Pauline

Hanson are mere celebrity impersonators on some comedy channel called Fox.

'The thing to look forward to is a country which is, in its soul, at peace with itself, that's not prospering at the dispossession of another people,' Keating tells an ABC caller gently. 'We are a unique multicultural country, we have lots of opportunity, we're located in the fastest growing part of the world. But to go forward together as a people means we have to go forward together on terms on which we all agree.'

Unfortunately for Keating, a future on which Australians could all agree was a fantasy. To the rural and regional voters living outside Sydney's optimistic halo, those people whom Keating had once famously quipped were just 'camping out', Labor's policies were divisive, elitist and changing too fast.

Hanson was one of these people. Dishing up fish and chips to the working families of Ipswich seven days a week, she was uniquely tapped in to the rising disaffection of regional Anglo-Australian voters, as the impacts of globalisation, multiculturalism and Keating's radical vision for change began to take hold.

'I couldn't stand a bar of Paul Keating, didn't like him at all!' snarls Hanson, in her lavish formal living room. 'I thought he was an arrogant man. He didn't understand how the Australian people were feeling.'

As Keating pontificated on the radio at Marsden's, Hanson battered dagwood dogs and kvetched with her customers. The prime minister's confident declaration that Australia was a 'unique, multicultural country' with a promising future in Asia meant nothing to the beleaguered workers of Ipswich. The city's once prosperous wool, coal and railway industries were floundering. Australia's manufacturing sector, the proud producer of Victa lawnmowers and the FJ Holden, was being eroded by cheap overseas imports. Factory men, employed for decades, were suddenly out of work. Down the road from Hanson's Silkstone shop, newly arrived Vietnamese migrants were taking on low-paid jobs outside the unions, while drugged-up teenagers terrorised welfare-dependent single mothers in the mall.

From behind her counter, Hanson ran a kangaroo court on the evils inflicted by Keating, and the woeful neglect of Australia's rural and regional centres by the 'jumped-up, private-schoolboy politicians' in Canberra.

'In the '90s, it was just complete shutdown of our freedom of speech,' she says in disgust. 'You couldn't criticise anything because you were seen as a racist, and if you were Aboriginal you get schooling paid for, you get the books paid for, you get all this done for you. And of course you had the immigration issue. Our rights as Australians were taken away from us and you had the threat of charges being laid against you, and it was just a complete shutdown of our freedom of speech. The whole system was not fair.'

A telling exchange between Keating and an ABC radio caller in 1992 reveals the stark divide between Australia's urban decision-makers and the radically different nation Hanson and her customers inhabited. The caller's anger about Labor's new Indigenous land rights legislation encapsulates the simmering indignation that Hanson would harness and transform into a populist revolt, turning the suspicion among many Anglo-Australians that things under the progressive status quo were just 'not fair' into a national battle cry.

'Look at the hysteria that you and your government have caused,' the man rails at Keating, referring to Mabo.

'That's a decision of the High Court,' Keating replies coolly.

'I have to buy my land. Why can't they? Why do you see Aboriginal people as more equal than whites? I'm not a racist, but . . .'

'They all say that,' Keating interrupts, tetchy now. 'Look, if you own a property, you can bet your bottom dollar that an Aboriginal person owned it at some point.'

'The average white Australian feels prejudiced against by your government!' the man yells, and hangs up. Keating studies the microphone wth regal tolerance, and lets out a patient sigh. There's a sense that the ABC producers recording him feel, as he does, that the caller is swimming against the tide. That this man, and unreconstructed Australians like him, will inevitably be brought into the fold. That Keating is on the right side of history, and, with persistence and a steady hand, he will take the nation with him.

As Hanson already knew from her customers in Ipswich, Keating and his ABC producers could not have been more wrong.

'Canberra has been out of touch with the general public for a long time,' Hanson declares now, launching into the anti-establishment diatribe she's been giving for two decades.

'They're arrogant. They're driven by the big end of town, career politicians, not grassroots. They go through university – they haven't done the hard yards. They have no idea of what it is to struggle and yet they pass legislation expecting the general public to deal with issues of life, when they can't even do it themselves. I believe we need to get our hands dirty and prove we can carve out a living for ourselves, before we can [make] tough decisions about other people's lives. The fish and chip shop put me directly in touch with the average Australian. It's a pity I can't say the same for a lot of pusillanimous career politicians that take up wasted space in our seats in parliament today.'

The forty-year-old Hanson was not one to stand around and whinge. Fed up with the stories of hardship, lay-offs and petty crime she was hearing from her broke and beleaguered customers, she decided to act.

Hanson's first foray into the cutthroat business of politics took place in 1994, when her then boyfriend, Ipswich councillor Rudy Guylias, encouraged her to stand for a seat on Ipswich City Council. Hanson mounted a persuasive case for candidacy, based on her close knowledge of the community and the fact that through hard work and acuity she had transformed her struggling business into a success. She campaigned aggressively against a proposal for a new public library, arguing it would be a waste of taxpayers' money – and won the seat.

Twelve months later, in March 1995, Hanson was booted off the council, the unwitting victim of an internecine preference war with the local Labor faction.

'They preferenced against me and changed the boundaries. I lost by 132 votes, and they got back their Labor council,' Hanson remembers, with that peculiar, figure-accurate recall all campaign-hardened politicians share. Rather than convincing her to stay in the fish shop, however, Hanson's skirmish on council whetted her political appetite. In August 1995, as Prime Minister Keating and conservative opposition leader John Howard prepared to do battle in the forthcoming federal election, Hanson joined the Liberal Party, determined to do her bit to help boot the 'politically correct' Labor powerbrokers out of office for good.

It's easy to see why Howard, with his old-fashioned family values, pride in Australia's military and colonial history, distaste for big government, squeamishness about Asian immigration and love of the monarchy, appealed to Hanson. While Keating was intent on taking the nation 'forward' into a new multicultural century, Howard was determined to take it back: to the traditional folds of the Menzies era, which he, like Hanson, cherished. Howard may have been fifteen years older than Hanson, with a Sydney University law degree and a twelve-year stint as a New

South Wales Supreme Court solicitor to his name, but ideologically the two politicians were peas in a pod.

Also from a big, lower-middle-class family, and also the youngest (of four boys), Howard had grown up near his father's service station in a modest bungalow in Earlwood. Like Hanson, he'd learnt from an early age to value self-sufficiency and the work ethic, and to respect the political opinions of uneducated people like his parents, both of whom had left school at fourteen. Like Hanson, Howard was inordinately proud of his family's military record: his father and grandfather had both served with distinction on the Western Front in World War I, helping to halt a German advance in the 1918 battle of Villers-Bretonneux. Hanson's grandfather had fought fearlessly at Gallipoli, surviving a bullet in his lung after a Turkish doctor found him half-dead in the trenches and gave him water. From the time they could walk, little Pauline and John had both risen at dawn every Anzac Day to cheer on the brave veterans who had given their all for the nation.

'You could already sense, leading into the '96 election, that he was very keen on taking us back to the Australia as he knew it and he loved,' Neville Roach observes of Howard. 'What worried me is that we were going to change from a progressive, very successful Labor government, to a very conservative one. Everything had been moving in the right direction. And the entire thing was going to change.'

'He is truly the most conservative leader the Liberal Party has ever had,' Keating thundered to the party faithful at the 1996 Labor Party election campaign launch.

'As a nation, we of course carry with us a projection of Western civilisation, of our relationships with so many of the nations of Europe,' Howard countered stiffly at a Liberal Party event, asserting his unfashionable fidelity to Australia's Anglo-European roots.

In November 1995, as the tussle between Keating's dynamic, Asia-focused future and Howard's Anglo-centric vision of a nation 'comfortable and relaxed' about its past began to heat up, Hanson made a fateful decision. Snatching a precious break from her fish shop and three younger children, she swapped her green uniform for a neat suit and heels, and fronted up to a federal preselection meeting at a local Liberal branch in Ipswich.

The way she recalls it now, no single incident finally compelled her to convince the Liberals she had what it took to wrest the federal seat of Oxley, safely held by Labor for thirty-seven years, out of incumbent Les Scott's hands. Rather, she was driven by an accumulating sense of frustration. Furious with Keating, she nurtured an unshakeable belief that she, not he, knew what was best for the people of Ipswich, and a burning conviction that the erosion of traditional Anglo-Australian values under Labor's multiculturalism had to stop. Hanson had simply had enough.

'Political correctness was shutting us down and people felt they didn't have a voice,' she reflects. 'One person can't change anything. But you can be the vehicle. If people want to sit back and stay around the barbecue and whinge and complain all the time, and see their rights and democracy slipping away, they've got no-one to blame but themselves.'

Hanson's belief that she could be a credible federal candidate was bolstered by her experience in local government. Many of her customers, impressed with what she achieved on Ipswich council, told her she was the right man for the job. 'When I was in the local government, I saw the waste that was happening and I thought if I could fix someone's driveway or whatever, I got the satisfaction. And that's what got me into politics. I'd gotten that many letters from people, and I said, "You're going to have to send this to your local member," and they said, "I do, but they don't do anything about it." I get a great satisfaction out of helping people.'

Two other Liberal Party members were vying – somewhat reluctantly – for federal preselection on the night of the meeting in Ipswich. The view was that someone had to front up for the conservatives, even if Labor, just as it had for the last fourteen elections, was going to win. Hanson's disillusioned competitors spoke dutifully of new car parks and better municipal services. Hanson, nervous but determined, spoke last. 'I was very new to the party and I had to get up and give a speech. I spoke off the cuff and told them I was going to put my money where my mouth is, and I won it!' she remembers with pride.

The Oxley Liberals hid their incredulity and relief, and wished Hanson luck. The fact that no-one thought she had a chance didn't enter Hanson's mind. 'Look, I didn't go into it thinking I couldn't win my seat. I don't have that attitude!' she says, with the same never-say-die spirit that would see her take on another 'unwinnable' election twenty years later, for the 2016 federal Senate.

'I went in to win my seat!'

Enlisting her devoted ex-boyfriend Morrie Marsden as campaign manager, Hanson photocopied a black-and-white flyer promoting her political bona fides as a true-blue, small-business-owning Aussie battler, hired a Laotian woman, Lilly Vichitthavong, to manage her shop, and began a gruelling grassroots campaign through the suburbs of Ipswich.

Hanson was facing an uphill battle. The vast majority of Oxley's 75 492 voters had voted Labor for generations. Disenchanted with the pro-immigration, globalist policies of Keating, they nonetheless still nursed a deeply ingrained, old-school Labor animosity towards the blue-chip conservatives of the LNP, and the 'exploitative capitalist bosses' who voted for them. Almost half of Oxley's adult population had left school by fifteen. Unemployment sat at 10.7 per cent, with the average income a lowly $673 a week. Oxley's embattled residents had witnessed the migrant population balloon to 26 575 under Labor, taking over one-fifth of the electorate. Of these new arrivals, 14 033 came from non-English-speaking countries, with 5712 from South-East Asia. Unable to communicate but determined to survive, Oxley's new wave of migrants worked harder than many Anglo-Australian locals to house and educate their kids.

Footage from the time shows abandoned factory buildings crumbling into the weeds, and shabbily dressed white families wheeling fretful toddlers through run-down malls. To the Australian-born voters of Oxley, the only thing worse than an out-of-touch Labor politician was an out-of-touch Liberal one. As Les Scott cruised the streets in his air-conditioned campaign van, assuring people that everything, under Labor, would be fine, Hanson went on foot from house to house, door-knocking, enduring scorn and derision, doors slammed in her face, and the unwanted attention of barking Rottweilers. Debriefing with Morrie over chow mein at the Marco Polo, Hanson quickly realised she'd taken on an impossible task.

Then, a month into her floundering campaign, four words changed everything. Watching the ABC in her cottage in Silkstone on 2 January 1996, Hanson saw the Minister for Aboriginal and Torres Strait Islander Affairs, Robert Tickner, an architect of the 1987–1991 Royal Commission into Aboriginal Deaths in Custody, implore the states to 'act on their responsibilities' and find alternatives to jail for Indigenous offenders, to avert a growing national tragedy. Hanson saw red.

'I was incensed by this because if you've done a crime there has to be a form of punishment. I saw it as a division between Aboriginal and non-Aboriginal. It just reflected back about how I felt about everything at the time. There was a struggle for small businesses to survive and especially Robert Tickner with his comments about Aboriginals, well, jeez, I'm putting my kids through school – why should they get extra money? The whole thing was not fair. The police never locked up the Aboriginals, and if the bike was stolen the cops would say, "How much is it?" and write you a cheque. You had escalating crime, and people felt it was becoming an unsafe society. Tickner's saying, "Let's not lock up Aboriginals," after $400 million being spent into Deaths in Custody, and it hadn't done a damn thing. So I got angry.'

Hanson sat down in her sunroom, and in the looping, painstakingly symmetrical cursive that had won her top marks at Coorparoo State, penned a letter to the *Queensland Times*. 'I didn't run it past anyone; it was my opinion and I still stand by it,' she says.

When it was published on 6 January, Hanson's letter to the editor caused a political firestorm. The Liberal candidate for Oxley had broken a major taboo: while a tolerant and generous approach to Indigenous policy dominated both sides of politics in the mid-1990s, she accused the Keating government of 'reverse racism' for awarding special privileges to Aboriginal Australians. Even today, Hanson's letter is shocking in its blunt refusal to acknowledge that Indigenous and non-Indigenous Australians do not, and never did, inhabit a level playing field.

'Imagine what type of country this would be to live in if Aborigines didn't go to jail for their crimes. One of these men was convicted for twelve years, and it wasn't just for speeding fines,' Hanson wrote, of one of the Indigenous men Tickner had tried to protect.

> The Indigenous people of this country are as much responsible for their actions as any other colour or race in this country. The

problem is that politicians in all their profound wisdom have and are causing a racism problem.

I would be first to admit that, not that many years ago, Aborigines were treated wrongly, but in trying to correct this we've gone too far. I don't feel responsible for the treatment of Aboriginal people in the past because I had no say but my concern is for the future.

How can we expect this race to help themselves when governments shower them with money, facilities and opportunities that only these people can obtain no matter how minute the indigenous blood is that flows in their veins, and that is what is causing racism. Until governments wake up to themselves and start looking at equality not colour then we might start to work together as one.
Pauline Hanson

The day Hanson's letter hit the local press, Paul Tully, an old Labor foe on Ipswich council, alerted the national media. The rookie candidate for Oxley was suddenly on the federal radar: a 'racist, red-headed redneck', gleefully held up by Howard's opponents in parliament as proof that the Liberal Party endorsed extremists, and lacked the centrist steady hand that was required to govern.

Howard was alarmed. Hanson's outburst followed hot on the heels of two other controversial statements by Coalition candidates. The National Party's Bob Burgess had cheerfully described Australian citizenship ceremonies as 'de-wogging' events, while the pro-assimilation, Lebanese-descended Bob Katter dismissed Burgess's outraged multicultural critics as 'little slanty-eyed ideologues who persecute ordinary average Australians'.

Determined to present as a moderate in the face of Keating's relentless accusations that he was going to take Australia back 'to the Dark Ages' and stood to the right of Genghis Khan, Howard was battling claims that he was a racist himself. Political commentators and the multicultural left had not forgotten his ill-judged 1988 observation that the pace of Asian immigration should be 'slowed down a little so that the capacity of the community to absorb [it] were greater'.

As Howard faced the blistering force of Keating's derision in Canberra, Hanson was mobbed by the press in Silkstone. Locals doing their errands on Blackstone Road were greeted with the alien sight of Marsden's sleepy shopfront bristling with camera vans and reporters baying for the candidate for Oxley's blood.

'The Liberal Party rang me up, told me to pull my head in, and released an apology on my behalf. And the media said, "They apologised for you," and I said, "No I won't," and I actually expanded on it,' Hanson remembers with satisfaction.

News reports of the event show the startled Hanson, in her double denim work gear, frozen at the fish shop doorway like a possum in a spotlight. It was the first time she'd faced a television camera since her childhood stint on *Jill and Beanpole Present*. Quavering but firm, she stared down her interrogators: 'A lot is given to the Aboriginal community that is not available to the white community.'

Hanson's refusal to retract her comments inflamed an already volatile situation. Anonymous callers threatened to vandalise Marsden's, Keating upped his attacks on Howard's 'backwards' candidates, and the media went to town. Campaigning in the Ipswich suburbs, Hanson received a distressed phone call from the 65-year-old woman who was minding her shop. Protesters were planning a huge rally on Blackstone Road if Hanson did not immediately apologise. Hanson, always protective of the most vulnerable of her tribe, rang the media and exploded.

'I said, "No-one threatens my business or my staff." I can't stand threats and bullying,' Hanson flashes, with the same lockjawed anger that played on her pale, pinched face as she climbed out of her boxy white sedan behind Marsden's and stomped past the yelling press pack in 1996.

Australians watched the unfolding Hanson saga with uneasy fascination. In Canberra, a rising star in the press gallery, Margo Kingston, took note. Rangy, iconoclastic and razor sharp, the chain-smoking, left-leaning Kingston had earned the respect of politicians, readers and journalists as a fearless crusader for the independence of the fourth estate. Kingston, then political chief of staff for Fairfax, recalls huddling around a TV set with elite reporters in Parliament House after long days on the federal campaign trail, marvelling at the 'redneck alien' from Ipswich. Uneducated, blunt and outrageously off-script when it came to the mid-1990s orthodoxy of inclusivity, Hanson was mesmerising to Kingston: a bizarre exception to the evasive, heavily scripted politicians she was facing daily on the hustings.

Hanson was 'a shot of oxygen for a jaded media reporting to a jaded public', Kingston says, remembering her disillusionment with federal politics at the time. The 1996 election campaign was one of the first American-style, spin-driven, aggressively orchestrated leadership contests in Australia. Keating and Howard announced their policies to hand-picked constituents in secret locations, to which journalists were bussed in packs. With little advance notice of the day's itinerary, and with Howard and Keating staying on message in glossy photo ops designed for the front page of the broadsheets, the print media were corralled behind the cameras at the back of the pack. Kingston, a strong believer in the crucial role a free press plays in a healthy democracy, had little autonomy, access or reach.

'We'd lost our ability to get questions answered. We were just characters in a play,' Kingston says of the campaign, which she and her colleagues quickly dubbed the Magical Mystery Tour. 'It's totally controlled, it's set up for the media, you don't get the policy till the doorstop, it is not a serious engagement at all. It was just awful – you never knew where you were going. If you thought about it as getting the story for the people, it just wasn't going to happen.'

Like Hanson, Kingston is a self-deprecating Queenslander, raised to value honesty and mateship over pretension and social grandstanding. In January 1996, when Hanson published her incendiary letter slamming so-called Aboriginal privilege, many of Kingston's relatives in the blue-collar logging town of Maryborough were expressing the same resentment. But they were doing so in the privacy of their kitchens. Hanson's outburst sent shockwaves through the political establishment not just because it contrasted so sharply with the prevailing orthodoxy. Just as shocking was the fact that the fish and chip shop lady, an uneducated, backwoods nobody, had dared to blaspheme out loud.

'My first response was, "Now John Howard's going to have to act." That's all I cared about,' remembers Kingston. 'I'm in the press gallery and it's all about power. I didn't think much of it at the time, except, "Oh well, she said something about race, John Howard will have to move."'

And move he did. Howard publicly chastised his two National Party candidates, Burgess and Katter, but declined to sack them. The Liberal Party reserved its ire for Hanson.

On the evening of 14 February, sixteen days before election day, Hanson was cleaning out the oil vats in Marsden's when she received a furious call from the state director of the Queensland Liberal Party, Jim Barron.

'He said, "We f-ing want you down here now. Do you

understand me? I want you f-ing down here!"' Hanson says.

Still in her grease-spattered uniform and boots and smelling of fish, Hanson drove straight to Liberal Party HQ in Brisbane. Morrie Marsden came with her for moral support. Barron, a moderate Liberal with a progressive bent on race, was livid.

'He started swearing again and my campaign manager said, "Cut your language," and he said, "She's gone too far this time, she's got to go." And all these people trampsed past into the boardroom and they called me in with Morrie, and said, "We want your resignation." And that is when [they] said it came from John Howard, that I had to go,' Hanson recalls. Howard 'was terrified of losing because of a female candidate who was standing for the Labor seat of Oxley. Katter was also being outspoken, [but] I was the only female.'

Howard's version of Hanson's removal from the Liberal Party, as one might expect of an elder statesman intent on preserving his own legacy, is more prosaic. 'I certainly remember the incident. But it didn't figure very large,' he says dismissively, seated at a gleaming mahogany table in his Martin Place office.

'I was told she'd asserted these views about Indigenous people, which were wrong, in fact. The Queensland branch of the Liberal Party as a result wanted to disendorse her, they asked me and I agreed. I didn't give it a lot of thought. I didn't think we'd win in Oxley. I accepted the judgement of the Queensland Liberal Party that she should be disendorsed, and that was that.'

Shattered, Hanson returned with Morrie to Doyle Street. The fact that the Liberals had been happy to dump her, even when it was too late under federal election rules to put up another candidate, was demoralising. Hanson's father, Jack, was deeply upset with his firebrand fifth child.

'Dad said, "Why did you open your mouth, you will never change anything. It's a dirty game,"' recalls Hanson. 'And I said,

"It's because of people like *you* that things don't change."'

As Jack and Hanson argued, Morrie quietly scoured the Australian Electoral Commission regulations. Then he interrupted them with startling news. Hanson could still run: as an independent. Jack was appalled. But Hanson, just as she had when she took over Marsden's, stood up to him.

'I said, "You know what, Dad? I am going to have a go,"' she remembers. 'It was the same thing when I bought the shop. He said, "You can't do it," but I thought how many sacks of spuds, et cetera, and I worked it out. And it was the same with politics.'

Listening to his headstrong youngest daughter, Jack may have regretted the lesson he'd taught her under the studio lights of *Jill and Beanpole Present*: that it doesn't matter if you win or lose, as long as you have a go.

I ask Hanson if the decision she made that night, to keep fighting her election campaign solo, came from a need to prove her father wrong. The theory annoys her. 'I didn't need to prove anyone wrong. It was all about my inner strength, self-respect, who I was, what I believed in. Not to prove my dad or anyone wrong. Dad was the quiet one, and Mum was the goer. And she said, "If I was younger, I'd be right up there with you!"'

The day after the Liberals disendorsed her, Hanson rose at 4 a.m. to drive to the fish markets at Colmslie. Her fisherman mate Rocco greeted her with a blaring newspaper headline – *Hanson Sacked!* Jim Barron had made sure the Coalition's divorce from Hanson and her dangerous views was all over the media. Greek and Italian buyers ribbed Hanson good-naturedly. Today's news is tomorrow's fish wrapper, after all – now she could add a personal touch to her Marsden's takeaway packs.

Heartened, Hanson drove back to the shop to unpack her weekly haul and put it on ice. Backing into her car space behind the skips, she was suddenly mobbed by a gargantuan media pack. She hightailed it out of the car park to her cottage in Doyle Street, and a press pack was waiting for her there too.

'The media frenzy was unbelievable. They were all outside the front of the shop with their cameras, every TV station, then they heard where my house was and they all came down here, and that's when I finally had to go outside and stand in the carport and talk to them.'

On the concrete slab under Doyle Street's lopsided awning, where Hanson's loyal supporter Jonathan now enjoys his nightly fag, the disgraced politician squared off against the cameras.

'I am not racist. I just want equality for all,' she told them shakily, and announced she was still running for Oxley.

'I just stood by what I said. Nothing had changed,' she says now, of her refusal to appease the Liberals and her decision to keep fighting alone, with her controversial views intact. 'I'd made up my mind. I didn't want to be in a party where I was a yes person. "Sit down, shut up, you know nothing, we know everything. You just put up your hand and shut up unless you're on the front benches." And I thought, this is not what politics is about.'

The national media immediately wrote Hanson off. Without the infrastructure and support of the Liberal Party, she was toast. 'I thought, as everyone in the press gallery and politics thought, that she was gone,' Kingston recalls. 'When Howard disendorsed Pauline Hanson, everyone in the elite in Australia thought, "That will be the last we'll ever hear of her."'

Hanson, unfazed, changed her corflutes from 'Liberal' to 'Independent' and continued her campaign outside the spotlight. If Jim Barron's media ambush had been intended to shame her into oblivion, it had the opposite effect. As Hanson walked from house to house in the downtrodden backstreets of Ipswich, doors that had once been slammed in her face were suddenly open to her. In the mall, on the footpaths, even in the changing rooms of her favourite dress shop, Hanson was approached by people of all ages, congratulating her on standing firm and shyly offering their help. Many had voted Labor all their lives. Others were Liberal supporters appalled by Howard's treatment of Hanson.

Oxley's 4246 Indigenous voters quietly kept their distance, as support for the little fish shop lady who'd stood up to the Liberal bigwigs steadily grew.

'I had to run [the campaign] from my shop because I couldn't afford to put staff on all the time. And sixteen days out from the election, the public momentum, people from all over came to help. We just changed the corflutes and I didn't have to do much. It just happened for me,' Hanson beams.

Oblivious of the surging support for Hanson, the national media juggernaut rolled on, focused on the only story that mattered: the momentous battle being fought out by Keating and Howard for control of Australia's future.

In cosmopolitan Melbourne and Sydney, the elegant Keating was mobbed by crowds of screaming, multiracial schoolgirls, like a rock star at Big Day Out. But in the back rooms and boardrooms of the corporate lobbyists and political strategists, the smart money was quietly moving to Howard. In the final weeks of the campaign, the opposition leader worked the wavering middle ground with cunning precision, alternating coin-toss photo ops with popular cricket players and patriotic statements about Australia's allegiance to Empire with carefully orchestrated appearances at multicultural events, designed to reassure nervous non-Anglo voters that he would not abandon them in power.

Archival footage shows the stark difference between the Keating and Howard campaigns. As Keating strides regally in front of Reichstag-sized backdrops, extolling Labor's bold vision for Australia as a new powerbroker in the Asia-Pacific region, the uncoordinated Howard stumbles off one-foot-high rostrums, framed by his folksy 'For All of Us' banners. Confident but modest, he delivers small-target statements in inner-city community halls, as sari-clad women and Chinese-Australian businessmen 'spontaneously' emerge from the clapping crowds to shake his hand and offer him flowers.

Kingston, unlike many of her staunchly Labor colleagues in the press gallery, was tuned in to the changing mood. She had already decided to award her own vote to the Liberals in the lower house and Labor in the Senate. 'Australia was over Keating and was looking for – John Howard picked it – Australia was looking for "relaxed and comfortable",' she explains. 'We wanted to settle down. Australians had been traumatised, there was a tremendous split caused by Mabo, particularly for country people. They had been through the republic debate – they felt that Keating was too hifalutin on social issues. Australians wanted to just get the economy sorted and do their own thing.'

Howard agrees, describing a nation that was hungry for change after five terms of increasingly self-satisfied Labor rule. 'There was a weariness in the Australian community with some of the political correctness of the Keating government. I think Australians had got a little bit tired of all the navel-gazing: were we Asian or part Asian or in Asia, involved in Asia, European, Western . . .' he reflects wryly.

'Fundamentally, Australia was always part of Western civilisation. We'd always been seen as Aussies. One of the big myths about Australia and Asia is that we got confused with the British. We didn't. Australians were always identifiable. Keating's biggest mistake was to believe we had to shun our British associations to ingratiate ourselves with Asia. That was nonsense. I never had any trouble with my relationships with Asia, saying we had close links to America and the British. They understood who we were, and knew our history better than a lot of us do. Just as they respected their own histories and traditions, they respected countries and leaders who did the same thing about their own history and traditions.'

'So which Australians did you mean, with your slogan "For All of Us"?' I ask.

'"For All of Us"? I think it's self-evident. You should govern for everybody,' Howard replies.

'Is that possible?'

'If you provide security, economic stability and national pride, the answer is yes.'

Behind Howard in the room where we're filming is a floor-to-ceiling bookshelf, laden with mementos that capture the unthreatening, homespun appeal he held for voters in 1996, as Keating's flashy pronouncements failed to gain traction. Bats, portraits and baggy greens signed by Merv Hughes and other cricket legends share pride of place with framed pictures of the diminutive Howard grinning like a fanboy with the towering athletes of Australia's world-class rugby and swimming teams. In photos taken during his third and fourth terms, Howard is more polished, his bearing more stentorian and powerful. But as he poses with the Queen, George W Bush, Bill Gates, Tony Blair and the Pope, his slightly goofy smile remains unchanged.

I suggest that one of Howard's chief attractions in 1996 was his underdog status, against the glamorous Keating's impressive cultural, legislative and global record. Australians love to take down a tall poppy, especially when they can replace him with someone they feel is more like themselves; someone like the sports-mad, accident-prone Howard, whose suburban persona, 'commonsense' statements and obvious discomfort in front of the cameras only increased his appeal.

'Can I correct your memory of the time,' Howard tuts. 'We need things in proper historical perspective. Mr Keating may have been cheered by some people, many leaders are. But it's a mistake to say I was the underdog. Most of the polls said there would be a change.' Howard, like Kingston, knew voters across the board were disenchanted with Keating. He classifies these people as 'mainstream Australia' – and positioned himself as their voice.

'"Mainstream Australia" were the views of the majority of Australians. And views that were not based on feelings of shame and guilt about our past, or in exuberant, xenophobic feelings about where Australia was in the world, but a confident belief that this was the best country in the world, and a confident belief that we got a lot of things, indeed most things, right,' Howard states. 'I used the expression "relaxed and comfortable" as a description of how people viewed where we'd been, where we'd come from, and what we'd done.'

On 2 March 1996, Australians queued up in schoolyards and community halls to decide the nation's future. That night, Hanson and her supporters gathered around a crappy television set in Morrie's backyard, to barbecue some snags and watch the returns. On the ABC, Kerry 'Red Kezza' O'Brien held court in the national tally room, as beloved Triple J commentators Rampaging Roy Slaven and H G Nelson provided comic relief. Kingston recalls the electricity and tension in the air as the count began. Seasoned press gallery journalists who'd built their careers covering the progressive legacies of Hawke and Keating stared at their TV screens in trepidation.

The verdict of the Australian people revealed itself with shocking speed: well before midnight, it was clear that Howard had stormed home in a bloodbath. Labor's visionary run was over. The jubilant look on conservative stalwart Michael Kroger's face as he stared down the barrel from the tally room contrasted with the sense of shock and foreboding in the mainstream media, as the Coalition seized power across the nation. 'John Howard is the new prime minister of Australia,' Kroger said, with quiet finality. To Keating's faithful, his words were a death knell.

News footage shows the triumphant Howard sweeping onto the stage of the gilt-edged 1980s Sydney Hilton ballroom to claim victory, with his wife, Janette, and three beaming children in tow. 'We have been elected with a mandate,' he declared – and the champagne-toting, black-tie crowd erupted in an ecstatic cheer.

'I feel a lot more relaxed and comfortable now, don't you, Roy?' H G Nelson drawled to the disheartened studio audience at the ABC. 'The new Mr Asia, John Howard!' Roy Slaven retorted, capturing the shocking magnitude of Howard's win with a rapturous punch of his fist.

Howard's 1996 'mandate' remains one of the few in Australian election history that is not up for dispute. Labor won 38.75 per cent of the primary vote: its lowest result since 1934. The Coalition picked up twenty-six new seats in the House of Representatives, with the ALP losing a staggering thirty-one. The thirty-eighth federal parliament would be run by seventy-five Liberals, eighteen Nationals, one Country Liberal Party member, and forty-nine Labor survivors. Five independents also secured seats in the lower house. The usual grab bag of colourful characters were destined for the crossbench: two disenchanted ex-Liberals (Allan Rocher and Paul Filing), one defected Labor maverick (Graeme Campbell), and a popular TV reporter turned rural-rights advocate, Peter Andren. But only Pauline Hanson succeeded in raising an eyebrow from the ABC's fastidious election analyst, Antony Green.

'Well, these are remarkable results and show some extraordinary things going on in Queensland,' Green observed to reporter

Maxine McKew, as the election graphic for Oxley showed the bold red pillar of Les Scott's vote rapidly descending.

'This is a seat that's obviously about as Labor as you can get!' McKew gasped, staring at the count in astonishment.

Footage of Morrie's election night barbecue, shot by the only TV crew that had the foresight to turn up, showed Hanson in a block-print dress, blushing and incredulous in a plastic chair, as her four children and the volunteers who had manned her polling booths spontaneously stood and cheered.

'Pauline Hanson has won the seat of Oxley,' Green noted with mild surprise, before returning to his analysis of Labor's ignominious demise.

'Pauline for the Lodge next!' yelled one of Hanson's supporters at the camera, waving a beer. The tableau of modestly dressed, underprivileged Anglo-Australians around him, cheerfully waving their sausages and corflutes, represented Hanson's support base in miniature: a snapshot of things to come.

'Hanson tapped in to Anglo-Australians, poor, disaffected and feeling like they did not have a say in their future or how the country was run,' observes the Labor member for Barton, Linda Burney. Oxley's disaffected voters had delivered Hanson to power in a landslide, making her the first female independent in history to win a seat in the lower house. She'd beaten Les Scott with a 19.31 per cent swing – the biggest swing achieved by any of the 148 candidates elected to the 1996 House of Representatives. The Ipswich fish and chip shop lady had found her demographic.

'I was very surprised to win. I was tired, absolutely worn-out,' remembers Hanson happily. 'I was blown away by the response.'

Professor Marcia Langton, on the other hand, sees Hanson's win as all too sadly predictable. 'I was not surprised when she was elected to parliament. That kind of whingeing and whining about Aborigines, for those of us from rural Australia, that was the norm.'

'I was a little bit surprised, but there were many surprises on the night of the March 2 1996 election,' Howard cautions, keen to place Hanson's win where it belongs: in the shadows of his own extraordinary triumph. 'We had a huge swing in Queensland, the highest two-party-preferred vote for our side since Federation. It was remarkable – the high-water mark. I actually think [Hanson's] disendorsement made the difference between her winning and just falling short, because it actually liberated a lot of disgruntled Labor voters from the obligation of not voting for an official Liberal candidate.'

Hanson flushes with pleasure when I tell her Howard admitted that the Liberal Party's treatment of her was a major factor in her election. 'The whole fact is, I won the seat. And maybe if he hadn't done anything about it, I wouldn't have been elected to parliament. So I've got to thank John Howard for that!'

Historic though Hanson's win may have been, no-one in the mainstream media gave it more than a passing thought on election night. 'The big story was the end of an era. We'd had a change of government for the first time in thirteen years, that was huge!' Kingston says. 'As far as any reaction to Hanson goes, I thought, "Ah well, Queensland does some funny things sometimes."'

But as Kingston and the press gallery dissected what a Howard government would mean for Australia, one man nursed a beer in a Kalgoorlie pub, 3771 kilometres from Morrie's barbecue in Ipswich, and watched Hanson frying sausages for her delighted supporters with tunnel-visioned focus.

John Pasquarelli was the notoriously brutal spin doctor for Hanson's new crossbench colleague, the anti-immigration Kalgoorlie independent Graeme Campbell MP. With a Sydney

University arts degree and a brief affair with superstar feminist Germaine Greer under his belt, Pasquarelli had a gift for words, and an uncanny ability to get uber-right politicians onto the air. Six foot three, big-boned and completely bald, Pasquarelli was the grandson of a Northern Italian migrant who'd worked in the Queensland cane fields, and the son of an army doctor who'd studied with the heroic World War II surgeon Weary Dunlop.

Fond of telling his left-wing mates in Melbourne he'd been successfully 'de-wogged', Pasquarelli had forged his idiosyncratic career with the machismo of Ernest Hemingway. He'd hunted for crocodiles, mined for gold, and served as a Papua New Guinea parliamentarian in the 1960s, before turning his unique talents to Australian politics. Rendered partially deaf by Ménière's disease and afflicted by random hallucinations, Pasquarelli was volatile, foul-mouthed and brilliant. In the influential political and media circles he inhabited, he was both feared and revered, and was known simply as Kojak.

'She's going to need your help,' Campbell told Pasquarelli the night Hanson was elected. Pasquarelli finished the fistfight he'd started with some snooker players in the Kalgoorlie pub, jumped in a mate's car to dodge the approaching police, and sped to the airport.

'One was part Abo. I gave him a smack in the ear, I think . . .' Pasquarelli recalls of the fight. 'Anyway, by the time the police arrived – I suppose they were going to charge me with assault – I was off and gone and in the air on the way to Ipswich.'

Together, Kojak and Hanson would craft a speech that would change the nation.

Chapter 5
The maiden speech

I believe we are being swamped by Asians. They have their own culture and religion, form ghettos and do not assimilate.
—Pauline Hanson, maiden speech, 10 September 1996

Since the arrival of TV in the decade Hanson was born, every twentieth-century democracy has produced a handful of audio-visual memories so powerful that they changed the political tide. Shocking archival flashes that once seen cannot be forgotten. Americans have JFK's assassination, Watergate and the naked Vietnamese girl fleeing a napalm attack at Trang Bang. The British have the Falklands War, Johnny Rotten snarling 'God Save the Queen' and Princess Di's fatal crash in the Pont de l'Alma tunnel. Canadians can visualise the day the red maple leaf graced their flag and the failed secession of Quebec. South Africans remember when Nobel-winning human rights activist Nelson Mandela was jailed for life and the day that apartheid died.

And any Australian old enough to be watching the news in the second half of the twentieth century can still see Gough Whitlam, sacked but defiant, raging against Sir John Kerr on the steps of Old Parliament House; Alan Bond's ingenious winged-keeled yacht,

Australia II, winning the America's Cup; and a sharp-eyed redhead in a brass-buttoned jacket standing in the near-empty House of Representatives to declare in a quavery voice that we were 'in danger of being swamped by Asians'.

'It was an electric shock to the political system. It changed politics,' says journalist Margo Kingston of the maiden speech Hanson delivered on 10 September 1996.

'She let the genie out of the bottle,' says the man who drafted it, John Pasquarelli.

'Hanson's basic instinct, being a fish and chip shop owner from Ipswich, was to hate Aborigines. She also hated Asians. She let the dogs out, basically. I don't think politics has been the same since,' says Professor Marcia Langton.

'A lot of people think [it] changed Australia. I still hear to this day that it has,' says Hanson of the words that ripped through the country like a thunderbolt, catalysing its gradual devolution from a multicultural success story to an increasingly divided society fractured by fear, suspicion and violence.

'I think what it did was open up debate,' Hanson continues, matter-of-fact. 'I dared say something that many other Australians were thinking. I think they got a shock to see someone standing on the floor of parliament and actually expressing this.'

Art critic Robert Hughes saw Hanson's speech as nothing more than 'the burps and farts from the deep gut of Australian racism'. But to Hanson's bullish adviser, Pasquarelli, it is 'the most significant maiden speech in Australian political history'.

The words delivered by the Member for Oxley two decades ago are now seared into the national consciousness. In twenty-one short minutes, Hanson wrote herself into history.

The process of getting her there, Pasquarelli attests, was tortuous. Being Hanson's spin doctor, he says, was like being 'a gun horse breaker, unable to get a bridle on a flighty and stubborn filly'. Their nine-month professional relationship, as the political hardman doggedly transformed his inexperienced new charge from a redneck pariah to a nascent populist force, would prove rocky, rewarding and treacherous.

Hanson and Kojak met on 3 March 1996, the day after she was elected. Media crews were camped in her front yard at Doyle Street, waiting for the startled new member for Oxley to emerge. They were like 'a swarm of blowflies trapped in a half-empty beer bottle', Pasquarelli growls. 'This media avalanche was a thing she couldn't understand. Pauline was, I think, desperate, trying to work out what had happened to her. Her voice was gone, all that sort of stuff. So first I cleared out the media maggots, then I gained entry to her house and we had a cup of tea.'

Footage of the day shows Pasquarelli in a cream safari suit, thudding towards the press pack like a bull elephant, murder in his eyes. 'I thought, "Am I in the right place or not? Is there a domestic going on here? Has someone been killed?"' he grimaces. 'There were people all through her yard and peering into her windows with cameras and everything, and I thought, "Oh shit, this is no good." And I saw [Channel 9 reporter] Lane Calcutt and thought, "I hope this bloke doesn't know judo," because I went right to him and said, "Get this mob and piss off back to the street where you belong. This is this woman's private property. It's a nice warm Queensland day, and the beer in the pub is nice and cold. So go and have a drink and calm down!" And I managed to broom them out.'

Hanson hired Pasquarelli on the spot. 'He was the right man at the right time,' she says. 'From the very first moment he stepped on my property, he took control of the media and was in my good books from then. He sorted it all out and gave me a break from it all. He had media savvy, a wealth of knowledge and experience with politics, he was spot-on, and I couldn't have had anyone better.'

Pasquarelli, as Hanson's senior political adviser, tackled an already hostile media by doing what he did best: attacking back. On 7 March, the ABC's *7.30 Report* shot a program with Hanson, brokering a meeting between her and leaders of the Purga Elders and Descendants Aboriginal Corporation in Ipswich. Hanson agreed to the meeting on the understanding it wouldn't be filmed.

'I said, "I want to meet the elders and have a talk with them but no media," and they agreed with me,' remembers Hanson. 'I turned up, [went] to the house, and immediately these women started pouring out, calling me racist and white trash!'

The report shows Hanson in a black-and-white cowboy shirt, shaking with indignation as two Indigenous women angrily tell her to leave.

Pasquarelli was furious. 'The Purga thing was a set-up. I told Pauline to speak to these people, of course, they were her constituents. But our mates in the media got an Aboriginal lady to be the stooge and abuse Pauline for the cameras and she called Pauline a white bitch. And that was the end for me. I said all bets are off, particularly the ABC, finito. You're gone. And I banned them. It worked a treat!'

The program that made Pasquarelli ban the ABC, reducing its female producer to tears, is in fact a balanced look at Hanson's 'reverse racism' claims about Indigenous aid, contrasting her views with opposing commentators. Whether the women who insulted Hanson at Purga were 'stooges' or justifiably angry is open to interpretation. What is not debatable is that Pasquarelli and Hanson, in banning a major news organisation, pulled off a counterintuitive volte-face that no major democratic leader would be brazen enough to contemplate until 24 February 2017, when President Trump blocked CNN, *The New York Times* and other leading media outlets from a White House press briefing, accusing them of running 'fake news'. By shutting out voices they didn't like, Hanson and Pasquarelli pioneered an unorthodox strategy that now reaps dividends for far-right populists across the globe: show voters you won't kowtow to the 'fakers' of the 'elite, leftist media' and you build your support.

The ABC was a powerful and dangerous enemy to have in 1996. When Hanson arrived in Canberra to begin her federal political career, the newly elected Howard had yet to wind back Keating's generous funding to the public broadcasters, and 'mainstream opinion' in both the public and commercial media sectors was, by today's standards, firmly left-wing.

Walking up to Parliament House to be sworn in as the member for Oxley in April 1996, with the proud Hannorah and her two younger children in tow, Hanson was greeted by a line of Indigenous protesters standing on the forecourt in dignified silence, holding placards denouncing her election. Asked by a reporter if she would stop to speak with them, Hanson, stiff and awkward in a new pink suit, lifted her chin and declared, 'No. I think it's a special day for myself and for the people of Oxley who've, um, elected me to be their representative, and for my children and my mother.'

Untroubled by the possibility that the protesters' grievances were legitimate, Hanson was free to enjoy her day. 'Going into parliament the first time was absolutely overwhelming,' she sighs contentedly. 'I felt honoured, I felt proud, I was very shy in some ways, too. I was absolutely blown away, you know. This is really outside my depth. This isn't behind the counter of the fish and chip shop. This is huge.'

The Ipswich fish shop lady was a fish out of water, both demographically and politically. Footage of the swearing-in ceremony for the thirty-eighth Australian parliament shows Hanson in her bright pink jacket surrounded by expensively suited men, isolated and alone. Her outsider status sits in stark contrast with the effusive reception she'd receive twenty years later, when powerful Coalition and Labor politicians queued up to bestow hugs and congratulations on the newly minted senator after her 2016 maiden speech.

'I was ignored by the other politicians. They didn't want to have anything to do with me,' Hanson says of her 1996 parliamentary debut. 'One explained to me, "A lot of these politicians hate you because they haven't had your publicity and they're jealous that they haven't achieved what you have." And I said, "Well, that's your problem."'

Shunned by her fellow MPs as politically toxic, scorned by the media as a racist throwback, and ridiculed by the left-wing chatterati as an irrelevant and uneducated 'Oxley moron', Hanson quietly moved in to her offices to hire new staff. Pasquarelli's ex-boss, Kalgoorlie MP Graeme Campbell, was one of the few independents to drop in and offer support. The security guards and cafe ladies were friendly to the new politician, but from the major parties only one man went out of his way to acknowledge her existence. The day after she was sworn in, Hanson heard a polite 'Excuse me' as she was walking to the Senate. She turned and looked down. It was John Howard.

'He said, "I wanted to congratulate you on your win." It was amazing he said that to me,' Hanson says, smiling. 'And I turned back and kept walking. Then I went up to the office and told Pasquarelli, and he said, "Oh my God, Pauline, you should have congratulated *him*!" Actually, I was pleased he won and not Keating, so I went back to him the next day and said, "I want to congratulate you."'

Pasquarelli was racing against a ticking clock with his headstrong new client. Hanson's political isolation was compounded by the fact that as a first-time MP she would be unable to speak

THE MAIDEN SPEECH

in the House of Representatives until she had been 'blooded' by her maiden speech. Labor and Liberal ministers could lambaste the rookie politician with impunity as Hanson sat unblinking on the crossbench, unable to answer back.

'Every politician has to have a maiden speech: a definitive speech that breaks the ice. You're not allowed to use the word "maiden" anymore; you have to use the words "First speech",' Pasquarelli snorts derisively. 'So I started to think about what Pauline had to say. And because of that letter to the *Queensland Times* about Abos getting too many benefits, the Liberals wet themselves. I mean, if you read that letter, it's innocuous, absolutely innocuous!'

Pasquarelli was determined to craft a speech that would accelerate the controversy Hanson was already causing; a speech Australians would remember. But Hanson, as the 'shyest' Seccombe sibling, was terrified by the prospect of having to speak, alone and uninterrupted in the House of Representatives, as the nation looked on. Pasquarelli threw his 'unbridled filly' into the deep end. He booked her to address municipal events in Oxley, to break her into public speaking as quickly as possible, and hired a speech therapist to correct her famously shaky voice. He used the hours he spent driving with Hanson around Ipswich and Canberra to research the maiden speech, trying to discover what made her tick.

'I told Pauline, make up your mind because you're going to sink or swim on this. If you want to go away and burble on about, "I come from such and such an electorate and I want to thank my mum and my dad," like a lot of these people do, that's all very nice but it's all so terribly *boring*! This is supposed to be about politics and connecting with people! The speech therapist, I think that was a failure . . .' Pasquarelli guffaws.

Hanson was not easily taught. She sacked the speech therapist after one lesson, appalled at what the woman charged.

Pasquarelli's wry observation that brain surgeons 'cost a hell of a lot more' fell flat.

'I was there for an hour and she said, "There's nothing wrong with you, not a problem." Five hundred dollars later!' Hanson exclaims. 'They used to pull me up on the way I said "Australia". Well, it's the way we were taught in school and it's the Aussie way. I'm sorry, that's how we pronounce it and that's me. I am who I am and that's what you've got. They say, you know, "Now you're going to hear the real Julia" or "the real Abbott", and you won't hear me say that, because I've been the real Pauline Hanson from day one that I got elected and I'm not going to change for anyone!'

'But you often sound like you're about to cry,' I say, coming to Pasquarelli's defence.

Hanson grows solemn. 'I can't help it. There's nothing wrong with my voice box, it's just me. Some people do say I sound very nervous and my voice shakes, but I can't do anything about it. People say, "That's who you are, the way you speak. Don't change yourself for anyone," and I haven't,' she concludes, with that tremulous, upward whine Australians now know so well.

Hanson and Kojak also locked horns over staff. Determined to stick with people she knew, Hanson appointed two women from her fish shop to administer her Ipswich electoral office: a university student and a short-order cook. She allowed Pasquarelli to hire Melbourne journalist Brett Heffernan as a researcher, but ignored his picks for the influential role of electoral secretary, insisting they take on an articulate, well-groomed blonde with strong Coalition ties, Barbara Hazelton. Hazelton had worked for the Queensland National Party senator John Stone and the Nationals MP for Fisher, the now disgraced former speaker Peter Slipper. Pasquarelli, keen to block any leaks to the powerful conservatives, was livid.

THE MAIDEN SPEECH

'Pasquarelli would walk up and down Doyle Street, screaming on his mobile,' remembers Hazelton, speaking to me in Queensland in 2009. '[He] wanted to put me on probation, but Pauline said, "No we don't." She liked me straightaway.' Hanson and Hazelton quickly established a cosy friendship, filling the office with pot plants and magazines, and gossiping over the ministerial desk as Hazelton glued acrylics to Hanson's nails. The oestrogen was too much for Kojak: he'd storm into the leafy office declaring, 'Christ, the only thing missing here is Tarzan and Jane!' and tore into Hanson about a new TV she'd bought with her parliamentary allowance. The $2500 state-of-the-art unit with in-built VCR, according to Pasquarelli, mysteriously vanished from Hanson's Ipswich office the day it was installed – only to magically reappear in the lounge room at her farm.

Hanson, for her part, was furious that her researcher, Brett Heffernan, was reading the newspapers all day on her payroll. 'Thank God someone is!' Pasquarelli shot back at Hanson, who, as Hazelton notes, never read the newspapers herself.

'Pasquarelli picked on Barbara. He used to make her cry,' Hanson says of the high-voltage environment in which the obsessive Pasquarelli thrived. 'He'd put his feet up on the girls' desks. He was very loud because he was partially deaf. I'd say, "This has got to stop. You're bullying and intimidating them."'

'Barbara was more interested in Pauline's lipstick and the seams in her stockings than real work, and it was pretty annoying what I had to put up with,' Pasquarelli counters. When Pasquarelli told Hanson, after one particularly volatile screaming match, that she was incapable of running an office, she was unbowed. 'If I can run a fish shop, I can run anything,' she retorted. No-one in Hanson's office that day was in any doubt that her 'anything' included Australia itself.

'Pasquarelli wanted to control me, and was very much a male

chauvinist,' claims Hanson, who still insists she's no feminist. 'I was on a big learning curve, by all means, but no man intimidates me...' She shoots me a take-no-prisoners glare. 'No woman, neither.'

Despite their office dramas, Pasquarelli and Hanson's first months together, in public at least, were productive. Pasquarelli squired the novice politician around Canberra, introducing her to Doug Blake, a former clerk of the House of Representatives, who told her that although she'd been a big fish in a small pond in Ipswich, in federal politics it would be the reverse. If she forgot her roots and let her head swell, he warned, she'd become 'just another politician'. Pasquarelli took Hanson to the Australian War Memorial, where she paid her respects to her heroic maternal grandfather, Frederick Webster. They stood at the top of Black Mountain, and Hanson reminisced about her paternal grandfather, Norman Seccombe, who she'd been delighted to discover had also been in politics, in the 1930s. DNA and a gift for connecting with strangers seem to be all the two Seccombes shared: Norman was a strong advocate for workers' rights and a loyal member of the ALP.

Surveying the Aboriginal Tent Embassy on the lawn of Old Parliament House, Hanson found herself in furious agreement with Pasquarelli. 'I don't like it and I don't think it should be there,' snaps Hanson of the symbolic monument to Indigenous sovereignty, first erected by Aboriginal campaigners Michael Anderson, Billy Craigie, Tony Coorey and Bertie Williams in 1972. 'I think it's an eyesore, and if it's their way of protesting, then I don't think it's the right way to go about it. I remember back then too, it was so dry in Canberra and they had a complete fire ban and anyone else would have been told, "You cannot have a fire burning here," but they didn't. They had their fires burning and it was so wrong. You can't have this inequality because you could've had trees and homes burning down and all the rest of it. You've got to treat everyone the same.'

To help her overcome her nerves at the podium, Pasquarelli ordered Hanson to imagine him standing at the back of the audience, completely naked. It was an image, she says, with a tiny shudder, that 'didn't inspire me at all'. But she was learning. On 21 March 1996, Hanson fronted the media and her vanquished Labor opponent, Les Scott, and shakily managed to deliver Pasquarelli's Orwellian doublespeak at the official declaration of the poll for Oxley in Ipswich, declaring somewhat ominously, 'I believe all members of society should be treated equally. Once some members of society are seen as being treated more equally than others, divisions are created.'

Bolstered by her performance, Hanson made what was then seen as a shockingly reactionary call for compulsory national service at an Anzac Day event. Three days later, on 28 April, an angel-faced loner named Martin Bryant gunned down thirty-five innocents at Port Arthur in Tasmania. Hanson confidently held her own at a Canberra shooting range, at a meeting Pasquarelli had brokered with the president of the 50 000-strong Sporting Shooters' Association of Australia, Ted Drane. With 100 000 outraged gun owners rallying against new gun reform laws announced by Howard in May, and with Howard sheepishly donning a flak jacket to face his angry opponents at a widely publicised protest in Sale on 16 June, Pasquarelli and Hanson knew they were riding a populist winner.

'I was angry with Howard banning guns. I'm not saying every householder should have a gun, by no means. But he treated every gun owner as an unlawful citizen,' Hanson says, as indignant as a child. 'That's not right! They spent half a billion on the gun buyback scheme!'

Thanks to her trademark directness and her surprisingly accurate amateur pistol skills, Hanson won over the powerful Ted Drane without a hitch. The gun lobby would become one of her first official backers, and a significant donor to her future campaigns.

By 8 July, Hanson's contentious progress as the new member for Oxley had earned her the moniker 'lumpenproletarian hag' in the *Australian Financial Review*. Pasquarelli was delighted. Four months on from her election, it was becoming clear that the more the mainstream media smeared Hanson, the more disenchanted voters rallied behind her. Hanson was now working the podium like a seasoned pro, rejecting Pasquarelli's carefully crafted sound bites to speak off the cuff. 'I had to be me, and I can't just stand there and read from a piece of paper. I'm no different to anyone else,' she says of the raw, unmediated delivery that still defines her political brand. 'It has to come from the heart and you can only do that by speaking to them – not from what's been put in front of you.'

Hanson particularly enjoyed addressing citizenship ceremonies as an honoured federal MP. 'There's this sea of different cultural backgrounds, different nationalities, with big grins on their faces, so proud to be Australians. But I would get up and say, "I welcome you to Australia. But if you don't give this country your undivided loyalty, I'll be first to put you on a plane and wave you goodbye." And they'd burst out laughing, and all the other bureaucrats would be shock-horror. But the [new Australians] would all line up after to get a photo with me, not with them, and I was always the latest one to leave that hall.'

Pasquarelli was grudgingly impressed with Hanson's growing independence. 'She was a filly, a maiden really, with this whole new world all around her. And then the filly has her first race and away we go. The times I got through to Pauline was when we'd go down very early to the fish markets, at sparrow's fart, down there in the dark, and she'd do her business and come back. And I thought, she's got it, physically and mentally. That's when we'd talk a lot, and I'd think I was doing okay.'

But the ticking clock was getting louder. By August 1996, despite her building media profile, Hanson was a standing joke in parliament, having sat mute on the crossbench for months. MPs on both sides of the house took turns to speculate whether the Member for Oxley was capable of stringing a single sentence together, let alone an entire speech. With the unfinished maiden speech 'growling like a beast' in his computer, Pasquarelli loaded Hanson up with political histories, desperate for a personal response to add to his draft. Hanson, he says, threw the books away in tears of frustration, confessing she couldn't 'retain'.

'She was intelligent; she had to be. She ran a fish and chip shop successfully for ten years,' says Pasquarelli, confounded. 'She liked a drink, she was a nonsmoker, and to hold all of that together, the intelligence factor, there's no doubt about it. [But] the education side of it she lost very badly, having left school so early. It's pretty hard to get Pauline to read something and assess it. So I'd mainly read out the draft to her. I had to say, "What do you think about this?" and, "How do you think this will go?" I gave her [Arthur] Calwell's biography – he was a great bloke even though he was a socialist – and I told her, "You can quote this bloke, because he is still very current with what you're saying now," and I remembered Calwell's infamous "Two Wongs don't make a White". But no, she couldn't read it. That's a great shame. I found myself continually trying to equate the intellectually indolent Pauline with the energetic and tireless fish shop lady.'

Hanson bristles at this accusation. 'From the beginning, I used to read lots of books on Aboriginal affairs, et cetera, to try to further my knowledge and educate myself on different matters. This country is built on lots of people who don't have a uni degree. Wisdom is picked up along the way; it doesn't come from textbooks. I have a commonsense approach to things based on my life experiences. Like the man on the land or farmer, his knowledge and experience is far greater than anyone else's. Pasquarelli did say I'd never read the classics, and I'll give him credit for that, so each to their own. But don't underestimate me or any other Australian. Most time people don't have a clue.'

Determined to prove her point, Hanson springs up from her chair and grabs a well-thumbed book from her hallway library. It's by Paul Hasluck, the mid-century Australian politician and historian whose conservative ideas she devoured in the weeks leading up to her maiden speech. Hanson puts on her glasses and leafs through the book to the words that inspired her. 'I was calling for equality, and the difference with what was happening with the government's policies and reverse racism. I was amazed with this line from Hasluck, about the 1950s,' she says excitedly.

'Hasluck said, "a social problem is one that concerns the way people live together in one society. A racial problem is a problem which confronts two different races who live in two separate societies, even if those societies are side by side. We do not want an Australia in which one set of people enjoy one set of privileges and another enjoy another." His vision was "of a single society in which racial interests were rejected and social issues addressed". He's saying here in reference to the white Australians and the interests there, and I thought how relevant it is to the Australians here today, and so I put it in my maiden speech.' Hanson shuts the book triumphantly, having demonstrated her intellectual nous.

If success has many parents and failure is an orphan, Hanson's maiden speech, for anyone who endorses its ultra-right, ubernationalist content, was a monumental success. But trying to get Hanson and Pasquarelli to agree who actually wrote it is like trying to get a pair of cutthroat Hollywood producers to share the credit for Best Picture Oscar. Hanson insists she 'basically wrote' the speech after rejecting Pasquarelli's drafts. Pasquarelli scoffs at this, declaring he wrote the speech 'in toto', and still keeps the original word processor and floppy disks, buried in the bowels of his Townsville study, to prove it. 'You don't let things like this disappear without being totally documented,' he growls.

'He wrote the original,' Hanson concedes. 'And I woke up one morning and read it and said, "This isn't me." I was rehearsing it and I just didn't feel comfortable with it. And I sat down in bed one morning with a pencil and an A4 piece of paper, and I wrote my thoughts on it. And I brought Barbara in and read it, and she was crying, and she said, "That is you. Don't let him change you. It's you." So I brought in Pasquarelli and said, "Just listen to it." And he said, "No, this is your speech," and I said, "No, this is. Now take it and clean it up." He didn't like it at all.'

'Of course she didn't write [it]. Nobody thinks she wrote her own maiden speech, the woman is a halfwit,' Professor Langton observes flatly. 'She was not capable back then of putting more than two or three sentences together in a logical way. She just had a number of catchcries, a series of racist statements. It was the normal abuse of Aboriginal people that was flung at you when you went shopping.'

'It was a bloody good speech,' Pasquarelli responds angrily. Hanson 'came back with a few ideas – what was that thing she had a bee in her bonnet about: child care, family allowances, that sort of thing – and as a concession I had to put [those] elements in'. Pasquarelli coped with the tortuous revision process by going to the cinema in Ipswich. He watched *Mission Impossible* and felt like Tom Cruise's framed American spy. Hanson's changes 'were giving me the irrits big time, but I keep my cool under fire, and we got there in the end', he says.

'It wasn't his speech, it was *my* speech,' Hanson snarls, determined to have the last word. 'I delivered that maiden speech on the floor of parliament, I am proud of it and I was the member for Oxley and not Pasquarelli. I know the truth. He knows the truth. And you know what? I don't give a damn. If it gives an old man pleasure in his later years that he wants the credit for writing my maiden speech, then so be it, but he won't be around for my next one. Knowing Pasquarelli, I am sure he's got my notes that were written by lead pencil in my writing on white paper.' She leans forward and sneers imperiously at the lens, in a clumsy attempt at arch sarcasm: 'So, John, please, will you put them in the will and send them back to me?'

Having filmed Hanson and her estranged spin doctor insulting each other like this for hours, it's clear to me that the speech was actually the brainchild of two uniquely suited collaborators. Pasquarelli's talent for simple, persuasive language melded perfectly with Hanson's defiantly lowbrow vernacular, creating a well-constructed but shockingly raw diatribe that would rip through peaceful 1996 Australia like a homemade Catherine wheel at a fete.

The infamous 'swamped by Asians' line, imaginatively inflated from Brett Heffernan's research on Asian immigration numbers in the mid-1990s, was Pasquarelli's, as were the brutal slap downs of globalisation and Indigenous reconciliation, and the xenophobic calls for Australia to halt immigration, end multiculturalism and ban foreign aid. Hanson inserted salty humour and emotion, slamming economists as men she wouldn't let 'handle my grocery shopping', advancing the proverbial 'feed a man a fish' line as a panacea for all Indigenous woes, and issuing a tremulous call for Anglo-Australian recognition: 'I am fed up with being told, "This is my land." Well, where the *hell* do I go?'

At 4 p.m. on 10 September 1996, as Hanson prepared to deliver these game-changing words, it was business as usual in federal parliament. Greens senator Bob Brown had given his maiden speech without issue, followed by the 31-year-old member for North Sydney, Joe Hockey. The speaker of the lower house announced Hanson was up next, and Coalition and Labor politicians swiftly left the chamber, determined to keep their distance from the unfashionably reactionary member for Oxley.

'They weren't going to listen to this fish and chip shop lady,' Pasquarelli snorts. Independents Graeme Campbell and Peter Andren stayed and waited for Hanson to arrive, along with a few curious Coalition MPs, including De-Anne Kelly and Joanna Gash. In the deserted public gallery, a lone tourist looked on. Bored witless by Joe Hockey's maiden speech, she'd been on the brink of leaving until a parliamentary usher begged her to 'give the lady from Ipswich a fair go'.

But Hanson was nowhere to be seen.

'Pauline went missing. She literally locked herself up in the room and she wouldn't talk,' remembers Pasquarelli. 'And we were starting to get nervous, because she was the last cab off the rank; everyone else had gone. And some smart-arse in the media was saying, "Where's your girl?" and all this sort of stuff.'

'I was terribly nervous,' Hanson recalls. 'I had no family; they weren't there. I had no-one. My knees were shaking. It was a big moment. I'd never even been in a debating team before.' Her jittery state was exacerbated by the tense hours she had just spent with Hazelton, deleting, by hand, the word 'homosexual' from a hundred advance media copies of the speech. At the eleventh hour, Hanson had spotted a homophobic comment inserted by Pasquarelli that she didn't agree with, and insisted it be struck out.

Finally, just before 5.15 p.m., with Kojak and her staff banging on her door, Hanson plucked up the courage to take her place beside Andren and Campbell on the near-empty benches of the lower house. As the chamber's automated TV cameras swivelled towards her, she shakily unfolded her notes and began to speak.

> I come here, not as a polished politician, but as a woman who has her fair share of life's knocks. My view on issues is based on common sense and my experience as a mother of four children, as a sole parent, and a businesswoman running a fish and chip shop. I won the seat of Oxley largely on an issue that has resulted in me being called a racist . . .

Australia was asleep at the wheel. In the press gallery, Kingston and her colleagues were busy filing copy for the 6 p.m. news, with half an ear on the tannoy. 'I don't think anyone in our office knew that she was about to give her maiden speech,' Kingston recalls. 'But when she started, it was just like, "Oh!" She's got this quality that you just, you have to watch it!'

> We have lost all our big Australian industries and icons, including Qantas . . . Now this government wants to sell Telstra, a company that will make a $2 billion profit this year. Anyone with business sense knows that you do not sell off your assets, especially when they are making money. I may be only 'a fish and chip shop lady', but some of these economists need to get their heads out of the textbooks and get a job in the real world. I would not even let one of them handle my grocery shopping . . .

'It did not register on my radar,' says John Howard, a tad huffy. 'It was not seen by me as any kind of dramatic thing. Obviously, I didn't listen to it. She was an independent. I had other things to do.'

THE MAIDEN SPEECH

But as Hanson's high-pitched whine continued to filter through the parliamentary corridors, stunned reporters and politicians began to gravitate around the House of Representatives feed. 'She was obviously nervous and looked quite dark, and it was compelling,' remembers Kingston. 'The entire office gathered round in shock, and Hanson introduced herself to the nation.'

> We now have a situation where a type of reverse racism is applied to mainstream Australians by those who promote political correctness and those who control the various taxpayer-funded 'industries'... servicing Aboriginals, multiculturalists and a host of other minority groups. In response to my call for equality for all Australians, the most noisy criticism came from the fat cats, bureaucrats and the do-gooders. They screamed the loudest because they stand to lose the most – their power, money and position, all funded by ordinary Australian taxpayers...

Among the 'fat cats' and 'bureaucrats' angered by Hanson's words that day were several senior Canberra trade officials hosting a friendship delegation of Hong Kong politicians in parliament. The group's leader, former Hong Kong Democratic Party chair Emily Lau JP, was riveted to the flinty redhead railing on the little TV in the corner of the room. 'The Australian MPs were very annoyed with what she was saying,' Lau recalls. 'And I was shocked that somebody, in what I'd call a civilised parliament, could make such an outrageous speech without blushing!'

> Present governments are encouraging separatism in Australia by providing opportunities, land, moneys and facilities available only to Aboriginals. Along with millions of Australians, I am

fed up to the back teeth with the inequalities that are being promoted by the government and paid for by the taxpayer under the assumption that Aboriginals are the most disadvantaged people in Australia . . .

Beyond the privileged bubble of Capital Hill, Australians from Broome to Brisbane to the Nullarbor started to gather round water coolers, pub counters and kitchen tables, mesmerised by the shockingly off-message words emanating from Canberra. 'I was in my car when I first heard it reported,' recalls Linda Burney MP, then a public school educator. 'I remember the intake of breath, if you like, that happened collectively across the country . . .'

> This nation is being divided into black and white, and the present system encourages this. I am fed up with being told, 'This is our land.' Well, where the *hell* do I go? I was born here, and so were my parents and children. I will work beside anyone and they will be my equal, but I draw the line when told I must pay and continue paying for something that happened over two hundred years ago . . .

Randa Abdel-Fattah, then a seventeen-year-old Muslim schoolgirl in Sydney, was hurt and furious when she heard Hanson's speech. Abdel-Fattah was no stranger to xenophobic abuse: she'd had her hijab ripped from her hair at the shops and had been told many times to take her 'nappy head' back to where it came from. But Hanson's words cut far deeper than random public slurs. 'As the daughter of a Palestinian migrant, I understood the trauma of dispossession and stood in solidarity with Indigenous Australians. What Hanson was saying wasn't new to us, as people from minority communities. What was new was that somebody was actually articulating it, very openly, in parliament.'

> The majority of Aboriginals do not want handouts because they realise that welfare is killing them. This quote says it all: 'If you give a man a fish you feed him for a day. If you teach him how to fish you feed him for a lifetime.' Reconciliation is everyone recognising and treating each other as equals, and everyone must be responsible for their own actions. This is why I am calling for ATSIC to be abolished. It is a failed, hypocritical and discriminatory organisation that has failed dismally the people it was meant to serve . . .

Professor Marcia Langton heard Hanson's call to abolish ATSIC with weary recognition. 'Of course she wanted ATSIC abolished: she wanted native title abolished; she wanted Aborigines to stop identifying as Aborigines,' Langton says. 'Her credo was that if you are Aboriginal and poor, that can't be attributed to your Aboriginality. What she did was take a series of hot topics that riled up that yobbo part of the population, and still upsets those white Australians who feel they are the victims of history. You know, "Aborigines get welfare, Aborigines get houses for free, Aboriginal dogs get welfare cheques, that's why they've got so many dogs," et cetera. String all those sentences together, get Pasquarelli to clean up the grammar, and there you have it, the maiden speech.'

> Arthur Calwell was a great Australian and Labor leader, and it is a pity that there are not men of his stature sitting on the opposition benches today. Arthur Calwell said: 'Japan, India, Burma, Ceylon and every new African nation are fiercely anti-white and anti one another. Do we want or need any of these

people here? I am one red-blooded Australian who says no and who speaks for 90 per cent of Australians.' I have no hesitation in echoing the words of Arthur Calwell.

> Immigration must be halted in the short term so that our dole queues are not added to by, in many cases, unskilled migrants not fluent in the English language. This would be one positive step to rescue many young and older Australians from a predicament which has become a national disgrace and crisis.

In a small flat in the heart of Sydney's pink mile, Simon Hunt, a soft-spoken sound lecturer with a Singaporean boyfriend, recorded Hanson's speech to VHS. 'I remember thinking, "I've got to see more of it, because this is just crazy stuff." It's not like she invented racism, but she was the first to say it out loud.' Hunt, who composed satirical pop-song mashups in his downtime, was as fascinated by Hanson's delivery as he was repulsed by her words. 'Like Adolf Hitler, Pauline Hanson had an unusual voice. It was distinctive; there was something idiosyncratic about the way she put it. Not since Hanson has there been someone that you can listen to a tape of them speaking, and you can say, "that's her"...'

> Immigration and multiculturalism are issues that this government is trying to address, but for far too long ordinary Australians have been kept out of any debate by the major parties. I, and most Australians, want our immigration policy radically reviewed, and that of multiculturalism abolished.
> I believe we are in danger of being swamped by Asians. Between 1984 and 1995, 40 per cent of all migrants coming into this country were of Asian origin. They have their own culture and religion, form ghettos and do not assimilate.

'My big surprise was when she said "swamped by Asians",' remembers Hunt. 'It was almost like a plague, the way she represented it.'

'"Swamped by Asians": people went ape over that,' says Pasquarelli, chuffed.

'I was shocked when she said "swamped by Asians", by yellow people,' recalls Emily Lau. 'That's very racist because she was talking about the colour of the skin. And she was also very disparaging about the blacks or the browns, anything non-white. It was quite devastating. If I'd met her when she came out of the chamber, she'd probably say, "Oh look, this is the yellow peril I'm talking about. She's already swamping Canberra!"'

'Oh yes, "we are being swamped by Asians"!' Dr Thiam Ang intones sardonically. In 1996, Ang was an obstetrician, servicing a bustling multicultural clientele in western Sydney. 'I did remember at that time saying to myself, "Well, it looks like we're going to be in trouble." It was like a signal: "Look! You can actually let loose on these people." The big fear I had is it would start the dehumanisation of people. So when the abuse came, it would be okay, because these guys are "subhuman".'

> Of course, I will be called racist but, if I can invite whom I want into my home, then I should have the right to have a say in who comes into my country. A truly multicultural country can never be strong or united. The world is full of failed and tragic examples, ranging from Ireland to Bosnia to Africa and, closer to home, Papua New Guinea. America and Great Britain are currently paying the price. Time is running out. We may have only ten to fifteen years left to turn things around. Wake up, Australia, before it is too late . . .

The Indian Australian chair of the National Multicultural Advisory

Council, Neville Roach, heard Hanson's words with deep foreboding. She was dog-whistling the haters, and the impact on minorities could be devastating. 'She saw multiculturalism as something that conferred special privileges to "new ethnics", and that was just palpably wrong,' Roach says. 'We were bringing them in because we needed more people, and the value they'd add would be limited if we didn't help them learn English, allow them to settle, let them send their children to school. All those things were necessary to get full value out of what was really the most precious resource. And it took us a while before we would value the diversity they were bringing with them, but everything done for them was applied to all migrants. I mean, the "ten-pound Pom" was helped by us!'

> Australians need and want leaders who can inspire and give hope in difficult times. Now is the time for the Howard government to accept the challenge. Everything I have said is relevant to my electorate of Oxley, which is typical of mainstream Australia. It is refreshing to be able to express my views without having to toe a party line. It has got me into trouble on the odd occasion, but I am not going to stop saying what I think. I consider myself just an ordinary Australian who wants to keep this great country strong and independent, and my greatest desire is to see all Australians treat each other as equals, as we travel together towards the new century.

As ordinary Australians across the country stood round their TVs and radios, mesmerised, revolted, exhilarated and stunned, Hanson wound up her speech. Wide shots captured on the House of Representatives cameras paint an interesting picture. In the almost empty chamber, Pasquarelli's former client Graeme Campbell stares straight ahead, implacable. But the independent for Calare, Peter

Andren, leans as far away from Hanson as is physically possible. His entire body seems twisted in revulsion. Andren would later request to be permanently relocated to a different part of the House.

> I will fight hard to keep my seat in this place, but that will depend on the people who sent me here. Mr Acting Speaker, I thank you for your attention and trust that you will not think me presumptuous if I dedicate this speech to the people of Oxley and those Australians who have supported me. I salute them all.

At 5.36 p.m., Hanson, with a little smile, gathered up her notes and accepted a warm handshake from Campbell. The lone tourist in the public gallery clapped loudly as Hanson exited the chamber, unaware of the powerful new adversaries she had just acquired. Lau, Abdel, Langton, Hunt, Ang and Roach would each work hard to stymie Hanson's rise over the next two years, as she attempted to wrest Australia away from the 'elites' and 'minorities', and return it to the picket-fenced 1950s haven she believed in. A land where traditional values ruled, Indigenous people knew their place, immigrants repressed their heritage, and everyone lived happily inside an Anglo-American melange, united by that unique Australian aspiration defined by novelist Patrick White and mercilessly lampooned by Dame Edna Everage: 'the exultation of the average'.

'I was just pleased that it was over!' Hanson says of the speech that changed the nation. As she and Kojak walked back through the whisper-quiet corridors of parliament, a strange cacophony started to build. On abandoned desks and in empty rooms, faxes and phones were whirring to life. By the time Hanson and Pasquarelli got to their office, the Parliament House switchboard was jammed with jubilant callers from Darwin to Hobart, congratulating

Hanson on 'having the guts' to say what they were thinking.

Pasquarelli relishes the memory. 'Almost immediately, it was on. The phone never stopped ringing. Back then it was those mobile phones you'd carry around like bricks. I started getting calls from people I didn't expect – Malaysians, Indians, Filipinos, all highly complimentary of Pauline. They were calling from across the country, and wouldn't identify themselves because they were frightened. You know, "How dare you talk to that Hanson woman?", that sort of frightened. The Indians were calling because they don't like the Vietnamese. Wake up, Australia, this is multiculturalism! She was getting support from a lot of different people.'

Alongside hundreds of calls from Anglo-Australians and second- and third-generation migrants, messages of support flooded in from Europe, Canada, Japan and the US. Australians were begging for a copy of Hanson's maiden speech, to pass on to their local federal members. Hanson would later give a teddy bear to the parliamentary switchboard operators, in thanks for the overtime they put in that night, working long after her fellow MPs had gone to bed.

As Hanson's staff worked the phones, panicked journalists huddled around their computers in the Senate wing, trying to work out what to do. 'I was horrified, totally horrified,' says Margo Kingston. 'There was a split in the gallery on how to report it. We knew this had the potential to blow a gasket on Australian politics, otherwise we would have said, "Oh, she's just another idiot backbencher." What she was saying was your standard far-right conspiracy crap, but there is something about Pauline that is mesmerising. Love her or hate her, you couldn't be indifferent to her. She's a charismatic person, and we knew that this was huge. Here's this woman who got an incredible swing after being racist, and here she is, saying her stuff. I said, "We won't report it." And my boss said, "Margo, we have to."'

Kingston and her Fairfax editor decided to bury Hanson's

THE MAIDEN SPEECH

explosive words in a back-page story, leading with Greens senator Bob Brown's maiden speech. The other broadsheets followed suit. But the tabloid reporters smelt money. 'They knew it would sell papers,' Kingston says of the decision by the Murdoch-led commercial media to give Hanson oxygen. 'Talkback went ballistic the next day, and from then on the tabloids went, "We've got ourselves a story."'

Oblivious to the media avalanche that was about to engulf her, Hanson left her parliamentary office near midnight, to celebrate her political deflowering. With her maiden speech freshly delivered, she wanted to dance. She shared a ride with Pasquarelli and Hazelton to the Grange, a popular political watering hole in Manuka. Pasquarelli, battling one of his Ménière's disease headaches, stayed in the bustling club long enough to deflect some abuse about Hanson's speech from rising Labor bullyboy Mark Latham, then stomped off home.

Hanson and Hazelton settled happily in at a corner table and kept drinking. Suddenly, a man from the left-faction of the Liberal Party came up and attacked them. Furious about the hateful words Hanson had just spoken in parliament, he unleashed a blistering, expletive-ridden tirade.

'This fellow came up to me, and he was so abusive,' Hanson says, frowning. As the man towered over her, screaming that she had disgraced the prime minister and every Australian with her racist speech, another man leapt to her rescue. Tall, dark and oddly handsome in a Clark Kent-meets-Albert Speer kind of way, Hanson's bespectacled knight in shining armour grabbed her attacker by the collar, shoved him against the wall and told him to leave. Then he smoothed down his impeccable suit and approached Hanson to apologise on her abuser's behalf.

Hanson was dazzled by her mysterious new suitor. 'He said his name's David. He was charming, respectful, and I thought it was nice, how he came up and said, "It's not everyone's thoughts,"' she recalls of the young man who would become her svengali, closest political confidant and rumoured lover. 'He wouldn't tell me who he worked for, and he congratulated me on the speech.'

David, as Hanson would discover weeks into their clandestine affair, was David Oldfield, the ambitious personal secretary of Howard's chief headkicker, the lapsed seminarian and Oxford boxing blue Tony Abbott MP. Known to his enemies as a ruthless sociopath who'd sell his own mother if it got him a vote, Oldfield, when it came to Machiavellian power plays, would make the thuggish Kojak seem as malevolent as a grandmother flogging baby knits at a church stall.

'I thought David was genuine at the time, and I do believe that,' says Hanson of the apparently random encounter that changed her political destiny.

'I didn't know she was at the Grange, but I saw this fellow getting stuck in to her,' Oldfield purrs, in the well-stocked bar he maintains at his spotless Sydney mansion. A little dog looks on from a pen in the corner. I wonder if it's Dinky, the Jack Russell who famously swallowed six condoms in 2009. 'I wouldn't have cared who it was abusing [Hanson], it was just wrong,' Oldfield continues. 'And I pulled him off – well, that's probably not the right expression – *dragged him away*, and that's how we met.'

Barbara Hazelton shudders. 'If you believe that, you believe in the tooth fairy. The Grange was definitely a set-up. Hanson was a vehicle for Oldfield to get into politics. With Pasquarelli, you knew your enemy. With Oldfield you didn't.'

Hanson and Oldfield's unholy alliance would produce one of the most violently contested political movements in Australian history.

Chapter 6
Please explain?

Hanson is no political messiah as far as I'm concerned. She just said what the ordinary Australian was thinking.
—One Nation co-founder David Oldfield, interview, November 2015

David Oldfield is often portrayed as devious and self-serving; a manipulative genius who mercilessly used, then dumped, Pauline Hanson to advance his own political career. But the man I meet in 2015 is driven by something far more potent than personal ambition: deep, heartfelt patriotism. 'I was not then, and am not now, a fan of multiculturalism,' he says passionately. 'I hate the idea of a melting pot. My wife is a Sioux, my kids are part American Indian. I don't think it matters what Australians look like in fifty years, what matters is what they think, what they're up to, and what their culture is like. We're all better off if Australians are Australians, rather than being caught up in where they've come from. I'm a bit "when in Rome", you know – one nation, one flag, one culture.'

Oldfield and his reality TV star wife, Lisa, are raising their two young sons on a heavily fortified, semirural block in the prosperous Sydney suburb of Belrose. Dumped from his drivetime gig on 2UE in 2010, after he declared the electric fence at the Christmas Island refugee detention centre 'should be turned on', Oldfield now lives in genteel semiretirement on an indexed parliamentary pension, courtesy of his eight-year stint as a New South Wales One Nation MP between 1999 and 2007.

The spin doctor whom Margo Kingston has described as an 'extreme narcissist', a 'mischievous devil' and a 'big-city carpetbagger using the One Nation roller-coaster as a fast track to power' is surprisingly fond of animals. Every morning, Oldfield hops on his quad bike and hoons down a bush track to the paddock at the bottom of his property, to feed his horses and chat with his chooks. 'It's probably hard to have a relationship with a chicken; I'm not sure where they are on the intelligence bird chart,' Oldfield muses, as he scatters grain for Gwyneth Poultry, Cluck Norris and Whitney House-hen. 'I say good morning and give them a pat. Animals get a bad deal from humans, so you give them the best deal you can. We rescue a lot here – tawny frogmouths, kingfishers, kookaburras. We got a possum so overwhelmed by paralysis ticks we had to take it to the vet.'

In the den of his imposingly minimalist, stone-and-steel mansion, Oldfield feeds live cockroaches to his sons' lizards, Bruce and George, and gently offers mice to his beloved pet python. Oldfield's obsession with cleanliness borders on OCD: the house, from its white-tiled floors to its gleaming white walls, is spotless. Upon arrival, we are instructed to leave our shoes at the door, and Oldfield follows us around for the rest of the day with a little stick vacuum, discreetly hoovering up our footsteps and crumbs.

The man who usurped John Pasquarelli as Hanson's political puppet-master is fanatical about security. He tells us calmly that he keeps firearms in the locked bedrooms, and Lisa, who doesn't seem to have a front-door key, has to call Oldfield to be let in. As we're setting up for his interview, Oldfield ushers me behind his bar and opens a mirrored panel to reveal a dark padded vault inside. The space is soundproof, and exceedingly chilly. Oldfield, with a pleasant smile, tells me it is his wine cellar. It could be a panic room. As I hesitate in the doorway, I have the irrational sensation that Oldfield's about to shut me inside.

Despite these unsettling traits, Oldfield also possesses a certain magnetic charm. At the end of our interview, he gives us each a bottle of red wine and a clutch of freshly laid eggs. He waves us off, smooth and self-assured, and I imagine how attractive this well-groomed and utterly self-possessed man must have been to the rough-edged Hanson on the night they met at the Grange.

Oldfield's enemies claim he operates inside an amoral, emotion-free zone, driven by a clinical obsession with power. They are wrong. Descended from two generations of military heroes, Oldfield sees himself as a patriotic warrior fighting an ideological war. 'My dad, grandad and uncle all fought for Australia – I feel they fulfilled a responsibility that I hadn't been able to do. They did their moral duty. This was my war,' he explains of One Nation, the anti-immigration, far-right party he established with Hanson in 1997. 'This wasn't about political opportunism. I passionately believed in the change we could have brought about. But hey, who would want to make David Oldfield "an okay guy"?' he quips.

The day Hanson delivered her maiden speech, Oldfield immediately recognised what the conservatives would continue to deny: Hanson had the charisma to amass a significant political following. Oldfield would fight for Hanson and their populist party with tireless conviction. His uncompromising patriotism and strategic political brain would make him a dangerous and powerful player in One Nation's meteoric rise. But when Oldfield began his incendiary quest to reshape Australia with Hanson at the helm, a large obstacle stood in his way: Kojak.

On 11 September 1996, the morning after her maiden speech, Hanson's office looked like 'a clearing room at Interflora', Pasquarelli remembers happily. Flowers and gifts spilt over desks and across the floor. But Hanson only had eyes for a bouquet of roses, sent by her mysterious new admirer from the Grange. Unbeknown to Hanson, Oldfield was working just a few doors down the corridor, in Tony Abbott's office.

Pasquarelli grabbed the bouquet and yanked the besotted Hanson out of her reverie, determined to capitalise on the furore exploding around her speech.

'The media really got that maiden speech up and running. They went hysterical about it, especially the ABC, they went absolutely fermented,' Pasquarelli beams. 'It made me want to give a few of them a good belt!'

As the public broadcasters slammed Hanson as dangerously divisive, demanding that Howard immediately condemn her speech, 2GB's popular shock jock Alan Jones lauded the Member for Oxley as a champion of 'forgotten battlers' everywhere. With her brassy, eye-popping outfits, no-bullshit delivery and audacious refusal to follow the prevailing social norms of decorum and restraint, Hanson was an instant darling on the chat-show circuit. The ecstatic Pasquarelli chaperoned her through the studios of channels 10, 7 and 9, as praise for Hanson continued to grow among Australian viewers sick of being told what to think by the 'politically correct' pointy-heads of the ABC and SBS.

First to give Hanson the star treatment was Kerri-Anne Kennerley's *Midday* show. On 11 September 1996, in front of an overwhelmingly white studio audience baying for blood, Kerri-Anne pitted the Member for Oxley against respected Indigenous campaigner and ATSIC deputy chair Charles Perkins, in a head-to-head stoush.

'I want all immigration stopped. We need to clean up our own backyard. Let's look after our own before we start looking after others,' Hanson began primly, immediately getting the audience on side.

'You're a racist, ignorant person – you don't know what you're talking about. You're giving this country a bad name!' Perkins retorted, and Hanson handed him a dubiously researched breakdown of Indigenous expenditure, demanding to know where the 'millions of taxpayer dollars' had gone.

'You're talking a lot of bullshit!' Perkins yelled, and flung the document back in Hanson's lap. The studio audience jeered as Hanson watched in righteous silence. 'That's right, now the blue-rinse set's piping up,' Perkins muttered wearily, and Kennerley slapped him down. 'Do *not* speak to my audience like that,' she told him with imperious contempt. She might as well have called Perkins 'boy'. When viewers of *Midday* were polled the next day, 94 per cent said they didn't think Hanson was racist.

Next to cement Hanson's new status as the most-talked-about politician in Australia was *60 Minutes*, then the highest-rating current affairs program on air. Prompted by Perkins's challenge to Hanson on the *Midday* show that she actually visit an Indigenous community before she criticised how Aboriginal funding was being spent, *60 Minutes* reporter Tracey Curro and producer Peter Wilkinson decided to take Hanson and Perkins to the Indigenous settlement of Palm Island, on Queensland's Great Barrier Reef.

Curro, unlike her chat-show and talkback colleagues, was no supporter of Hanson. Aware that Pasquarelli saw *60 Minutes* as a chance to promulgate his anti-minority, anti-Indigenous credo, she resolved to hold the new politician rigorously to account. 'The Hanson Phenomenon', which aired on *60 Minutes* on 13 October 1996, was a well-researched and convincing rebuttal of everything Hanson stood for. When Hanson, in one of many tense face-offs with Curro, complained she was finding the interview process 'very hard, because I have to sort of clarify all my, what I think and how I feel about things, isn't it?', Curro cooly replied, 'Precisely, because you are a federal politician. We're not just sitting around in a pub.'

Curro's critical treatment of Hanson sits in stark contrast with the fawning tone *60 Minutes* reporter Liz Hayes would adopt with the politician two decades later. In August 2016, Hayes' *60 Minutes* 'exclusive' was promoted as an 'in-depth encounter' with the controversial senator but turned out to be little more than a chummy puff piece, in which the sympathetic journalist sipped beer with the newly elected Hanson at her farm, giggled at Hanson's daughter's quip that her mum was nicknamed 'Johnny Farnham' because of her endless political comebacks, and wandered around Parliament House with the emotional Hanson, gushing about the battleaxe survivor's extraordinary Second Coming.

'The note Hanson struck was inflammatory and mean-spirited,' Curro says, summarising the radically different response Hanson triggered in the political media in 1996. 'Her maiden speech seemed fashioned to divide, and it didn't seem to me to be terribly well aligned to the values of contemporary Australia. If she had been some fat old bloke giving that speech, I dare say it wouldn't have attracted quite the attention. Pauline, without Pasquarelli's wordsmithing, may have gone largely unnoticed, but he crafted a beautiful speech designed to grab attention, and it absolutely did.'

During their *60 Minutes* shoot, Curro and Wilkinson accompanied Hanson to her mother's home, where Hannorah proudly remembered warning her daughter about 'the yellow peril' when Pauline was still a toddler on her knee, and to Melbourne, where Hanson addressed a boisterously supportive Shooters Party event. Then, on 22 September, John Howard, who had refused to denounce

Hanson's maiden speech for twelve days running, revealed his true colours. At a state Liberal Party function in Queensland, Howard declared he was glad the 'pall of censorship' had been lifted, and that Australians could 'now talk about certain things without living in fear of being branded as a bigot or as a racist'.

With the prime minister's veiled endorsement of Hanson hanging in the air, Curro and her *60 Minutes* crew followed Hanson through the dilapidated streets of Palm Island, capturing the politician's first exposure to an Indigenous community. The degradation and malaise inflicted on the island's largely transplanted inhabitants by the Queensland government was all too tragically clear. Plagued by alcohol, poverty and violence, Palm Island had been used as a dumping ground for 'disruptive' and problematic 'mixed-blood' Indigenous Australians for the majority of the twentieth century. Hanson, tight-lipped with disapproval, was unmoved.

'All Pauline could see was there was rubbish on the street,' Curro recalls. 'The only contribution she could make to a very complex issue was "clean up the rubbish, then you'll have some pride". think that's pretty typical of the very simplistic, homespun solutions that she's trotted out for twenty years.'

Hanson remembers it differently. 'I spoke to the schoolkids, and I travelled round the island and saw the houses falling down, full of mess and rubbish. People had no pride in themselves or others. Two men came up intoxicated and said, "Pauline, we want to work." Then after I met them, I was sitting down with Perkins and the [Indigenous] women. And he said, "You have no idea how in tune with the land we are," and I said, "Well, if you're that in tune, why don't you clean it up?" And he didn't know what to say.'

The *60 Minutes* footage of the meeting between Hanson and the Indigenous elders of Palm Island confirms Curro's more nuanced reading of the encounter. The women agree with Hanson that not all of ATSIC's funding is being spent properly, but vehemently disagree that the solution is to shut down ATSIC, and all Indigenous programs with it. 'You've opened up a can of worms. That's fine with us, but we want something positive coming out of a negative statement,' one of the women tells Hanson.

'The administration has been given the dollars to look after their own people. And they haven't done their job!' Hanson counters angrily.

'Hang on a minute,' the woman replies. 'Europeans have had control of this country for two hundred and nine years. You've made a mess of it, and you expect ATSIC to clean it up in six?'

Hanson glares at her, and an older Indigenous woman graciously interjects. 'You are still a very young person,' she tells the 42-year-old politician gently. 'Not so much in years, but in knowledge. What I'd like to see you do, Pauline, is to be educated.'

Hanson's lack of formal education was fully exposed in Curro's searing *60 Minutes* critique. The underlying implication was that Hanson's intolerance was the result of her ignorance: as someone who'd left school at fifteen, and was largely politically illiterate, the Member for Oxley's credibility was suspect. When 'The Hanson Phenomenon' went to air, its treatment of Hanson caused a seismic shift in 1990s class politics. The fish shop lady's unlikely rise from suburban backbencher to celebrity politician confirmed the egalitarian ideal the majority of Australians cherished: that theirs was a largely classless society, unfettered by the stuffy pretensions of British entitlement and American money. But a Keating-era belief in the value of a good education still prevailed. That was until Curro asked Hanson, in their most heated exchange on the show, if she was xenophobic. And everything changed.

'There are 866 224 Asian-born Australians out of a population of over eighteen million. Now, is that in danger of being swamped?'

Curro began, in the interview that would define her journalistic career.

'I don't believe those figures. They're just book figures,' the denim-shirted Hanson snapped back.

'They're just book figures!' Curro repeats to me now. 'I mean, that's just bizarre. That characterises Pauline. This inability to accept anything outside your own very direct experience, no matter how narrow that might be.'

'All I know is what's here inside.' The young Hanson tapped her heart proudly, staring Curro down.

Appalled that the politician felt it was acceptable to trust her instincts over facts when disparaging Australia's immigration policy, Curro then asked the question that birthed Hanson's most famous phrase, enshrining her place in the national lexicon.

'Are you xenophobic?' Curro purred. Hanson stared at her blankly.

'I distinctly remember [thinking], if she has read anything written about her in the past three weeks, she will have come across that word,' Curro recalls. 'So it will mean one of two things: either she doesn't read the commentary, or if she comes across a big word she just skips right over it.'

'Everything's racing through my mind,' Hanson tells me at her farm, reliving the agonising four seconds she spent gazing unblinkingly at Curro, trying to work out what to say. 'Do I bluff? What do I do?' After an eternity of dead air, Hanson opted to play it straight.

'Please explain?' she shot back. It was Curro's turn to pause.

'I needed a moment to go, right, okay, something has just happened there, and for a couple of seconds it was like time stopped,' Curro says. 'We certainly didn't anticipate the kind of reaction that it would have.'

'Well, Pasquarelli is on the couch and I can see him, and he puts his head down and he shakes his head, as if, "My God, what has she done now?",' Hanson says with a grin.

'I thought, "This is going well, la di da di da," and suddenly I heard, "Please explain?"' Pasquarelli laughs. 'Absolutely brilliant, couldn't have scripted it better myself. Laid it right on the line. Please explain! It was the sort of thing ordinary Australians want to say to their bloody politicians. These pollies who are not interested in the national interest, they're interested in their entitlements, their travel lurks, their study abroad which is rubbish, they are a mob of spivs. Never been off the bitumen, wouldn't know what the real world is. None of them have run a business properly, and people are saying, "Please explain. *Why* are we spending money on that? *Why* have we got bureaucrats everywhere costing a fortune? *Why?* Please explain!" The fish and chip shop lady strikes again!'

If the producers of *60 Minutes* thought Hanson had just dug her own political grave, they were quickly proven wrong. 'They got so much mail from the public. I think it was 98 per cent didn't know what the word "xenophobic" was,' Hanson says of the viewer backlash that besieged Channel 9 the next day. 'The media were a bunch of smart-arses, trying to belittle me. But the more they bashed me or tried to denigrate me, the more public support I got.'

'Please explain' is now a daily feature on Google Alerts, trotted out by everyone from bloggers to sportscasters to parents whenever something a tad suspect occurs. The night Hanson uttered the phrase to Curro marks the moment Australia realised it had a new class divide: between those who valued deep knowledge and those who resented the status such knowledge conferred. Suddenly, a lack of education was not a thing to be concealed or ashamed of, but something to 'be worn like a badge of honour', Curro reflects. 'And if you did have an education, that was something people could rub in your face derisively. It was very strange.'

Years later, Hanson tried to trademark 'Please Explain' as a clothing label, and Curro approached her for an interview. Hanson replied archly that she'd bring a dictionary. 'I don't know that she entirely intended it as a joke,' says Curro, smiling.

After her triumphant 1996 debut on *60 Minutes*, Hanson's support base ballooned. Joining the thousands of Australians already converted by her maiden speech, a new wave of believers, stalkers and zealots flooded Hanson's offices with fan mail. 'It was mad. The correspondence, there was a twenty-foot container full of the bloody stuff!' Pasquarelli remembers. 'The girls used to bring me handwritten 300-page treatises from Joe Bloggs in Cunnamulla on how to fix Australia's problems. We're still on faxes and word processors and all the paper, that was phenomenal!'

In malls and halls from Townsville to Gatton, Hanson was mobbed by emboldened new admirers. Teenage girls in Townsville's casino begged for the politician's autograph, telling Pasquarelli, 'We love her. We're racists and so are the Abos, and now we can say it!' Hanson, bolstered, took to jumping into taxis to deliver her favourite spiel, telling her immigrant drivers that if they didn't give Australia their 'undivided loyalty', she'd pack them off home. The drivers, out of either delight or fear, would laugh and pledge her their vote.

On the airwaves, Hanson was now working the talk shows and pressers with beguiling skill. The performer inside her revelled in the attention, and the politician she was becoming sensed that her instinctive, straight-talking persona was a unique asset no opponent could buy. 'There are three certainties in this world,' the jubilant Kojak told one of the press packs that now followed Hanson's every move, 'the rising and setting of the sun, and Pauline Hanson on the six o'clock news.'

Hanson's Ipswich and Canberra offices were as chaotic as a red-carpet premiere. Besotted voters began lining up for an audience with their new hero, like 'winners at a TAB', says Pasquarelli. 'It was real Hollywood stuff!' With the anti-Semitic, ultra-right League of Rights distributing Hanson's maiden speech across the country, and with her face plastered all over the tabloids, the Member for Oxley was the pin-up girl du jour for extremists, loners and the generally disaffected – particularly men. The sacks of mail Pasquarelli pored over each day contained hundreds of handwritten marriage proposals from toothless farmers, burly labourers and bow-tied accountants, posing with their utes and Harleys in front of rusting sheds and hedge-fringed semis, and pledging their undying love.

But Hanson stayed blissfully ensconced in her celebrity bubble and gave her new admirers a wide berth. She had already found the kind of love she craved, in the arms of the younger, and surprisingly attentive, Oldfield. Behind Pasquarelli's back, the pair began to rendezvous at the Sundown Motel on the outskirts of Canberra, where the kitsch honeymoon suite boasted a discreet walkway through a gnome- and flamingo-studded yard.

Cosmopolitan, articulate and raised in the blue-chip Liberal enclave of Manly, the classy Oldfield was a demographic step up from the men Hanson had dated before. When he seduced her with his signature dish, filet mignon in red wine sauce, Oldfield may well have triggered a nascent aspirationalism, in the working-class mother who'd battled so hard to get ahead.

'Pauline was totally enamoured of him,' Hazelton remembers. 'She bought pâté and swish things on the nights he came around, not Pauline-type stuff.' As Hanson sought culinary and sartorial tips from the sophisticated Hazelton, the puzzled Pasquarelli detected a 'whiff of snobbery' in his previously self-deprecating client. When he teased Hanson that the chips in her fish shop were cut too short, she corrected him tetchily: 'It's a *fresh seafood takeaway*, John.'

A few weeks into her secret affair with Oldfield, Hanson asked Kojak, straight-faced, if an independent could 'become prime minister'. 'Like a faulty firearm that discharges milliseconds after it should, those words took longer than they should have to penetrate,' Pasquarelli says of the moment he realised Hanson was forgetting her roots and becoming what Doug Blake had warned her on her first tour of Canberra not to become: 'just another politician'.

Hanson and Oldfield's political pillow talk at the Sundown was largely to blame. 'Middle-aged men wanted to protect her and wrap her in cotton wool,' Oldfield says disparagingly, making it clear he wasn't one of them. Oldfield, a renowned Lothario with unusually catholic tastes, once described his perfect woman as 'a cross between Jayne Mansfield and my mother'. He has always denied the affair with Hanson, even taking (and failing) a lie-detector test in 2007, after Hanson spilt the dirt in her autobiography, *Untamed and Unashamed*.

'There was never any romance as far as I was concerned,' he insists. 'I was very fond of Pauline, and I accepted her for her faults like people accept me for mine, but there are no sex tapes on David Oldfield because none have been filmed. We were very friendly, and people can draw what conclusion they like. I don't publish my conquests. That's bar-room talk for blokes on the piss. Pauline was a simple, unaffected person who stood up and said what a lot of people would have liked to have said, and I admired that, and I thought it could be used in a positive way.'

Oldfield, unbeknown to the smitten Hanson, had an agenda. A gifted over-achiever whose father was a World War II fighter pilot and a personal friend of John Howard's, Oldfield had learnt early to value the nexus between contacts, salesmanship and power. 'Politics is just good salesmanship,' Oldfield explains. 'I wasn't naturally a good salesman, that doesn't require much honesty. I was a good salesman for things I believed in. If I had a good product, I could sell it.'

The Manly diving equipment store Oldfield ran in the 1980s was the perfect political training ground. It placed him at the centre of the suburb's conservative culture, and face-to-face with the Liberal powerbrokers who ran it. In 1991, fed up with the new wave of non-Anglo-European 'blow-ins' moving into Manly, Oldfield put his connections to good use, running an ingenious campaign for the local council in which he only leafleted streets where the demographics matched his goals. By 1994, Oldfield had acquired enough influence for a budding Liberal hopeful, Tony Abbott, to seek his support in the by-election for the federal seat of Warringah. By 1995, Oldfield had risen to become a Liberal candidate himself, in the New South Wales state election.

Selling his diving store, Oldfield threw himself into a turbo-charged, slogan-driven campaign, reassuring voters that 'Dave cares' and that he was 'Manly through and through'. Then, at a multicultural community event hosted by the Chinese-Australian New South Wales Liberal MLC Helen Sham-Ho, Oldfield declared that the Aboriginal flag should be removed from Manly Town Hall. His support collapsed. Oldfield's fondness for politically incorrect jokes, like 'I don't discriminate along colour lines – I dislike all people equally' and 'I have no problem with gay marriage, as long as both chicks are hot', hadn't helped his vote. With his political ambitions in tatters, Oldfield sank into a black depression.

The conservative old boys' network swiftly came to his rescue. In February 1996, as Hanson doorknocked Oxley with her home-made flyers, and Keating and Howard faced off on the federal campaign trail, Oldfield, with Howard's endorsement, was back on the hustings for the Liberal Party machine, helping his old mate Abbott campaign to hold Warringah. Setting out A-frames on the Manly Corso, the two men discussed what kind of country Australia should become under the conservatives, and realised they shared the same radical vision.

'I've always been a fighter for things I believe in, and I thought there were things that should be changed,' Oldfield says now of his ideological bonding with Abbott.

'People were understandably angry about little sections of Asia popping up in Australia, and the signs would be in a different language, and the people working in the shops would not speak English. Multiculturalism separates us into tribes. When you develop policies that keep people in their own language, whether it's Chinese or Vietnamese or even that nonsense of teaching Aboriginal languages, is that going to get a child a job? No! When people are primitive, you have a problem getting them into a modern society. And if you have multiculturalism, there's no way a person from a primitive background will finish up with everyone else, because the policy stops them. I'm a nationalist. I don't particularly care if the Maldives sinks into the Pacific; I am concerned about what is going to happen to Aussies. A few thousand people from the paddy fields of Cambodia don't have much to offer. The seventh century has no place in twentieth-century Australia.'

Abbott listened closely as Oldfield shared his worries about 'primitive' Asians diluting the true-blue Aussie culture he loved. If Howard won government, Oldfield insisted, he would 'need to integrate them, not encourage them to stay separate. Otherwise, in a few generations, the fabric of Australian society will be torn apart.' Abbott's response was reassuring. When the Coalition won power, he told Oldfield, there would be a better 'balance' in who was allowed to call Australia home.

Eight months later, the conservatives were in power, and Oldfield and Abbott's ideological bromance was flourishing in Canberra. Oldfield had solidified his position as Abbott's 'trusted right-hand man', the only staffer who wrote letters the member for Warringah 'didn't have to change'. He was also deep into his clandestine relationship with Hanson, and keen to share with Abbott how she could be used to advance their mutual cause.

'I suggested to Tony that we use Pauline as a preference feeder, to influence the Liberal Party in the right direction for what the nation needed to have changed,' Oldfield recalls. 'She was a lightning bolt. She was saying a lot of things, not very well, but she was saying a lot of things people were already thinking. And Tony said, "No, no, no, no, no, ma-a-ate, stay away from her!" He just didn't want to know. He told me to steer clear of it.'

'And did you?' I ask.

Oldfield feigns anguish. Or maybe he's genuine; it's hard to tell. 'No, I couldn't! There was too much that needed to be done! My loyalty was first and foremost to what needed to be done for Australia. If that wasn't going to be done through the Liberal Party, I needed to find another way, and the opportunity presented itself with Pauline. It was always about getting the best outcome by whatever means. Once it became evident I couldn't even have a conversation with Tony about it, I had to decide if I would leave his office or stay with him. I am always portrayed as devious and disloyal, but I am the opposite of that. I was the only person Tony could rely on. And there was a substantial tug of war for me at the time, because I actually didn't want to leave Tony.'

Oldfield, with Machiavellian pragmatism, decided to stay on Abbott's payroll and continue seeing Hanson on the sly. He and Hanson slipped into a double game, working closely with the innocent Abbott and Pasquarelli during the day, and conspiring with each other at night about how to best harness Hanson's growing support. Oldfield stealthily persuaded Hanson she had the talent to lead her own political party, and that he had the smarts to run it. He also suggested Pasquarelli's 'storm trooper image' was not the best fit for her brand.

In public, Oldfield soldiered on as Abbott's trusted lieutenant, writing briefs for the minister's Abstudy and Austudy portfolios. 'I just did what I needed to do for Tony, and when I was able to do other things for Pauline, I did that too.' He shrugs. Hanson, the honest battler who had always said 'my word is my bond', faced the press packs with duplicitous ease, declaring, as the unsuspecting Kojak stood by her side, 'There are two things I never leave home without: my mobile phone and John Pasquarelli.'

By mid-October 1996, as Hanson plotted with Oldfield, the damaging effects of her divisive rhetoric and Howard's continuing refusal to denounce it had begun to be felt on the streets. Just as hate crimes against Muslim and Jewish Americans escalated after the election of Donald Trump, Hanson's maiden speech and the publicity bonanza that followed it generated a shocking spike in assaults on Asian and Indigenous Australians.

Dr Thiam Ang, then the president of the powerful Chinese Australian Forum, began to receive distress calls from Asian Australians across Sydney. 'I was getting reports of men in suits in Chatswood and Turramurra stations spitting on Asian people. And even worse than that, beautiful children of mixed marriages were called mongrels. Now, I am an obstetrician, I deliver babies, and for the life of me I can't imagine people can be so racist as to call these children mongrels!'

'It was a frightening time for people who hadn't been on the receiving end of blunt-force trauma of that kind,' recalls Professor Marcia Langton. 'I don't think Australia was ready for the emergence in Australian politics of that kind of right-wing nut-job, Ku Klux Klan–inspired racism, and it took everybody by surprise. Being from Queensland, for me it was quite normal, but for people from Sydney and Melbourne, it came as quite a shock.'

'All of us found ourselves in positions where we had to defend ourselves,' agrees Indigenous Labor MP Linda Burney. 'I remember having to fend off constantly the sort of rubbish Hanson was espousing. It gave permission for those ugly, old, stereotypical racist views to be aired again. Aboriginal people were abused and derided because of the views she was throwing up. Views we thought had gone away a very long time ago. There were many occasions in schoolyards where Aboriginal children were called names.'

A friend of Burney's, then working for the Council for Aboriginal Reconciliation, recalls the 1800 information line the council had set up for Australians to discuss Indigenous issues being flooded by Hanson supporters phoning in violent abuse and death threats. 'It reminded me of the Australia I knew as a little girl in the late '50s,' Burney reflects. 'A time when racism was normal and acceptable. Where Aboriginal people were openly denigrated, and racism was not hidden. And being Aboriginal was the worst thing that could happen to a person. It was a very difficult time.'

'I was a member of the Liberal Party, a humble backbencher,' says former Chinese Australian MLC Helen Sham-Ho, now an enthusiastic patron of Sydney's multicultural community. 'I got letters to say, "Monkey come from tree, you know where you should go back to."' Sham-Ho's staff were attacked by anonymous callers, and her car tyres were slashed. Deeply disturbed, Sham-Ho wrote to Howard, urging him to speak out against Hanson. With her impeccable Liberal credentials and invaluable ties to the wealthy Chinese-Australian business community, Sham-Ho expected a reply.

'He didn't respond.' She shakes her head sadly. 'All the time during Hanson's rise, I had been asking to see our prime minister, who has a duty to see constituents like myself if we're concerned about a national issue. I wrote many letters. I requested to see him and discuss it. My office must have rung him about three or four times. Usually members of parliament reply to their constituents. He didn't even reply. He did not say Hanson was wrong; he actually said, "Oh, this is freedom of speech"! Come on! That's not condemning, that's condoning! That's why, in private, I said he's a latent racist himself.'

Footage of Howard caught in a media scrum at a commemorative military service a few weeks after Hanson's maiden speech appears to confirm Sham-Ho's suspicions. Clearly annoyed at being asked, yet again, to 'please explain' why he won't rebuke the Member for Oxley, Howard yells above the blaring trumpets, 'Anyone, including Pauline Hanson, has the right to be heard!'

'It was expected that Howard, who shared Hanson's politics, wouldn't say anything, because there was political mileage to be enjoyed in what she was saying.' Randa Abdel-Fattah shrugs, recalling the schoolyard bullying she endured as a young Muslim Australian in the wake of Hanson's rise. 'Hanson was a litmus test to see what would work and what would backfire. It was very strategic on Howard's part, and not surprising given that culturally and politically, they were on the same page. Of course it's disappointing the leader of your country isn't going to immediately condemn that damaging and ugly rhetoric, but it wasn't surprising.'

'I felt that if the prime minister had come out and condemned Hanson's remarks, things would die down,' Dr Ang says quietly. 'I was at a barbecue, and this Jewish work colleague says, "Thiam, we're glad you guys are here. You've taken the heat off us a bit!" When you look back at it, in the '50s it was the Italians and the

Greeks who were getting it, and after that the Continentals from Eastern Europe, and then after that the Asian people. Now, of course, it's the Muslims.'

Neville Roach, then the Indian-Australian CEO of Fujitsu, is adamant that Howard's stubborn silence created a media vacuum, in which Hanson's hate speech was able to flourish. 'The reason she got more oxygen than she deserved was that Howard was very quiet about what she was saying, and he certainly did not condemn her,' he says flatly.

When I present these accusations to Howard, he is unfazed. 'The speech had an impact on the Australian people because sections of the media beat the daylights out of it. That's why it had an impact. It didn't, of its own momentum, have an impact,' he adds with an edge of irritation.

I'm lucky Howard's speaking to me at all. Minutes before our interview, he tore into me about my film's central premise: that Hanson, and her speech, changed Australia. Unimpressed by the fact that, apart from broadcaster Alan Jones, I was not interviewing any conservatives whose stature matched his own, Howard threatened to walk. Rattled, I quoted glowing phrases from his autobiography, *Lazarus Rising*, back at him, pleading with him to stay. Having reduced me to a state of sycophantic subservience, Howard then calmly faced our camera. This exchange confirmed for me why this fearsomely intelligent man managed to hold power for eleven years. Mr Teflon, as the media would dub him, distanced himself from Hanson's racist rhetoric with cunning precision while successfully adopting her policies. Howard is brilliant at intimidating his critics.

'The reason I didn't [denounce Hanson] was because I thought it was an overreaction,' he continues now, confident I'm no longer in any state to challenge him. 'I felt that it would have magnified the impact she had on the community. I also understood, very early in the piece, that beyond her statements about Indigenous people and Asians, she was, however inadequately, articulating a sense of feeling left out on behalf of a lot of Australians, who felt that economic progress and attitudes at a national level were leaving them behind, and that somehow the older Australia with which they felt very familiar was being attacked and undermined. Now, I understood that and thought the wrong thing to do was to launch an all-out attack, labelling all the people who supported her as racist.'

Howard's controversial appeasement strategy is now lauded by conservative commentators as the 'right way' to deal with Hanson. But when Howard first test-drove his approach in late 1996, he was under siege. As Hanson monopolised the media, vilification of multicultural and Indigenous Australians intensified. In parliament's increasingly volatile question time, the Liberal member for Moreton, Gary Hardgrave, demanded that Howard denounce Hanson, receiving several cheers from his own side of the House. Seizing on the disunity in the conservative ranks, Labor opposition leader Kim Beazley excoriated the prime minister for his inaction:

> Has the Prime Minister seen a letter in yesterday's *Daily Telegraph* from a Sydney mother who wrote: 'I was extremely concerned and ashamed when my six-year-old son returned home one day from school to proudly tell me he had told an Asian classmate to leave Australia. When I asked him how he could say something like that he replied, "That's what that lady on TV said."'
>
> Has the Prime Minister also seen reports of comments by the New South Wales upper house Liberal member Mrs Helen Sham-Ho calling on the Prime Minister to make a strong statement supporting the Asian community and cultural

diversity because after living here for thirty-five years she felt quite personally attacked by the views of the Member for Oxley?

Will the Prime Minister now agree it is time for him to exercise leadership on this issue and state clearly and unequivocally that the Member for Oxley's views on racial issues are hurtful to a great many Australians, are damaging to our interests in the region and do not reflect the kind of society that Australia is or wants to be?

Without once referring to Hanson by name, Howard calmly replied, 'In my view, there should be robust debate in this country about the size of our immigration policy. People who exercise free speech have an obligation to do so in a sensitive and caring fashion. That has always been my credo. But it has also been my credo that, if someone disagrees with the prevailing orthodoxy of the day, that person should not be denigrated as a narrow-minded bigot.'

'There was a deep split in the Liberals about how to handle Hanson,' recalls Kingston of the tumultuous weeks of debate that followed Hanson's maiden speech. 'On one side was the "appease and understand side", which was Tony Abbott and John Howard, and on the other side was the "disprove and rebut", which was the [Jeff] Kennett and [Peter] Costello side. It was obvious she had to be handled, but there was a major split about how to handle this phenomenon.'

On 30 October, in a lukewarm compromise, Howard moved a 'racial tolerance' motion. Originally proposed by Beazley, the motion upheld the government's commitment to equal rights for all Australians, rejecting 'racial intolerance in any form'. In a lengthy speech laden with platitudes, Howard commended the Australian people for their ability to 'understand things in a mature and open fashion'; upheld their right to vigorously debate 'all issues';

and rejected the 'black-armband view of history', asserting that Australia's past had been 'very generous and benign'. Once again, he deliberately avoided mentioning Hanson by name.

Not that it mattered: Hanson was not there. With Kojak in tow, the Member for Oxley was playing hooky. Keen to distance Hanson, in the eyes of the public, from the 'politically correct' status quo in Canberra, Pasquarelli took her to a market in Melbourne, to rub shoulders with 'real people'. When they got there, he says, 'we had the Aussies and wogs and Italians – the Vietnamese steered clear of her because of the "swamped by Asians" stuff – but the wogs and Greeks loved her!'

News reports of the day show Hanson in one of her feminine suits, blushing under her eyelashes like Lady Di as overall-clad Mediterranean men line up to pay their respects. 'Don't worry about those MPs, they're just a bunch of shirt-lifters,' says one. 'Good on you, give them heaps!' says another. Then a lone dissenter steps out from the back. 'You're about to wreck the country, the way you're going,' he says. There's fear in his eyes. Hanson, every inch the polished politician, doesn't blink. 'The country's already in a mess!' she snaps, and moves on down the line of adoring men. All of them successfully assimilated, '50s- and '60s-era Anglo-European migrants. Exactly the kind of 'de-wogged' patriots Pasquarelli knew Hanson was attracting, with her calls to stop the new Asian immigrant wave.

On their way back through Tullamarine, a press pack ambushed Hanson and Pasquarelli on the airbridge, demanding to know why the MP wasn't doing her job and voting for the 'racial tolerance' motion in parliament. 'I'm there to make a difference, not a record,' Hanson retorted, using a phrase Oldfield had taught her during one of their clandestine trysts. Pasquarelli, oblivious, wielded his Samsonite like a battering ram to get Hanson into the business lounge, and several onlookers cheered. In 1996, one national trait showed no sign of being swamped: Australians still loved a wagger.

Hanson and Pasquarelli's little holiday made the headlines. Meanwhile, Howard and Beazley continued to trade insults, competing for the moral high ground on race. But as the politicians pontificated in Canberra, Dr Ang found himself on the bloody front line of the hatred Hanson had unleashed. An emergency call summoned him to a food court in Sydney's Chinatown, where an elderly Chinese woman lay in the ladies' room in a pool of blood. 'She had been followed inside by a Caucasian woman, who hit her on the head with a hammer,' Ang remembers, still shocked. 'She said, "Why is this happening to me?" What do you tell a woman, "I'm sorry, you got hit on the head because of the colour of your skin?"' As he bathed the woman's wounds, Ang knew he had to overcome his ingrained Chinese reticence about making a scene. He had to, as he puts it, *jiǎng chū lai:* speak out.

On 14 November 1996, Ang appeared on the *Today* show with an explosive survey. Collated by the Chinese Australian Forum, the survey revealed that attacks on Asian Australians had doubled in the two months since Hanson's maiden speech. 'This is not about "free speech", this is about hurting people,' Ang told reporter Tracy Grimshaw. 'The attention she's getting distracts from the real problem. Everyone is talking about her views, but blood is being spilt. Some of these attacks are happening to old and weak people, and this is tragic when we pride ourselves on looking after the weak.'

'Are you sure this is happening because of Pauline Hanson?' Grimshaw prompted.

In response, Ang quoted the survey's central question: '"After Pauline Hanson's speech, have you had any written, verbal, physical abuse or been spat at by non-Asian people?" We had 1055 valid responses, and there were a doubling of physical and verbal abuse, and three times the number of people being spat at,' he said.

'You can never discount the possibility that whenever there's a controversy, there can be some mean-minded people who will use that as a trigger for abuse and criticism,' Howard says gravely. 'It was an allegation easily made, and there could well have been incidents of it, but I don't recall having seen any hard evidence of that.' I offer Howard a copy of Ang's survey, and he refuses to look at it. 'There are lots of surveys, and I'm not especially denigrating that one, but the hard evidence of which I speak is based on surveys conducted over a period of time by an utterly disinterested source.'

On the *Today* show, Dr Ang criticised Howard with courteous restraint. But his trembling voice betrayed his anguish. 'Encouraging free speech needs to be equated with not hurting other people,' he said. 'Some leaders are sitting on their hands and not speaking out, so I encourage people to vote in the streets.'

Ang's heartfelt plea was lost in the media static. On 19 November 1996, Howard was busy entertaining the re-elected US president, Bill Clinton, on a widely publicised state visit. And Hanson was busy entertaining one of Clinton's bodyguards, a beefcake named Steve. It was a month of 'developing intrigue, an escalating media offensive against Pauline, and just plain madness', recalls Pasquarelli. 'Pauline had three men on the go in November 1996,' says Hazelton: 'Oldfield, Clinton's bodyguard and an ex-prisoner who chatted her up in a piano bar. He had no idea who she was, for obvious reasons.'

'That was interesting stuff when they'd turn up, the toy boys, root rats, and that bogan from Wollongong,' Pasquarelli says with a grin. 'He was flavour of that month. But that's her business. I told her to hold back on the lovers and keep it out of the media. My line was, we're here to do a job, and don't bring your private life into the office. In the office, work's the lurk. In your own time, that's your time. Good on her, I'd say in retrospect.'

Hearing her former staffers tally up her impressive sexual conquests, I remember Hanson sitting outside Marsden's Seafood, chatting with Luke. 'I was not much older than you, and can you imagine being tied up in that shop twenty hours a day with no social life?' she'd said. Hanson's cushy new parliamentary job and sudden access to clothes, clubs and men previously out of her reach must have felt like a five-star holiday to the hardworking mum from Ipswich. It's not surprising that Pasquarelli and Oldfield, as they competed for the politician's attention, found Hanson frequently distracted. The chance to let her hair down and party must have been too good to refuse.

In early December, as negative media coverage continued to drive 'a tidal wave of support' Hanson's way, Pasquarelli was preparing to set up an entity called the Pauline Hanson Movement. He wanted to raise political donations so Hanson could field candidates for the Senate. 'I said, "Pauline, you don't have the ability to organise a party. You'll have every idiot coming out of the woodwork and the whole thing will fly apart. You've got enough meat to get a Senate quota. Then you're upstairs, you're there for six years." And she warmed to that,' Pasquarelli recalls.

Hanson played along, visiting a bank with Pasquarelli to co-sign the Hanson Movement account. But she had already committed to Oldfield. Their secret plan to establish a nationwide political party was well under way. Kojak's time was up.

'Oh, getting rid of Pasquarelli was just a requirement,' Oldfield says smoothly of Hanson's dramatic dismissal of her first spin doctor on 9 December 1996. 'It was an entirely different direction we were going. He'd dissuaded her from starting a party. I reversed that. Pasquarelli just had this idea of Pauline anointing people for the Senate; she'd tap them on the head and say, "I like you." It was rubbish. One of the things Pasquarelli didn't understand was marketing. He was not a great image for what we were trying to do – he looked like Skull Murphy in black. Completely shaved head, wide eyes: he reminded me of the wrestler from the old days. Basically, he bullied Pauline and tried to use her as a mouthpiece for what he wanted to say. I was more genteel. There's no possibility he and I would've lasted five minutes together.'

Pasquarelli's Townsville bungalow is filled with photos of him and Hanson, back in the glory days. He heaves his huge bulk over to a bookcase bursting with artefacts from his croc-hunting past and pulls out a diary as big as an encyclopedia. 'At three-thirty in the afternoon, she said, "I want you to clear your stuff out and leave",' Pasquarelli reads with a scowl. Then he chuckles. 'Would've liked to see the look on my face! And I said, "Pauline, why are you sacking us?" and she said, "I am not telling you." And she called security, and two officers turned up in thirty seconds. You see, it was all set up. He was determined to get my job. Very successful, Mr Oldfield. The only bright thing was the next day I went on *Today Tonight* and got paid three thousand dollars!'

Pasquarelli was frogmarched out of parliament, and Hanson, under Oldfield's instructions, immediately changed her office locks. In the press gallery, ABC reporters popped champagne. Hanson's beleaguered female staff were just as delighted. 'We were so thrilled Oldfield was getting rid of Pasquarelli, we didn't even wonder what sort of person Oldfield was,' Hazelton says with a shiver.

When I relay Pasquarelli's version of events to Hanson, she's livid. 'He doesn't know why I sacked him – that's unbelievable! No-one knows the damn truth; they are speculating. *I* am the central person here. *I* know the story. And I'm sick of these people who jump on my coat-tails, the would-bes if they could-bes but never-have-been.

Pasquarelli was setting up the [Hanson] Movement with Graeme Campbell and Ted Drane, and I was furious they were treating me like a figurehead, to get my support. I had a confidential conversation with Pasquarelli on the Thursday, and then that could be relayed word for word by someone in WA on the Sunday, and that's when I sacked him. I couldn't trust him anymore. Pasquarelli lost his job because he wanted to manipulate and control me.'

Hanson's decision to replace Kojak with Oldfield would cost her, and Australia, dearly.

Chapter 7
The rise of One Nation

Australians can no longer afford the luxury of apathy. We must win this battle, or lose the war.
—Pauline Hanson, One Nation launch speech, 11 April 1997

Hanson is an instinctive creature: she likes to live in the moment. But when we take her into the auditorium of the Ipswich Civic Centre, site of the infamous 1997 launch of One Nation, she becomes unusually reflective.

'People when they saw me come through this door, they all stood and cheered, and it was absolutely amazing,' she says wistfully as she wanders through the empty hall, stroking rows of grey chairs facing the stage like ghosts. 'We had a band playing "We Are One" ["I Am Australian"], and I was so proud to be using a song that unites us as Australians. And I remember giving my speech, and that's when I looked down and Dad was sitting there with tears rolling down his face. It was a very emotional time for me. It's one of the highlights of my life, to have stood there and launched a political party.'

News footage of the night captures a less harmonious picture. Hanson, in her scarlet gown, was lifted out of her limo and raced into the hall by leather-clad bodyguards as a screaming mob of protesters tried to block her path. Inside, 400 Queenslanders in formal dress sat at long banquet tables to hear their idol speak, as furious activists yelled anti-racism slogans outside. By the end of the night, a window had been smashed and several people were arrested. The violent schism between Hanson's supporters and the massive army of protesters who mobilised against them would mark 1997 as the year in which multicultural Australia was plunged into a state of pseudo civil war. One Nation, the party that claimed it sought to unite the country, would divide it in two.

'The launch was exciting because we all had that sense that this was the day that we wanted to happen,' beams David Ettridge, the administrative and financial brain behind One Nation's extraordinary rise. 'The first thing that hit me was the street was full of TV cameras and OB vans, and hundreds of people. And we knew this was something special. It was like the birth of a child – the period of pregnancy was over, and we were telling the world about it!'

Of all the rogues, manipulators, ideologues and schemers who took part in the rise and fall of One Nation between 1997 and 2002, Ettridge knew Oldfield the best. The two had met on a 1979 scuba tour Oldfield was running through his Manly diving shop, and bonded over a shared love of Monty Python, small dogs, music and girls. Their eighteen-year friendship had not always been smooth. Oldfield, whom Ettridge says 'often offended people with his tactlessness', met Ettridge's Yugoslav son-in-law and declared, 'Your kids are a bunch of wogs.' During a diving session at the Dee Why ferry wreck, Ettridge ran into problems with his regulator and discovered that his buddy had abandoned him.

'David left my side. I stuck my head in a window and my air ran out. David was swimming around the wreck and I had to catch up with him to show him my air was gone,' Ettridge says, frowning.

Oldfield's recollection is more heroic: 'I wasn't his partner; we were in a group. Ettridge was suffering nitrogen narcosis. His eyes were big; he was running out of air at 150 feet. I had to dive down and give him another regulator. It took half an hour to bring him up. He gave me a shoulder tap, to say, "Thanks, mate." But Ettridge is not the sort of person who'd like to think he owed me anything. The idea that I saved his life would be horrible for him.'

Whatever the truth of their aquatic skirmish, Oldfield trusted Ettridge enough to ask for his help setting up Hanson's new party, months before its launch. A salesman-for-hire with an easy, low-key charm, Ettridge had worked as a model, band manager and talent agent before making his mark as a professional fundraiser for UNICEF and World Vision. Media reports would later speculate whether the entrepreneur maintained his office in Vanuatu for tax purposes.

When Oldfield introduced Ettridge to Hanson in a secret meeting at Sydney's Hotel Nikko, she was won over.

'It was very difficult to have a clandestine dinner with Pauline Hanson,' recalls Ettridge. 'Everywhere she went, she was recognised. I brought along a portfolio of the work I'd done for large children's charity organisations. I'd raised millions in publicity for these groups, which she liked. I also showed her my "Buy Australian" campaign, because I was annoyed the federal government had abandoned it. I thought we should encourage Aussie farmers and food growers. People were losing their businesses, and this was not good for the prosperity of the country.'

Swearing his old scuba-diving buddy to secrecy, Oldfield, still publicly working for Abbott, engineered a series of undercover strategy sessions with Hanson and Ettridge in hotel rooms, apartments and airport members' lounges. Together, the One Nation Troika, as they would come to be known, would cook up a party constitution like no other.

'We had an agreement between us that we'd be the national executive, a loyalty agreement that we'd move forward together,' says Ettridge of the document the Troika signed at Sydney Airport on 23 February 1997, in which Hanson, as president, signed over control of her new party to the Davids, making Ettridge the national director and Oldfield the national campaign director.

'It allowed us, as a partnership, to make it happen,' Oldfield explains. 'I was the principal adviser, in control of everything from media to candidate and campaign preparation. Anything to do with politics was me, and, of course, taking care of and guiding Pauline. Anything to do with administration and party structure was Ettridge. Pauline was the titular head.'

'We started with a standard sports club constitution, and I got lawyers to change it. I put a structure in place for the business side of the party,' says Ettridge. The unorthodox membership registration system he devised would eventually see him and Hanson thrown in jail for electoral fraud.

'We knew we'd be a threat to the existing parties, and there was nothing they'd not do to stop us,' Ettridge says. 'There was a turf war for voters and the money that flows from winning votes, so when we were starting out, we had to have a means of control.' To guard the new party from major-party infiltrators, political extremists and common or garden kooks, Ettridge invented an ingenious way of guaranteeing membership loyalty. Each person who joined the party would also have to sign an undated resignation letter, which Ettridge could later date and post back if the Troika decided they were dispensable.

'It was like a skink,' Ettridge says with a smile, pleased with the effectiveness of his punitive system. 'The party had the ability to drop its tail, so if one part of the organisation became contaminated – and there were a lot of people seeking to do that – we could discard it, and the party would remain intact. By having a letter where I could remove them, I could make them think twice about their behaviour.'

A large part of the new party's 'tail' was the Pauline Hanson Support Movement, an amateur, nonpartisan group set up by an ardent Hanson fan, Bruce Whiteside. Distinct from the Senate-focused political entity Pasquarelli had tried to form, the PHSM boasted 6000 members who'd been throwing their voices and hard-earned cash behind Hanson ever since her maiden speech. With its thirty-nine branches and energised followers, the PHSM was an attractive prospect to Ettridge and Oldfield, who wanted to kick-start their new party with a bang.

'We decided the PHSM had a function as something that people on pensions who didn't have a lot of money could join, to help out on election day and functions and things like that. Like a huge social club,' explains Ettridge of the decision to hijack Bruce Whiteside's beloved baby. 'But the way I restructured it, it was fully controlled by the party. If we ever wanted to drop the Support Movement and have done with it, it wouldn't affect us. It wasn't an essential element of the party itself – it would be a bit like losing a hand and keeping on going.'

With their unique party structure established, and its launch at the Ipswich Civic Centre fast approaching, the Troika brainstormed the party's title. 'I was the one who insisted it had to be Pauline Hanson's One Nation,' insists Oldfield of the name that protesters would gleefully feature, in acronymic form, on 'PHONey' placards for the next three years. 'Pauline wasn't wild about using her name – she was quite humble in the beginning, and thought it was pushing herself forward too much. But it was about identification. The name is the brand. In 1997, she was the only politician who was recognisable by her first name. So we sold this concept – when you tick the box, you're voting for Pauline. The long-term concept was that once the party was established, Hanson's name would drop off and it would just become One Nation.'

Hanson's contrary account of her party's genesis illustrates the competitive, distrustful and ultimately disastrous relationship she and Oldfield would endure over the next five years as they built, then mutually imploded, One Nation's electoral brand. 'Oldfield's got a very big ego. I am the type that gives credit where it's due,' she says crossly. 'It was Ettridge came into my office with a couple of names, and I picked out One Nation out of that. There was One Australia and Hanson's One Australia, and One Nation grabbed me to actually use that name.'

Ettridge is amused that his former colleagues are still arguing, twenty years on. 'David and Pauline are a pair of divas. They're melodramatic and reactive and emotional. David is a narcissist, and Hanson has the attention span of a flea. She wanted to keep everyone happy. She retained whatever the last person had said to her, a bit like a jug that kept needing to be filled up. I liked her but didn't respect her. She was unreliable, chaotic and self-destructive. She preferred me to David because he was a control freak and gave her lots of stress. I used to make her laugh.'

Pauline Hanson's One Nation, as a name, would not succeed in inspiring the universal patriotism the Troika were hoping for. With Hanson's divisive credo, it was wide open to satire. But the image she and the two Davids chose to advertise the party was a stroke of marketing genius.

Like many things in Hanson's political career, it happened by accident. A parliamentary photographer thought it would be fun, in an ironic kind of way, to snap Hanson in front of an Australian flag. In 1997, the flag was not the cherished symbol it is today, emblazoned on stubbie holders, T-shirts and tattoos. Malcolm Turnbull's republican campaign was in full swing, and the Union Jack's position in the top-left corner was hotly debated. A parallel debate about the right of the Aboriginal flag to coexist with, and even be incorporated into, the Australian one meant that only the most hardened Aussie patriots dared to wear the flag out in public.

That was until Hanson's staff put a secret call through to Oldfield, working three doors away in Tony Abbott's office. The Member for Warringah's two-metre flag was swiftly removed from its pole and delivered to the waiting Hanson. As the photographer started snapping, Hanson, overwhelmed with love for her country, instinctively grabbed the corners of the flag and wrapped it around herself like a bathrobe. The minute he saw the proofs, Ettridge knew he'd hit the jackpot.

'It was a brilliant photo for marketing purposes and to build the party brand around, because she looked ethereal – she was this Joan of Arc, innocent person, who was glowing. It was an amazing photograph,' Ettridge says of his split-second decision to snap up the copyright for $750.

'They gave me the flag and said, "Hold it out like this," and I thought, no. And put it around myself.' Hanson smiles. 'I don't give these things great thought. I don't contrive or plan. They happen on the spur of the moment. I'm just proud of the Australian flag, and when I saw the photo I loved it, because it's everything I love about this country. And it became the picture of One Nation.' She laughs and waves at the lens. 'So thanks, Tony – thanks for the loan of your flag!'

Hanson does look ethereal in the One Nation poster image, her profile tilted upwards and her red hair backlit as she gazes with heroic purpose into the distance. With the Union Jack folded protectively over her right shoulder, she resembles the 1936 Columbia Pictures logo, a torch-bearing nymph who graced the studio's opening credits with sparkling patriotism, draped in the American flag.

'She was never the Messiah or Joan of Arc,' says Oldfield, nonplussed by the sentimental patriotism Hanson's most famous portrait inspired. 'Realistically, Hanson is a myth created by other people. We usually say politics attracts the insane, the ambitious and the lonely. I don't think Pauline was insane or ambitious or lonely – she was just projected into all this by an electoral accident. It started with a letter written by her campaign manager that got her disendorsed. It moved on to the maiden speech written by Pasquarelli. Then it moved on to the speech written by me that launched the One Nation party. Pauline Hanson actually was the vehicle for events created by other people.'

'And you're one of them?' I ask, curious if Oldfield ever does self-deprecation.

He's unequivocal. 'Yes.'

The speech Hanson gave at the Ipswich Civic Centre on 11 April 1997, surrounded by images of her flag-wrapped self, was Oldfield's political battle cry. Her words had been designed to provoke and incite, taking the politician and her followers into altogether darker, more dangerous terrain. Oldfield took the racial hand grenade Pasquarelli had lobbed into parliament with Hanson's maiden speech and refashioned it into a mini nuke.

The political backdrop against which Hanson delivered Oldfield's explosive words was volatile. National tensions over immigration, Indigenous policy and Australia's cultural and economic identity were near breaking point. The High Court's Wik decision in December 1996 had allowed native title rights to coexist with pastoral leases, generating anger from farmers and a desperate 'ten-point plan' from Howard to water the legislation down. At the big end of town, CEOs from the prosperous education and tourism sectors were beating at the government's door, alarmed by the plunging numbers of Asian students and holiday-makers in the wake of Hanson's ascension, and demanding the prime minister end the Member for Oxley's damaging rhetoric for good.

Oldfield seized on these tensions to up the ante. At the One Nation launch, Hanson repeated the calls she'd made in her maiden speech: to stop immigration, to end multiculturalism and the 'Aboriginal industry', and to restore tariff protection for farmers and manufacturers. What made her speech new was the way Oldfield positioned Hanson herself. No longer the humble, fish-shop-owning Ipswich mum speaking up for the 'ordinary' folk of her tribe, Oldfield's Hanson was a nationalistic Valkyrie and a prophet of doom. Painting a dystopian vision of what Australia would become if its citizens didn't fight back, Hanson issued a sinister call to arms. She was the people's fearless leader in a dangerous new war.

'Ladies and gentlemen, who of you would not join this fight? Who of you would not stand up for your country?' Hanson asked her mesmerised audience, many of them war veterans proudly sporting medals from Vietnam, Korea and Ambon on their carefully pressed lapels. 'And yet there are so many people in Australia who do not think of themselves as Australians,' Hanson continued ominously. 'They have simply transplanted the problems of their way of life to our country. Where will they stand in any future crisis? Beside us, or behind us, or will they themselves be the crisis?'

Footage of the speech shows Hanson illustrating her question with laboured, wooden gestures. Oldfield, incognito in a baseball cap, was sitting in the balcony at the back of the auditorium. He remembers wincing. He'd spent hours rehearsing Hanson, performing his speech with Stanislavskian prowess. 'She had to be entertained, like a kindergarten child,' he laments. 'I couldn't even get her to read her press releases; I had to perform them for her. You couldn't convey anything to her unless you read it to her. So I crammed the speech with facts. To somehow penetrate her brain.'

'David appeared magically in the upper back row of the building,' Ettridge says, chuckling. 'He was always afraid Pauline would make mistakes, and this was part of the management of his protégé.'

'Actually, I wasn't terribly happy with it – I am still not,' Hanson says of Oldfield's speech. 'I think it's too clinical. I don't think it's me. It's very repetitive. It's got content, but it lacks heart and soul, what I feel about the real issues.'

Whether Hanson thinks Oldfield's militaristic language and threatening tone are to blame for the speech's 'heartlessness' is unclear. What is clear is that the politician, with her awkwardly honest charisma, managed to make Oldfield's paranoid vision of an Australia under attack by malevolent forces her own. Hanson's riveted audience were in no doubt they were fighting an enemy on two fronts: Asian migrants invading from the outside, and Asian criminals, Aboriginal powerbrokers and the politically correct multiculturalists already inside the citadel:

> What will the future of Australia be, if we continue to be the world's immigration soft touch? Do you want it to be like another place? Indonesia perhaps? Cambodia or Vietnam? How about Iran or Iraq or maybe Lebanon? Do you want race riots, religious fanaticism, gang and drug wars? Do you want civil war?
>
> We have a chance for Australia to be the best place in the world, but we won't achieve that by aspiring to be like so many places people want to leave. We won't achieve it by throwing our

money and our land at so-called reconciliation. We won't achieve it by allowing heinous crimes, previously unknown to us, to be imported along with so many cultures so alien to the Australian way of life.

We cannot continue pursuing the failures of multiculturalism. We cannot just give away what we all know to be so valuable. Australians can no longer afford the luxury of apathy. We must win this battle, or lose the war.

It is the truth that will save Australia, not the lies. I am about the truth. When you next hear them call me a racist and a bigot, remember that it is not just me of whom they speak, but everyone who believes these things of which I speak. It is an insult shared by millions of decent patriotic Australians.

By the time Hanson raised her fist for her rousing final line, her predominantly white-bread audience was on its feet in a rapturous ovation:

Ladies and gentlemen, it is with a sense of great purpose, pride and patriotism that I officially launch the voice of the people, the party of truth, fairness and equality for all Australians, Pauline Hanson's One Nation!

Hanson's followers clapped and cheered, and her two youngest children, Adam and Lee, walked onto the stage to give her a huge bouquet. Two young women in cocktail frocks turned on a backing track to belt out a tortuous version of the anthemic 1987 ballad 'I Am Australian'. Hanson led the chorus, singing with exuberant, sweeping gestures.

Outside the hall, the diverse faces of multicultural Australia yelled back in horror: 'Asians are welcome! Racists are not! Asians are welcome! Racists are not!'

Bruce Woodley, the man who wrote the song that launched One Nation, watches footage of Hanson lip-synching his verses, visibly repulsed. 'She didn't understand the first thing about what that song meant. As a matter of fact, I notice, she didn't even know the words,' the Seekers frontman sighs. 'They just didn't get it. Her approach is exclusion, whereas mine is total inclusion.' Woodley's lawyers immediately issued a cease-and-desist order, telling Hanson if she used his song again, he'd sue.

Reliving her jubilant performance of 'I Am Australian' on the empty stage of the Ipswich Civic Centre, Hanson is miffed. 'He threatened me, "Never use the song again." Isn't it funny, I'm calling for equality and bringing us all together as one, so proud to be using a song that unites us, and yet he opposes it being used here. I thought it was a way of expressing what we, what I stood for.'

Woodley's slap down was the one sour note on an otherwise glorious night for the One Nation Troika. Hanson's galvanised audience snapped up $40 party memberships like hot cakes. They also bought copies of the party's new manifesto, *Pauline Hanson: The Truth*. Written by four anonymous Support Movement members, *The Truth* was an ad hoc compilation of Hanson's speeches and ultra-right polemical essays. It slammed Howard's new gun-control laws, the Mabo and Wik decisions, and native title. Denouncing multiculturalists, Indigenous leaders and left-wing intellectuals as the 'new class elites', *The Truth* depicted 'political correctness' as a spectre of pure evil, the tyrannical force driving the wholesale 'assault on Traditional Australia'.

With an urgent tone lurching between hysteria and black satire, *The Truth* underpinned its racist invective with illogical arguments, dubious 'historical facts' and alarmist prophesies. The chapter on political correctness reads like an environmentalist sci-fi thriller passed through a lunatic right-wing filter:

> Imagine now the republic of Australasia 2050. A country once known as Australia. It is part of the United States of Asia, formed first by various free trade and open migration agreements, and later by an official world government proclamation. Australia's deteriorating environment had a heavy impact on its people. As punishment by the world court for acts of racism because of the White Australia policy, and for acts of genocide against Asians and Aboriginals, Australia was made the seat of the dirty and polluting industries of the world. And the country's name was changed to Australasia.
>
> Australasia's new President is Poona Li Hung. Ms Hung, a lesbian, is of multi racial descent, of Indian and Chinese background and was felt by the world government to be a most suitable President. She is also part machine, the first cyborg President. Her neurocircuits were produced by a joint Korean Indian Chinese research team. In the near future, given the present rates of technological success, Australasian Presidents are likely to be purely synthetic cybernetic systems. That will be real progress, as they will be more suitable to Australasia's harsh environment and polluted air. But there are problems in paradise.
>
> The Greenies and environmental doomsayers were right in all their predictions. Global warming is occurring at an alarming rate. The reason that this occurred was China's massive industrial expansion around 2005. The United States of America, as it was called before its financial collapse and breakdown into warfare between various ethnic states, even at the peak of its industrial output, would be no match for the new China.

Unfortunately, China chose to develop using its vast coal and oil reserves. This pushed the biosphere to the brink. Now President Hung must act to show the people of Australasia that something is being done about the pollution problem.

Replace China with Trump's America, and *The Truth*, on global warming at least, came close to the truth. But when Hanson unveiled the book on 11 April 1997, the media focused on a far more explosive claim: that Aborigines had been cannibals and were therefore not worthy of Australia's support, respect or protection.

'They killed and ate their own women and children, and occasionally, their men,' *The Truth*'s authors thundered, referencing 'eye-witness accounts' in an obscure 1967 history by Hector Holthouse, *River of Gold*, about the Cape York Peninsula Palmer River Goldfields:

> The older women were often killed for eating purposes like livestock. When a gin was to be killed she was taken away to a secluded spot. One man seized and crossed her hands in front of her, while another hit her on the back of the head with a nulla-nulla or wooden sword. Then she was disembowelled and cut up for roasting. A woman who was unfaithful was killed and eaten. If a man fell from a tree, or was in any other way seriously injured, he was generally killed and eaten. Plenty of food to eat was the mainstay of the peninsula Aboriginal's existence.

When I confront Hanson and Oldfield with this excerpt from *The Truth*, they are quick to disassociate themselves from it. 'It was a stupid book. I didn't read any of it; I thought it was garbage,' says Oldfield. 'It was nothing to do with us. It was produced by a branch in South Australia. It was an example of a pitfall created by

Pauline's naivety. It was utter nonsense, the worst possible example of a high school kid's sci-fi project. Pauline wouldn't have read it – it was hard enough getting her to read a paragraph, let alone a whole book.'

Hanson, sitting at the kitchen bench at her farm, carefully studies the pages I've scanned for her. 'The only time I really saw this book *The Truth* was after it was actually published and edited.' She frowns through her glasses. 'I wasn't aware of it at all.'

But archival footage reveals that Senator Hanson, like the 'polished' politicians she once derided, has learnt to bend the truth. At the 1997 One Nation launch, she is shown autographing copy after copy of *The Truth*, as enamoured supporters wait their turn. Hanson's smiling face graces the cover, under a simple header: *Pauline Hanson: The Truth*. Hanson's former webmaster, Scott Balson, walks us through his vault of One Nation memorabilia at Brisbane's Fryer Library, and tenderly unwraps the Moroccan-bound hardback copy he bought for $290 on the night of the launch. The inside sleeve is dedicated to Balson in Hanson's florid cursive, 'for Australia's future'. At a One Nation fundraiser shortly after the launch, Hanson spruiked *The Truth* like a meat tray in a pub raffle, encouraging members to buy 'my book, *Pauline Hanson's The Truth*. It's a very informative book. And it's only twenty dollars.'

On 22 April 1997, when he was challenged by *The Age* to defend the cannibalism claims made in *The Truth*, Ettridge, the only member of the Troika who still defends the book, stood firm: 'the suggestion that we should be feeling some concern for modern-day Aborigines for suffering in the past is balanced a bit by the alternative view of whether you can feel sympathy for people who eat their babies'.

The Truth caused outrage and horror among mainstream

commentators, politicians, and Indigenous and multicultural communities. But it did not damage Hanson's credibility with her supporters, nor did it curb One Nation's rapid rise. In the weeks immediately following the party launch, One Nation branches popped up across the country like fleas, sucking support from the major parties at a staggering rate of 2 per cent per week.

'We were amazing. There was so much support out there,' Ettridge beams. 'I got caught up in how fast this thing was growing. We were the new game in town, and the media were very interested in us. Every time we had meetings, there'd be people recording, because they wanted a faux pas, something that could be shown on the 6 p.m. news. We were travelling in new territory after years of political correctness.'

'Slowly, they're waking up. And that one voice is becoming ten, it's becoming a hundred, it's becoming thousands,' the resolute Hanson told a gobsmacked *Four Corners* journalist on 16 June, after One Nation's first two months of extraordinary unbroken growth. 'I bet Howard regrets sacking me now!'

Reports of the exploding Hanson phenomenon ricocheted across Asia, prompting concerned Australian and Asian business leaders to sign a petition in Hong Kong imploring Howard to act. News broadcasts from Singapore to Jakarta picked up alarming stories from the Australian media that Asian–Australian relations had sunk to a new low, with the formerly lucrative Japanese tourism market plunging to less than 5 per cent of its former size. In Tokyo, Japanese government ministers asked a visiting DFAT delegation from Canberra for a 'Please explain'.

On 8 May, nearly a month after the One Nation launch and eight months after Hanson's maiden speech, Howard finally succumbed to the pressure. At a black-tie dinner hosted by Dr Ang and the Chinese Australian Forum, the prime minister stood up in front of Australia's multicultural powerbrokers and denounced the Member for Oxley.

'I was satisfied that the way in which the controversy was being reported in sections of Asia was probably doing some damage to our relations in the region,' Howard says of his decision to break his silence on Hanson, careful as always to blame the media and not the politician herself.

'In his oblique way, he renounced Hanson's views,' Dr Ang concedes.

'When he did it, he used words that were good, but it somehow just didn't seem to come from the heart,' recalls Neville Roach, who is not surprised that it was the damaging economic impact of allowing Hanson to continue unabated, and not the anguish and pain she had already caused, that finally motivated Howard to act.

'She is wrong when she says that Australia is in danger of being swamped by Asians,' Howard read mechanically from his notes. 'She is wrong when she denigrates foreign investment, because its withdrawal would cost Australian jobs. She is wrong when she claims Australia is headed for civil war. The political campaign by the Member for Oxley offers fear without hope. She has no positive response to the need for jobs and growth. None of these goals will be achieved through populism, divisiveness, recrimination and cheap sloganeering.'

Ang watches Howard's 8 May speech play back on my laptop and shakes his head sadly. 'I felt by that time it was too late.'

Ang was right. Within eighteen months, the One Nation juggernaut would bloat to 350 branches, with 18 000 members nationwide – a following on par with both the major parties. Less than six weeks after the party's launch in Ipswich, and despite Howard's public denouncement, Hanson's populist revolution – and the massive resistance movement it spawned – was already dividing the country.

On one side was Hanson's growing army: rural and urban Australians, emboldened by One Nation's expanding profile and catalysed by Hanson's incendiary attacks on minorities and elites. 'She was a magnet. All ages, they just seemed infatuated with her. She was their pin-up girl,' says Ettridge of the panoply of voters who signed up to the Hanson crusade. Suburban battlers, disgruntled old-school Labor supporters and disenchanted Liberals, hardened nationalists, threatened farmers, elderly traditionalists, white supremacists and proudly assimilated European Australians packed out halls and gymnasiums across the country wherever Hanson was booked to open another One Nation branch.

On the other side of the battle were the students, civil rights activists, multicultural and Indigenous community groups, and thousands of ordinary mainstream Australians. These people were not a minority in 1997; they were the majority. They treasured the tolerant, pro-diversity policies the Hawke and Keating governments had worked so hard to establish, and were deeply alarmed that Howard's eight months of silence had allowed Hansonism to flourish. Mobilising in the tens of thousands, and vastly outnumbering One Nation supporters, Australians of all ages, backgrounds and political persuasions rallied at the launch of each new party branch, determined not to let Hanson rise without a fight.

'She made us into an Australia of two different countries,' Linda Burney says.

'It wasn't just city versus country,' Margo Kingston adds. 'She had country support, but also in working-class city areas. It was two nations geographically, but also ideologically. It was like the "Hanson nation" was a repressed minority. It had once defined who we are, but didn't anymore. And when Hanson voters screamed, and we screamed back, the screams got louder.'

Footage of Hanson's branch launches between 9 May and

31 July provides a startling illustration of the 'two Australias' that One Nation created. In Hobart on 9 May, the day after Howard's lukewarm rebuke in Sydney, thousands of angry anti-Hanson protesters, many dressed as Nazis, broke into the hall where a few hundred One Nation supporters were waiting for Hanson to speak. It became a full-scale riot. As scuffles between long-haired activists, skinheads and crew-cut veterans erupted across the hall, police were forced to cancel the event and whisk the furious Hanson, who had been hiding on stage behind a curtain, back to her hotel.

At the Newcastle One Nation launch on 30 May, Hanson addressed 1500 defiant supporters in the city's town hall as a chopper waited on the roof to evacuate her, and 350 riot police kept 2000 screaming protesters at bay. Bloody fistfights broke out in the melee, with furious One Nation supporters asserting their right to free speech while protesters pelted them with tomatoes and eggs, chanting, 'Racists, fascists, anti-gays, right-wing bigots go away!'

When Hanson and her bodyguards arrived to open the Dandenong branch of One Nation on 7 July, the party's comparatively genteel launch back in April was a distant memory. News crews were covering Hanson's appearances not as political events but as a blood sport. The largest anti–One Nation protest in Victoria, Dandenong elevated the war between mainstream Australia and Hanson's army to new levels of violence. Mounted police galloped through a heaving crowd of 4000 protesters, beating them with truncheons as One Nation supporters struggled through the fracas and helped each other over barricades, taking refuge in the safety of the hall. An elderly Hanson supporter was beaten unconscious as he left the launch. Footage of Keith Warburton, pale and bleeding in a gutter as protesters and cops skirmished around him, dominated media coverage for weeks. The image captured a horrific fact: Australia was at war with itself.

The conflict and violence escalated, as Hanson moved on to Adelaide and the Gold Coast. By the time she launched the Ipswich branch of One Nation on the night of 31 July, she was fed up. She stood at an open-air podium and yelled back at the hundreds of Australians gathered to denounce her, as a line of Ipswich's finest in Kevlar vests formed a protective barrier between her and the screaming rabble.

'I am not going anywhere! You *won't* get rid of me,' Hanson spat in the torchlight, her arm stiffly outstretched, looking eerily like the tirading Hitler at the night-time rally in the Berlin Sportpalast in 1933. 'The only people that are going to get rid of me are my constituents! Not you! Never, *never you!*'

Who was to blame for the violence at One Nation events – and why it was happening – became a hotly contested topic. The national convener of the anti-Hanson 'Resistance' movement, Sean Healy, justified the aggressive tactics Resistance used on the grounds that 'if it weren't for the counter-demonstrations, anti-racist sentiment would remain passive, and Hanson would get away with presenting her racist politics as in some way legitimate'. *Green Left Weekly*, in a largely ignored report, pointed out that the Warburton attack was an isolated incident, asserting that anti-Hanson protesters were largely peaceful and that the rallies proved something important: 'many more people are opposed to Hanson's racism than support it'.

A mere one hundred One Nation supporters came to see Hanson speak in Dandenong. The 4000 people who gathered to demonstrate against her proved that opposition to One Nation was both diverse and broad. Along with student-led socialist and civil rights groups, there were members of the expanding Campaign

Against Racism, as well as ordinary citizens of the municipality of Greater Dandenong City. A street away from the violent scenes at Hanson's launch, Dandenong mayor Greg Harris hosted a silent vigil and a multicultural concert.

'The wave of hatred that she unleashed was felt in all of our communities,' recalls Professor Marcia Langton. 'But at the same time, a bit of a silver lining, and that is, Aboriginal people and Asian Australians got together and started talking about how do we deal with this new wave of racism?'

To combat One Nation's escalating influence, Langton joined forces with New South Wales MP and Council for Aboriginal Reconciliation member Helen Sham-Ho and a number of other Indigenous and multicultural leaders, to fight Hanson in the media. With the support of New South Wales premier Bob Carr, Sham-Ho organised a large Rally Against Racism on the Manly Corso, directly outside One Nation's Sydney HQ. Philip Ruddock, the minister for Immigration and Multicultural and Indigenous Affairs, led the clapping crowd as an eight-legged Chinese lion danced under Ettridge's office window to chase the 'evil spirits' of Hansonism away.

In Melbourne, Muslim Australian student Randa Abdel-Fattah joined Australians mobilising under the banner of the newly formed Unity Party, which was preparing to field ethnically diverse candidates nationwide to run against One Nation in the polls. At a widely televised Chinese Australian Forum event, Dr Ang gave an impassioned speech to his politically cautious but financially influential members, imploring them to take a stand:

> Firm words a year ago would have been enough to dispel any lingering doubts that we still have the White Australia policy. But we have squandered the opportunity – talk is now cheap.

> A sceptical world is now watching to see whether we will match our words with deeds. The Pauline Hanson One Nation Party's efforts are very similar to the Nazis. We must not forget history, we must not forget Nazi Germany. If we do, we could end up more than wearing black armbands, we could end up weeping on the grave of Fair Go.

Langton, Sham-Ho, Ang and Abdel-Fattah were just four of the hundreds of thousands of Australians who rallied against One Nation between 1997 and 1998. But Hanson categorically rejects the suggestion that her opposition was a broad church.

'A lot of my rallies were organised by the Liberal or Labor Party, paying people to come and protest,' she says angrily. 'It was the same old signs, the militants and the other groups. The Labor Party bussed them down. In Tasmania, a woman told me her daughter was paid ten dollars to protest against me. They thought they had every right to stop freedom of speech in this country!'

John Howard, who would later dismiss the one million Australians who marched against the Iraq invasion in 2003 as a mere 'fringe group', is quick to take Hanson's side. 'Those largely left-wing Socialist Alliance demonstrations were very ugly. People are entitled to demonstrate energetically but never violently, and there was certainly a lot of blame that could be attached to the socialist left.'

Pasquarelli agrees. In his mind, the anti-Hanson protesters were the usual marginal suspects: 'the loony and hysterical socialist left, Aboriginal gravy-trainers, taut-faced technocrats and the pointy-heads from academia and the public service. All those scumbags out there in the streets, the GetUp! sort of people. Drongos throwing tampons and condoms of urine at her, packages of human excreta, absolutely disgusting.'

Hanson is still furious at the harassment she and her supporters were forced to endure. 'The protesters were the violent ones, not One Nation members. The police had to put up with these thugs and vermin. The way they pushed elderly people around who could have been their mothers, it was disgusting, and it went on time and time again. But Australians didn't desert me; they said, "We're not frightened, we're going to back you!" And people were spat on when they came out, and people said, "She's not racist if you listen to her!"'

In response to the escalating violence in 1997, Howard repeatedly recommended that Australians simply 'ignore' Hanson's public appearances rather than rally against her. He still blames the conflict One Nation generated, and the accelerating support Hanson received, on the protest movement itself. 'I think that a lot of the sympathy that Pauline Hanson got derived from the image of a battling woman being harassed in a violent, vile and bilious manner at meetings,' he says. 'I thought that was attracting sympathy towards her. And if the objective of those who conducted the rallies was to demonise her, then they failed miserably.'

In the turbulent months following One Nation's launch, Howard was embroiled in a battle of his own. Determined to stop Hanson from luring disgruntled Coalition voters into the One Nation fold, he toured the country, promoting his plans to wind back the High Court's contentious decisions on land rights and native title, and asserting the Liberal Party's credentials as a responsible, mainstream party of the centre. Footage of Howard's speeches between April and June 1997 reveals the eerie extent to which his messages on race and identity were morphing into Hanson's own.

'I do not believe in intergenerational guilt when it comes to Aboriginal affairs,' Howard told farmers in Queensland. 'I do not feel a sense of shame for our history,' he reassured voters in Townsville. 'Don't believe the fearmongering! Native title can't throw you off your property, we'd never allow that to happen!' he implored graziers in Longreach. 'Now, I find it offensive for my colleagues to be likened to membership of the Ku Klux Klan,' he railed at Labor MPs in Canberra when accused of being too cosy with Hanson and her fans, one of whom was the American KKK leader, David Duke. 'The Wik decision pushed the pendulum too far in the Aboriginal direction,' he soothed Australia's angry pastoralists, promising to bring pro-Indigenous legislation back to the 'middle'. By 27 May, when Howard addressed the Australian Reconciliation Convention in Melbourne, his credibility with Australia's First Peoples was on the brink of collapse.

'We must not join those who would portray Australia's history since 1788 as little more than a disgraceful record of imperialism,' the prime minister asserted, as his predominantly Indigenous audience listened with apprehension and disbelief.

'Such an approach will be repudiated by the overwhelming majority of Australians, who are proud of what this country has achieved, although inevitably acknowledging the blemishes in its past history.'

As Howard continued to speak, audience members, one by one, began to stand and turn their backs on him. Instead of adjusting his stubbornly unapologetic tone, the prime minister lost his legendary self-control. Launching into a red-faced, spitting tirade about the Wik decision and his plan to water it down, Howard bashed his lectern like a tantrum-throwing toddler: 'I repudiate the claim that my plan involves a massive handout of freehold title at taxpayer expense! That is an absolute myth! It is absolutely contrary to the fact and I absolutely repudiate it!'

Howard's outburst marked the beginning of the end of positive relations between the conservative government and Indigenous Australians.

'I was in the audience,' recalls Helen Sham-Ho. 'And when Howard was standing up it was just terrible. Almost everyone turned their back to him. I think he was upset, and he was really worked up because people were very rude to him. He was just so badly received, but I think he deserved it at the time.'

Linda Burney is less sympathetic. 'You cannot tell me that John Howard did not cash in on the sentiments being stirred up by Pauline Hanson. Hanson rode the perfect storm. Her views were Howard's best ally. What they unleashed in this country fed perfectly into his agenda. When Howard banged the podium and yelled at 2000 Australians about native title, that was a definitive turning point. You only have to look at the culture wars, at what Howard unleashed on the population with the lies and the divisiveness of the native title debate. It was a time of high unemployment, the economy wasn't too great, and a lot of social welfare benefits had been wound back. It all fed absolutely into Hanson's narrative. The narrative that Aboriginal people somehow get advantages over the rest of Australians. That's the real story of this era. Hanson's ascendancy was very useful to Howard. She fitted in perfectly to the Howard view of the world.'

By mid-1997, polls were indicating that 13 per cent of the voting public endorsed One Nation's platform, with up to 95 per cent of talkback callers feeling that Hanson was 'speaking for them'. Cartoonists, songwriters and satirists lampooned Howard and Hanson as a happily married couple. 'Hanson is a puppet! Howard pulls the strings!' was now a common chant at the protests that continued to dog Hanson across the country. In parliament, Labor MPs gleefully accused Howard of being 'in bed' with the Member for Oxley.

Delighted that the One Nation effect had penetrated as high as the prime minister's office, Ettridge and Oldfield persuaded Hanson to register One Nation in Queensland for its electoral debut in the 1998 state election.

'I didn't want to stand [in Queensland] because we were coming up for a federal election in 1998, and I argued if we get candidates who are not up to the job, the media will make mincemeat of them.' Hanson frowns. 'And I didn't want to show the major parties the support we had.'

Hazelton agreed with her. 'If you build a house without a foundation, it will all fall down – and that's what will happen to One Nation,' she warned. But the Davids overrode them.

'Pauline didn't want to run in Queensland. I don't know why.' Ettridge shrugs. 'David and I had to tread carefully with her, to convince her this was a necessary part of the growth of the party. You couldn't just have a party running one candidate from Ipswich – you needed members running in all states, and even in local councils.'

'We used to call Pauline "the sea anchor",' Oldfield groans. 'You had me and David in the rowboat, and Pauline kept plunging in and stopping us. She was afraid and often cried about what she was doing. She was insecure. She had no confidence. She'd cry on my shoulder and I'd reassure her and give her pep talks.'

Hanson was under severe emotional stress when she registered One Nation with the Queensland Electoral Commission on 27 June 1997. Her meteoric public rise as party leader masked the vicious backstage power struggles she'd been embroiled in since One Nation's April launch.

Oldfield's refusal to quit his job with Abbott had presented the first challenge. For weeks after the launch, he continued to advise Hanson on the sly, briefing her interim media manager,

David Thomas, via anonymous phone calls.

'Oldfield comes across as confident but he suffers from cowardice,' Ettridge observes. 'All his rhetoric is about war but he never served. He didn't leave Abbott until he was sure One Nation was a goer. In the end, I just said, "David, I need your help. You gotta quit."'

'He waited, and when he saw the time was right, he jumped,' recalls Hanson with distaste. On 9 May, having already secured a glowing recommendation from the unsuspecting Abbott, Oldfield finally said goodbye. 'I gave him one month's notice,' Oldfield insists. 'I don't know if it's ever going to go down in history correctly, but the Friday that I was leaving Tony's office, he said, "Ma-a-ate, it's nothing to do with Hanson, is it?" And I said directly, "Tony, we've been friends. I've done everything I can for you. It's the one thing I can't tell you." On the Monday, I was in Pauline's office.'

One week later, the triumphant Oldfield outed himself on prime time as Hanson's new mastermind. The blindsided Abbott was besieged with calls from irate Liberal MPs, furious that he'd allowed Oldfield to spawn the One Nation Frankenstein under his nose. Mortified, Abbott compared Oldfield's and Hanson's mobile phone records with Pasquarelli, tallying up the shocking extent to which he had been duped. The Oxford boxer and future prime minister was not one to let betrayal slide. Hanson and Oldfield had just acquired their most dangerous enemy.

'David's a very loyal, credible, honest person, and I am happy to have him on my team,' a simpering Hanson told the ABC's Tony Jones, as her new spin doctor sat smugly beside her.

'You can't make a move without him?' Jones asked cheekily, and Oldfield mimed pulling invisible puppet strings above Hanson's head. The gag was not an empty one: with Oldfield in the driver's seat, their relationship started to fray. Oldfield was determined to save Hanson from herself, for the good of One Nation. Hanson, who had always seen herself as 'no-one's puppet', was furious at being told what to do.

'He used to stay in the back wing,' Hanson remembers, of the long weeks Oldfield spent advising her at the farm. 'My daughter used to get so frustrated, she'd say, "What does he do in the bathroom all this time?" He was plucking this or putting cream on that, and I thought, "My God, he's worse than any woman!" No-one could deal with him! Everyone thought he was so egotistic. He wouldn't stop and listen to other people. It was all about David Oldfield. That's the difference between him and I. I don't care about being the head of a political party. I started it to give people a voice and someone to vote for. David wanted power, recognition, his name in lights. I couldn't care less. Even today if someone came along and could do a better job representing One Nation than me, I'd say go for it!'

Oldfield, on the other hand, felt like a top-flight salesman shackled with a political product that was not up to scratch. 'It was a running sore with me and Ettridge,' he sighs. 'This woman who'd never been captain of a netball team was now running the most powerful independent party in the country. You were always walking a tightrope with Pauline, because something could pop into her head which is irrelevant or wrong, and she'd blurt it out. And you were always having to explain what she meant.'

As Hanson battled what she saw as Oldfield's belittling, micromanaging style, she was also fending off increasingly vicious attacks in the media. David Thomas, the man Oldfield had deposed, denounced One Nation as 'a party founded on deceit. It is going to have a lot of problems. Oldfield will take the party out too far racially. He's a racist.' Speculation that Hanson had lost control of her party began to escalate, as One Nation branches arced up against the dictatorial directives issuing from Ettridge's Manly HQ.

Hong Kong politician Emily Lau fronted an excoriating *60 Minutes* critique, inflaming public perceptions that Hanson was Oldfield's pawn. She portrayed the One Nation head as an ignorant bigot who was out of her depth, and leading her gullible followers down a dangerous path. 'We have been hearing it loud and clear for ten months now,' said Lau. 'More and more Australians are anti-Asian. They want to shut the gate on us, people whose main concern is the colour of our skin.'

'Even in the House, [Peter] Costello and [Alexander] Downer tried to belittle me in parliament and the media of what type of person I was,' Hanson complains. '"Far-right wing", "Wants to take us back to the '50s", all these derogatory comments, because I was getting a lot of support and they had to counteract that.'

But far more harrowing than her ongoing public humiliation were the death threats Hanson had begun to receive on a regular basis. Sorting out the threats from the fan mail had always been part of the administrative load in Hanson's office, but what had started as a trickle under Pasquarelli was now a daily torrent.

'Pauline used to get really ugly death threats – not that there's a good-looking death threat.' Oldfield smirks. 'People wrote about not just killing her, but doing some really ugly, serial-killer type stuff. Like you see in movies, where people cut out newsprint and stick them on pieces of paper! They were constant. We had a secure section in the office where they'd be opened with gloves. And whatever was serious would be taken by police and fingerprinted. There were some stand-out ones that would make your blood run cold.'

'I had a price on my head. I think it was about $10 000, and it was from the Vietnamese that it came from – that's what they told me,' Hanson says quietly.

'Well, isn't that funny?' Pasquarelli says, grabbing his 1998 memoir, *The Pauline Hanson Story... by the Man Who Knows*. 'The ones I took, they weren't from Asians. They were good old Anglos!' He flips through to the book's picture inserts, where the vilest threats have been reprinted in full.

'"You are my favourite I want blood!"' he reads. '"Hanson you are a fucking cunt!" "Everyone has rights in this country, and I'm telling you, you fucking whore, that I will marry who I want." "I will rape your mother and your kids, and blame the Asians." That's a nice nutter, writing that!'

The Australian Federal Police (AFP) responded swiftly, tripling Hanson's security detail. They installed surveillance cameras throughout her house, bombproofed its foundations and set up a 24/7 surveillance van at the bottom of her farm. By June 1997, Hanson was the most heavily guarded politician in Australia. ASIO judged her to be a higher security risk than any other public figure, including the prime minister. A *Sun-Herald* report revealed that the annual cost of protecting the Member for Oxley was more than double her annual parliamentary wage.

'They put in bulletproof glass. All my mail was checked before it came here,' Hanson says tiredly, as she sits in our van outside her old electoral office in the W G Hayden Humanities Centre in Ipswich. 'It was dreadful! I had my entire privacy basically taken away from me. They didn't want me leaving the property without someone being with me constantly all the time. I had a van on my yard, security screening, alarm systems. A couple of workers I met one night said, "We've been working in your office, and we found a bug in your ceiling." It's quite evident it was a bug in my office. And this is all conspiracy, whether [the threats] were true or whether the federal government set it up to monitor where I was going, and who I was talking to, because I was watched 24/7. And yeah, it was extremely hard.'

Hanson's children also felt the toll. Hanson moved them into private boarding schools, where their new classmates terrorised them about their controversial mother. 'At least they were safe there,' sighs Hanson. 'I had many moments where I was torn about the kids. Lee would be in tears; she wasn't coping. Adam was being bullied – he's a deep thinker. He'd say, "Mum, they don't know you. They don't know the person you are."'

The most sensitive of Hanson's sons, Adam, now a singer-songwriter, reassured his mother he'd cope, writing her a letter encouraging her to 'follow your dreams and make the world a better place'.

On 16 June, Hanson hit breaking point. Visibly stressed, she told the ABC, 'My life's become like a goldfish bowl.' Two weeks later, the politician's wavering resolve was finally shattered – by an unknown Sydney drag queen. At a queer underground concert on George Street, a creature in a garish yellow jacket and a bright orange fright wig announced herself as Pauline Pantsdown, and lip-synched a pop-song mashup of Hanson's most famous pronouncements. Simon Hunt, the man beneath the make-up, had remoulded the Hanson sound bites he'd been collating since her maiden speech against a funky nightclub beat. His song, 'Backdoor Man', featured Hanson's quavery voice declaring, among other things, that she was a proud homosexual, a 'caring potato', and in league with the KKK.

'Backdoor Man' was an instant sensation, playing on high rotation on the ABC's Triple J and soaring to the top of the mainstream charts. The horrified Hanson immediately slapped an injunction on the song, and, within ten days of its unveiling, it was off the air. Oldfield blasted the song as 'the biggest sex scandal of the decade', proof of Australia's misogynistic treatment of female politicians.

'It was disrespectful. It associated her personally with sexual acts she didn't undertake,' Oldfield says, with some authority. Hanson's lawyers went to town.

'Her case was that people would take the song literally,' explains Hunt of Hanson's ultimately successful defamation action. 'So lines like "I'm a backdoor man with the KKK", Hanson's lawyers defined as "the plaintiff is proud to engage in unnatural sexual acts, including anal sex with members of the KKK". "I'm a very caring potato" is probably the only line in the song with no meaning at all, yet here it is, defined in the Supreme Court, as "a potato, which is understood to be a word for a male engaged in sexual acts with another male, who has his genitalia voluntarily inserted into his anal passage" – which is probably the broadest definition of a vegetable that we're ever likely to see in Australian law.'

'What a joke Pauline Pantsdown was. He was an absolute idiot ratbag!' Hanson seethes when I ask her about her singularly un-Australian decision to censor Pantsdown's larrikin piss-take. 'I think the words in it, that's what I found offensive: "couch potato", and I thought, "No. Crossed the line." I have no problem with having a laugh at yourself, but I am a member of parliament, and I have a right to be heard, and I am not going to let a ratbag try to shut me down. And that's why I proceeded to actually have the song banned, and it was never to be played again.'

After the humiliating 'Backdoor Man' debacle, Hanson fled from the public eye. Pilloried by the press, ridiculed in parliament, abused by protesters, stalked by lunatics and worried about her kids, she informed Oldfield she was quitting all media and retreated to her farm. On 31 August, when Lady Di, pursued by paparazzi, crashed and died in the Pont de l'Alma tunnel, the teary Hanson watched with quiet recognition. She too had tried to fight for her people. She too had been ridiculed by the media and attacked by the status quo. 'We'll never change anything. They'll kill us before we get there,' she told Oldfield.

With Hanson out of the media spotlight, One Nation's approval rating plummeted. Oldfield was beside himself. His ambitious plans to field a One Nation candidate in every electorate in Queensland were in tatters. 'I said, "Pauline, I don't think you understand: if you were Coca-Cola and you stopped doing advertisements, by next week Pepsi would be dominating the sales!" Ultimately, we got to a point towards the end of 1997 where Pauline hasn't been seen, the polls start to go down, and basically it was all over for the One Nation party by November. The hurrah and the yippee and the whoopee had all fizzled out of it, and we were looking at about 3 per cent in the polls. I had to resurrect it.'

To get Hanson back in the headlines, Oldfield devised a stunt straight out of a Hollywood thriller.

'Pauline was under a substantial level of personal threat, and I thought, people should be aware of this,' he says. 'The first ever political assassination in Australia – it was very much a possibility!'

In a stroke of marketing brilliance, Oldfield persuaded Hanson to record a tape 'for her people', to be shown as a voice of encouragement from the grave if she was murdered.

'I was very hesitant about doing it, and I said to him on the proviso it would never be released, and he assured me it wouldn't,' Hanson says, scowling.

'Yeah, I'm not sure that's the case,' Oldfield says with a grin. He had already brokered a deal with Channel 7's high-rating *Witness* show to air the tape on prime time. 'There was never any issue with them playing a small section of it – that was agreed to. But sadly, a lot of things that you say to Pauline don't register for very long.'

On 25 November 1997, the softly lit Hanson, wearing a pretty pastel blouse, faced millions of viewers on prime time and calmly announced, 'Fellow Australians, if you are seeing me now, it means

I have been murdered. For the sake of our children and our children's children, you must fight on.'

It was one of the most surreal events in Australian political history. The fallout was immediate, and vicious. The media compared Hanson to cult leaders Jim Jones and Charles Manson. Her political enemies tore her credibility to shreds.

'Everything Hanson does is bizarre,' scoffed Victorian premier Jeff Kennett.

'This is pathetic behaviour from a real political desperate,' sneered deputy federal Labor leader Gareth Evans.

'It's very weird,' John Howard said, barely able to conceal his glee.

'She's in a tragic redneck celebrity vortex that she doesn't want to escape. And then you have these *Triumph of the Will*-style film productions by David Oldfield. It's a joke,' declared respected Indigenous advocate Noel Pearson.

In the House of Representatives, Hanson was eviscerated by ageing Liberal patriarchs, who urged her fellow MPs to 'turn their back on her', thundering, 'The threat suggesting she might be assassinated is such a breach of privilege, it brings this place into contempt!'

An ad for a popular takeaway chicken outlet featured a cartoon chook squawking, 'Fellow Australians, if you are seeing this, I have been roasted.'

The universal consensus was that Hanson had murdered herself. The Member for Oxley and her fledgling One Nation party were dead.

'The ridicule he put me through in parliament: I didn't need that!' Hanson rages in her kitchen, still furious at Oldfield's deception. 'They demanded I apologise for this tape and I wasn't going to. They weren't wearing my shoes, they didn't know what I was going through! The media made me a laughing stock of the country!'

Hanson's death tape is now burnt into the national psyche, alongside 'Please explain' and 'swamped by Asians'. Even the most bizarre media stunt Senator Hanson has pulled since her 2016 election – swimming in the last unbleached corner of the Great Barrier Reef to disprove global warming – fails to eclipse the magnificent absurdity of 'I have been murdered'.

But as far as Oldfield is concerned, Hanson's fake death produced her greatest triumph. In early 1998, as Australians enjoyed their summer holidays, secure in the knowledge that Hanson was safely buried, the people of Queensland stubbornly rallied around their poor, pilloried Pauline and her seventy-nine fledgling One Nation candidates.

The death tape 'worked perfectly', Oldfield says, grinning. 'It propelled the party straight back into the media, and the polls just went up and up. And they never stopped. They just went up and up, bit by bit, until the night of the Queensland state election, where political history was made.'

On 13 June 1998, One Nation won an unthinkable eleven seats in Queensland, decimating the conservatives. The Liberal National Party's decision to give preferences to One Nation, on the assumption that the amateur party's own electoral chances were close to nil, had helped seal its fate. With a shocking 22.7 per cent per cent of the primary vote and 784 590 Queenslanders behind them, Hanson and her underdog army had leached the conservative base and delivered power to Labor.

The fish shop lady from Ipswich was no longer 'the accidental tourist of politics'. She was a major political force.

'I think they're going to take me a little bit more seriously now,' a glowing Hanson told the shocked election night press pack.

She was right.

Chapter 8
The fall of Pauline

We were a real threat. I was! They had to stop me!
—Pauline Hanson, interview, November 2015

One Nation's extraordinary triumph at the 1998 Queensland election made Hanson a political superstar: the leader of the third most powerful party in the country. John Howard and the conservatives scrambled to address the massive threat the seemingly invincible Member for Oxley and her emboldened supporters now posed in the looming federal election.

'It was a day of euphoric [sic]. I felt vindicated. They knew I was a threat; they had to stop me,' says Hanson, both angry and proud. In four short months, her enemies would collude to force her out of office. But the Big Party machine would not stop there. In 2003, the disgraced politician would find herself strip-searched and shivering on a cold cement slab in the suicide-watch cell of Wacol prison, facing a nine-year sentence for fraud.

Yet Hanson's incendiary fall from grace only served to make her a martyr to her devoted followers. A decade after her conviction, in January 2015, the flame that Hanson's battlers still carry for the Ipswich underdog who stood up to the bigwigs of power is on full display at the Gatton Shire Hall. Hanson, fighting her tenth election campaign – this time for the Queensland seat of Lockyer – is holding an American-style town hall forum to understand how 'grassroots Australians' are feeling. Nestled in the fertile valley between Ipswich and Toowoomba, eighty kilometres west of Brisbane, Gatton is Hanson heartland.

We've been filming volunteers carefully taping Hanson corflutes and One Nation banners to the auditorium walls for hours, as they wait for their idol to arrive. On a table to one side, Hanson's social media manager, Saraya Beric, lays out party merchandise and readies her laptop to monitor the Pauline Hanson's Please Explain Facebook page, when the forum goes live. At the foot of the stage, a big-boned Hungarian and his Malaysian Australian mate are on their knees, making sure the Aussie flags they've bought at the Waynes World discount barn over the road are hung just right.

'I thought it would be a good idea to make her more patriotic, because she's a very proud Australian,' says the Hungarian. 'It's from watching old town hall meetings in America. They're very patriotic over there. I'm trying to get some of that back into Australia.' To him, the fact the flags are made in China just supports Hanson's anti-globalist stance: 'If nothing else, it will win her a few more votes. I'm a country boy brought up in the city. My parents were migrants. My grandfather worked on the Snowy Mountains scheme. They were running away from communism. We're losing more of our civil liberties all the time. I believe in less taxes, small government and a stronger economy. We're seeing the death of the middle class. I definitely think Pauline should be in power. Having an independent in parliament keeps the bastards honest.'

An Ipswich accountant and his well-heeled wife declare themselves 'middle-of-the-road voters', curious to hear what 'Pauline has got to say'.

Doug, a retired labourer, remembers handing out how-to-vote cards for Hanson when she made her first historic bid for power back in 1996. 'Labor were saying she's racist, and I was counting the votes, and the little Labor fella turned to the other and said, "We're gone," and I went through the second preferences, and I yelled out, "She's won!" And that's when Pauline realised she'd been elected to parliament! I just care for this place, you know? I cry for what's been done to this country since 1972. It's a disgrace. I'm not a gambler, but I bet that we'd win nine seats in 1998 in Queensland, and I won nine hundred dollars. I haven't placed a bet since.'

Rusty, a leather-faced cockie in a 1970s tie, has championed Hanson in every election she's fought. 'I've been saying for seventeen years they're controlling all of us by stealth, and it's all run out of Washington, DC, and I have their ABN numbers. They're brainwashing our kids at school. I have a lot of time for Pauline, and these other bastards, like [Hanson's LNP opponent] Ian Rickuss. I call him "Lick Ass". Then we've got that halfwit Labor bloke. I hate to get fired up about all this and hate to think what our grandkids are going to get. Sixty years ago, this wasn't a bad country. A bloke could make a decent quid. Now they've taken away our freedom of speech – and I read the constitution every day.'

Hanson's line-up of speakers caters perfectly to the paranoid alt-right conspiracy theories that tend to appeal to Rusty and the hundred Gattonites now taking their seats. Promoting Hanson's bid for election are the constitutional monarchist and conservative lawyer Professor David Flint, the virulently nationalist leader of the Food Producers Landowners Action Group (FLAG), Peter Manuel, and, in a media scoop we all completely miss at the time, an unknown ex–coal miner named Malcolm Roberts. A last-minute ring-in when global-warming denier Professor Ian Plimer cancelled, Roberts is alleged to be a member of the anti-government outfit Sovereign Citizens. He has written many reports claiming that climate change is a scam by the United Nations and international bankers to impose a socialist world order. Roberts cites several anti-Semitic scholars and Holocaust denier Eustace Mullins as his 'primary references'. No-one, including Roberts, has any idea that in eighteen months' time he will be joining Hanson on the crossbench in federal parliament as One Nation's most outlandish senator.

Hanson strides into the hall, determined to ensure the tech check runs smoothly for the august company she's assembled.

'I think I should sit here,' she tells a young guy mixing sound levels as she climbs onto the stage. 'It will look better, and it will break up the men – you've got three men all lined up like ducks in a row!' Hanson repositions the name cards on the speakers' table, as the blushing Hungarian, too shy to speak, makes a little adjustment to the 'Give Us Our Country Back!' sign taped to the dais at Hanson's stiletto-clad feet.

Miked up and satisfied, Hanson retreats to a side door to await her grand entrance. The hall's orange plastic chairs fill up fast, and Hanson winks at our camera, pleased. With an actor's expert judgement, she listens for a lull in the buzzing crowd then sweeps in to greet her people, graciously accepting their congratulations, handshakes and smiles. 'Hi! . . . Hello there . . . Thank you.' Hanson beams as she moves through her clapping followers to join the three men already lined up on stage.

Manuel, Flint and Roberts may be a who's who of the burgeoning alt-right movement in Australia, but as the forum gets under way it is clear they have none of Hanson's magnetism or appeal.

People listen politely to Flint and Manuel making the case for laxer racial discrimination laws and tougher restrictions on Chinese buy-ups of Australian land. They clap in all the right places when Roberts depicts climate change as a government-funded conspiracy that lines the pockets of mendacious scientists with wasteful taxpayer-funded grants. Then Hanson chimes in, and the atmosphere instantly warms. A sea of expectant faces, wizened and youthful, defeated and hopeful, turn to her with wide-mouthed hunger, lapping up her every tremulous, grammatically mangled word.

'In 1998, we won the Queensland election, and it changed the face of Australia. Then I got 36 per cent of the vote in the federal election, and the major parties preference against me, and that was enough to put a Liberal in my seat,' Hanson begins shakily, anguish in her eyes. 'Every election, even last time with the nude photos, they are colluding against me, and that's why they are so determined to keep me out of parliament, and you have to ask yourself the reason. Why?'

Hanson's captivated audience shake their heads as one.

Manuel leans close to his mic. 'I'll tell you why, Pauline, because they're scared of ya.'

The crowd erupts in a righteous, foot-stomping cheer. This is the story they've come to hear. Pauline the battler, who rose from their ranks to make a difference, and was beaten down when she got too close. The never-say-die underdog mum, who, with the help of true-blue Aussies like themselves, will rise to fight the bastards all over again. Hanson receives their love with stoic dignity. She's magnificent and fierce, working her voice-of-the-people persona with indignant pride.

'I'm sick of these boys – it's a boys' club – you have to be a yes person. I saw it when I was in parliament, twenty years ago. They would come into the chamber when the bells were ringing and a minister said to me – an *independent* – what are we voting for? They have no idea, believe me. I want to reduce the number of ministers by half!'

The Gatton hall fills with laughter, and Hanson grows serious, switching tack with evangelical skill. 'It's been one hell of a job, but this is only the start. I want to rebuild the party and send a message to the major parties to bring it back to the people. And it will be people power. I will tell you now, I will not lie to you, I will tell you the truth. I am not perfect and don't have everything right all the time but I am passionate about our culture and I am not turning my back, to walk away and see some lily-livered, pusillanimous politician come in and take away what I love so dearly: my country!'

Afterwards, Hanson is mobbed. Men queue to shake her hand. Children ask her to sign flags and posters. Women fawn around her in awe-struck wonder. Doug, the man who helped Hanson get elected in 1996, spins her into his arms, covering her with kisses as he twirls her in a body-hugging slow waltz. Hanson hugs him right back. Then her mobile rings – a right-wing community radio show in America wants to know how the independent politician's tenth tilt at power is going.

'If I win the seat, I'll be screaming from the rooftop and I'll be the proudest of Australians to be speaking up for Queenslanders on the floor of parliament,' Hanson trills. 'And I'm sure they won't want to see me there again! But I'd like to say to your American listeners, come on down here, we have a great country, it's still unique in many ways, Australian hospitality is wonderful and I have a great and close bond with America. And I know if I win, it's all thanks to Alan and the Safe Worlds team, so thank you, Alan, for all your help . . .'

Safe Worlds appears to be Hanson's latest sponsor: an ambitious ecommerce start-up run by a Queensland octogenarian with serious alt-right credentials, Alan Metcalfe. According to Metcalfe's Jetson-esque, FX-laden YouTube videos, the concept for Safe Words came to him in a God-induced epiphany in 1999, when he realised the law of universal logic, as it is known in the IT world, mirrored the 'law of thought' in the Bible. Metcalfe, who has fraternised with American Christian and far-right figures since the Cold War, believes his revolutionary platform will usurp Facebook, Twitter and eBay as 'the home of Free Enterprise, a level playing field that all the world can use!' Designed to unite conservative Western political groups through community channels linked to its commercial arm, Safe Worlds is Metcalfe's Noah's Ark in a digital Babylon. With 'the flood of electronic information inundating the world with increasing confusion', Metcalfe writes, 'the end of the world, as we know it, is nigh'.

Hanson, two decades on from *The Truth*, obviously still has a knack for attracting kooky far-right polemicists. Having dutifully given Metcalfe his plug on American radio, she shuts her mobile and joins a cluster of adoring women.

'My dad helped you back in 1998, and there was a ten-grand bounty for any journo who could make you look bad,' a pink-shirted pensioner tells her. 'They were trying to get pics of you going to the loo! This country is run by the media, and you won't sell out to them, so they try to destroy you! I am here to help you any which way I can.'

'Well, thank you,' Hanson says with a smile. The complicity of Big Media in her political destruction is one of Hanson's favourite themes. In her mind, the biased press pack tracked her downward spiral, from One Nation's Queensland triumph to her devastating 1998 federal defeat, with merciless derision. And leading the evil cabal that hounded her into oblivion is one journalist: Margo Kingston.

'Margo was whispering in my ear and telling me what was going on. And a couple of things that came out afterwards that were untrue, so I've had a gutful about the media that have not reported the truth, or manipulated what was behind me,' Hanson says crankily. 'You had the media mongrels like Packer and Murdoch, and the journos were told they had to write negative stories about myself, and even today they're still doing the same. I am so angry with the media, how they have portrayed me over the years. I see Margo as the media. That's it.'

Kingston, when I pass this on, lets out a weak chuckle. Between 1998 and 2003, the star reporter's downhill trajectory loosely mirrored Hanson's own. Kingston became embroiled in controversy for positioning Hanson as a politician to be engaged with, rather than scorned. Branded by Tony Abbott and some media colleagues as the journalist who got 'too close' to Hanson, Kingston was also, paradoxically, seen as 'too left for Howard's world' by the new editorial team at the *Sydney Morning Herald*. By the time Hanson began fighting the legal battle that would eventually see her jailed, Kingston had been 'demoted' to the *SMH* online.

'I can't remember how I ended up in her bathroom. I think it was to go to the loo,' Kingston says of the night she slept over at Hanson's farm during One Nation's 1998 federal campaign. 'My memory is there was a hell of a lot of make-up all lined up, and I don't use make-up and haven't seen a lot of women's bathrooms, but it just seemed a hell of a lot. And she's made the point, in several articles, that I was a liar, because I said there's a lot of make-up in her cupboard. Of all the things I've written about Hanson, it's just a *classic* that that's the one thing that gets her freaked out. Really.'

Covering Hanson's rise and fall, then reliving it in her book *Off the Rails*, caused Kingston 'a three-point burnout: financial, physical and mental'. She needed years to recover. The political and emotional stakes, as Hanson fought to hold on to power and Kingston fought to make sense of the fractured country Hanson had created, were high. Hanson and the media, with Kingston at the helm, were 'locked [in] an embrace which both parties don't want to be in, but they're there', Pasquarelli has observed. The Hanson/Kingston saga is a tragicomedy of divided loyalties, broken boundaries and betrayal. It played out like an antipodean version of the 1949 political drama *All the King's Men* – with Kingston as the conflicted reporter Jack Burden and Hanson as the populist hick politician Willie Stark.

It was Hanson who made the first move in her tortuous relationship with Kingston. In early June 1998, a few weeks before the Queensland state election, *The Australian* published a poll indicating that One Nation, contrary to all expectations, could win several seats. New South Wales MLC Helen Sham-Ho and the Labor opposition had repeatedly implored Howard and the Queensland LNP to preference One Nation last, to prevent just such an outcome. But Howard had steadfastly refused, declaring himself 'comfortable' with the LNP's preference strategy. One random poll was not going to change his mind. Buoyed by the conservatives' arrogant refusal to see One Nation as a threat, Hanson issued a gloating warning in parliament:

> Queenslanders will be the first Australians in living memory to have a chance to elect a real alternative to the multicultural and politically correct Labor and Coalition parties . . . The winds of change blow ever stronger, as the ballot box draws ever nearer.

The following day, recalls Kingston, Hanson 'took the walk' through the Canberra press gallery, eager to spruik One Nation's goals for

Queensland. To everyone's surprise, she singled out Kingston, an openly gay progressive and one of the harshest critics of Howard's plan to water down the Wik ruling on native title.

'Margo, I know you think different to me,' Hanson told the incredulous journalist with a smile. 'But I like you, you're direct. You say it to my face. All I want is a fair go.'

Kingston, suddenly the anointed one, reluctantly interviewed Hanson about her intention to back a National Party government in Queensland in exchange for looser gun laws and the abolition of native title. Kingston's article, 'Enter the Powerbroker', ran on the front page of the *Sydney Morning Herald*. Her colleagues reacted with horror. Hanson was a flash-in-the-pan populist and her amateur candidates were unelectable, they told Kingston. One Nation was not worthy of serious analysis or attention.

But Kingston's instinct said otherwise. Alarmed that *The Australian* poll had listed her hometown of Maryborough as likely to fall to One Nation, Kingston hotfooted it to Queensland to cover the last week of Hanson's campaign.

'It was a working-class Labor town facing hard times, so to swing behind One Nation must mean something fundamental was going on,' Kingston explains. 'If I couldn't understand and empathise with it, I felt, I would have lost touch with my roots.'

Kingston's first exposure to Hanson's messianic, cult-like pull with the forgotten people of the bush knocked her for six. 'Following her into areas that had just been devastated, I could see the sense of the Hanson scream,' Kingston says of the frenzied scenes of mass adulation that followed the One Nation leader through the neglected backwaters of the deep north. 'It was just wild. It was like, "Ohhh! Here is our voice!"'

Hanson swept into country showgrounds in open-topped limos, waving to thousands of cheering supporters like the Queen.

She kissed newborn babies held up by mothers to be blessed. She signed the foreheads of rugged loggers hell-bent on immortalising Hanson's name in tattoo ink. She was showered with flowers as farmers bent to place their jackets over muddy puddles so Hanson's shoes could stay dry. In one outback pub straight out of *Deliverance*, mad-eyed timber cutters threw darts at a map of Aboriginal tribes, as a bearded bear of a man swept Hanson into his arms like a doll and declared his undying love.

Hansonland was an ominous new frontier to Kingston, a 'wake-up call that we in the media had no idea about the nature of the people we were meant to be representing'. In *Off the Rails*, Kingston's wild account of her time in the One Nation trenches, the journalist explains her early – and unpopular – realisation: Hanson would become more dangerous if she was ignored. 'There didn't seem to be any point in persisting with the media myth that she was some kind of monster who needed to be slain,' Kingston writes. 'There was often a nagging grain of truth in Hanson's half-baked simplicities. And maybe if the powerful, including the media, had engaged with the scream rather than returning it, the monster of One Nation might not have grown to terrorise us all.'

Kingston returned to Canberra just before election day, to find the political punditry asleep at the wheel. On 13 June, as Queensland began to vote, a Brisbane editor assured David Oldfield that if One Nation won a single seat, he'd 'run naked through the Queen Street Mall'.

Hanson, in no-nonsense denim, cast her ballot and told a sceptical press pack, 'I think a lot of people are going to get a big surprise.'

Kingston warned her disbelieving *Sydney Morning Herald* readers that Hanson was 'no longer the stumbling, gauche, ordinary woman at whom educated and politically aware Australians can afford to sneer'. But as the returns started trickling in that evening, many tally room commentators were still predicting a narrow first-term victory for the Queensland LNP.

That night, Hanson's fledgling candidates made history. In her yellow and black 'Bumblebee' suit, the politician claimed credit for One Nation's bloody routing of the Liberals, embracing her eleven newly elected MPs in front of the blindsided press and jubilant, flag-waving supporters singing 'For She's a Jolly Good Fellow'.

'It was completely unexpected by everyone, except perhaps me,' says Oldfield, who immediately told the gobsmacked Brisbane editor to make it eleven laps.

'There's no doubt coming out of Queensland, One Nation was strengthened, and that was seen as a challenge to us,' Howard says with cool understatement. But footage of harrowed LNP ministers and panicked Queensland MPs scrambling out of their limos in Canberra to confront the looming One Nation threat depicts a party in crisis.

'She decimated the Liberals in Queensland thanks to John Howard,' Kingston observes. 'And now we have all the ingredients of an effing nightmare: the possibility that Howard could lose power as a result of One Nation.'

'The whole tone of the party changed,' former Liberal MP Sham-Ho agrees. 'I remember in party room discussions, they were afraid of losing the support which was given to Pauline Hanson. That was really scary.'

Howard's counterattack was swift. In the turbulent two months following One Nation's Queensland victory, he backflipped on preferences, announcing that the federal Coalition would do 'no preference deals with One Nation'. Sensing that a race-based campaign would be a disaster for his government and a bonanza for Hanson, he shelved his threat to force a double-dissolution election over his controversial ten-point plan to water down the Wik decision, negotiating with independent Tasmanian senator Brian Harradine to devise a compromise on native title that the Senate would accept.

The Australian Electoral Commission rejigged the boundaries of Hanson's seat of Oxley, incorporating more urban, left-leaning and ethnically diverse voters. They named the new electorate Blair.

Across the country, the Coalition aggressively promoted its conservative credentials to Australians leaning One Nation's way. Several Nationals MPs, already privately predisposed to Hanson's views, came out in public, making it clear that they were no slaves to the multiculturalists or the bleeding-heart left. In New South Wales, Sham-Ho was ordered by senior Liberal officials not to nominate for the presidency of the New South Wales Legislative Council, as doing so would risk the LNP 'losing the support of, and credibility with, One Nation supporters'. Shocked and offended, Sham-Ho resigned from the party she had faithfully served for sixteen years, announcing the LNP was 'a racist and bigoted party'. Howard was unrepentant.

As One Nation fought off these public salvos, it was mired in internecine battles of its own. Hanson's call-out for loyal foot-soldiers willing to fight Labor and the LNP in the polls saw her offices deluged by a panoply of nutters, comedians and criminals. Oldfield took a call from an 'Imperial Wizard' of the Ku Klux Klan, who told him, 'I want to let you know we understand the code. We really like what Pauline is saying.' Another man accosted him in a car park with a boot full of handguns, insisting 'we need to protect people. I can get you submachine guns, F1s, you name it. I got rocket launchers too.' Ettridge ran into the neo-Nazi

Australian National Socialist Party's David Palmer, who confided that several of his members already belonged to One Nation, adding, 'If it gives you comfort, we have members in all the political parties.' Hanson received a fax from a prospective candidate who wanted to 'make the Big Parties accountable', signed Andrew Far-Carnhell.

To the media's delight, Hanson's freshly anointed candidates began to implode in spectacular fashion. A One Nation hopeful in Noosa announced that the Catholics had given cyanide to the Nazis, while another divulged that Jesus had appeared to him on a piece of toast in 1963, and asserted that the Pentagon had invented AIDS. A prominent South Australian candidate distressed his staff by carrying guns around the office. A Queensland contender told a female reporter he'd like to 'knock her off', while a Perth candidate was dumped after his backyard pornography business came to light with a bestiality video starring a German shepherd. In Toowoomba, one virulently pro-gun One Nation candidate took to driving around with a sticker on the back of his ute declaiming, 'Under God's Law, the only rights gays have is the right to die.'

Alarmed at the company One Nation was keeping, Barbara Hazelton locked horns with Oldfield, demanding he honour Hanson's original vision of a 'party of the centre'. But the Troika needed candidates. The strategy of keeping One Nation firmly on the right – within the bounds of sanity, of course – was working.

'One Nation was like a zoo, we had so many kooks in the party,' Ettridge grins. 'But Pauline kept them under control, because they liked her. Some idiot came out as a member of the KKK, and Pauline kicked them out.'

'People looked at her and saw what they wanted to see,' adds Oldfield. 'Pauline's an abortionist, pro-gay and an atheist, but she attracted the gun nuts, Christians, poofter bashers and the League of Rights people.' Under Oldfield's careful tutelage, Hanson's relaxed attitude to homosexuality took a sharp turn to the right. One Nation renounced the rights of gays and lesbians to marry, adopt or access IVF. When asked what she thought of Sydney's Gay and Lesbian Mardi Gras, Hanson snarled, 'No, the whole thing is wrong, and it stinks, and I don't like it.'

'I kept waiting for Pauline to wake up and become the person she was at the beginning,' Hazelton sighs. 'I wondered if she ever stayed awake at night, and wished she'd listened to people who cared.'

But Hanson was in the Davids' thrall. She stood by Ettridge as he quietly purged the party of 'white ants': sending pre-signed resignation letters to anyone the Troika considered ideologically suspect, too close to the major parties or too critical of the orders emanating from One Nation's Manly HQ. 'People saw David and I as the people who prevented them from getting what they wanted from Pauline,' Ettridge says smoothly. 'Because we were growing at such a rate, a lot of people wanted to be close to her, and there were times where I said, "Pauline, let me look after this." It was like children running to their mother because Dad would not give them what they wanted.'

As the conflict between the autocratic Troika and Hanson's grassroots supporters intensified, several 'white ants' went public. In what Hanson saw as a shocking betrayal, Hazelton joined them. Fed up with Oldfield's domineering style and tired of playing surrogate mother to Hanson's bullied children, Hazelton quit. When Hanson's mild-mannered biographer, Helen Dodd, was frogmarched out of the office for challenging Ettridge's assertion that he owned the Pauline portrait on the cover of her book, Hazelton blasted One Nation in the media. 'Hanson has allowed herself to be used,' she announced on 24 June 1998. 'The Australian people are being hoodwinked if they think they are voting for Pauline, because she has no control at all. Oldfield called One Nation members "fucking halfwits". He declared he was the only one capable of writing policy. Oldfield is a manipulative, hypnotic, hugely narcissistic individual who has taken complete control of Pauline's life – whether she realises it or not.'

Hanson immediately slammed Hazelton as a political Judas, and stood by the two Davids. 'Any damage I could do to Pauline paled in significance against what Oldfield could do to her, and she knew it.' Hazelton shakes her head.

But the Troika's heavy-handed approach to dissent produced a far more dangerous enemy. Terry Sharples, a disgruntled One Nation candidate, had been sacked for refusing to obey Oldfield's orders on preferences in the Queensland election.

'He upset Oldfield because he wanted to put his how-to-vote cards as he wanted. And that's when the jackboots came in and they trashed his office,' recalls Scott Balson. 'One Nation was a dictatorship. The dictator was Ettridge, Oldfield was the powerbroker, and Pauline was the stooge. I think she thought she was invincible, and she had people close to her who protected her from what was going on in the branches, and she thought she could say anything.'

Facing a press pack hungry for One Nation gossip, Sharples announced, 'If you speak out against Oldfield, you're gone the very next day. We need a new party. Just not this one!' Livid that the Troika refused to reimburse the $11 000 he'd spent on his campaign, Sharples quickly found a sympathetic ear in another man Oldfield had wronged: Tony Abbott. In a secret meeting, Abbott promised to underwrite Sharples's civil suit against One Nation. And in public, the politician put on his boxing gloves. 'The Member for Oxley says that she is not a politician, and that is true to this extent: no other politician in Australia would go on national television with her minder by her side as a kind of human autocue!' Abbott railed in parliament on 29 June:

> One Nation is not a democracy but a dictatorship, and the dictator is none other than David Oldfield. I ask the Member for Oxley: why has she allowed her party to be taken over by a charismatic psychotic whose activities most resemble those of Rasputin? Either the Member for Oxley is just another hypocritical politician – or she has been completely duped by the two Davids who have hijacked her party.

On 2 July, as Hanson glowered on the backbench, Abbott intensified his assault on her integrity and the credibility of her party:

> Over the past fortnight, questions have been raised in this House about the real nature of One Nation. Is it a party or is it a business? Is it a democracy or is it a dictatorship? Is it really an unstable political ménage à trois linking the two Davids, D1 and D2, with an antipodean version of Eva Perón? Is One Nation a constitutional entity ... or is it just a couple of political and financial brigands, trying to hoodwink decent patriotic Australians in the way Jimmy Swaggart once tricked pious Americans? I call on the Queensland government to urgently consider whether One Nation can be a registered party at all under its existing, highly undemocratic constitution. One Nation Ltd is not a political party in any meaningful sense; it is a business where no-one is allowed to ask questions. The best thing the Member for Oxley could do, if she has any concern for the decent Australians who might be tempted to support her, is ... get rid of D1 and D2!

'I can't understand why Abbott became so angry and vitriolic over the whole thing. I thought it was overkill,' says Ettridge, miffed.

But Oldfield is philosophical. 'Tony is the sort of person who likes to fix his mistakes. Having been blamed for One Nation being born out of his office, he went, "I have to correct it," and I'm quite sure that's why he went after Pauline and me with the vehemence that he did. If he hadn't felt the shame put on him, he wouldn't have pursued it.'

Abbott's attack hit its target: on 10 July, Sharples lodged a challenge to One Nation's constitutional validity in the Queensland Supreme Court, arguing the party was not properly registered, and therefore not entitled to the $502 589.74 due to it from the Queensland Electoral Commission following the state election. When Abbott was asked by the ABC on 31 July if he or the Liberal Party had made any financial contribution to Sharples's costly civil suit, he flatly denied it.

Hanson was unbowed. Convinced of the Troika's innocence, she wrote off Sharples's legal tantrum as yet another attempt by the Big Party machine to sabotage One Nation's federal chances. She had $100 000 from the Shooters Party in the campaign coffers and a nationwide army of true-blue Aussie patriots raring to go. 'You have to understand, at the height of One Nation we had 18 000 members. The other parties were pushing 9000. We were a major threat!' she says happily.

On 30 August, Howard called the election, confident that 'once One Nation was put under pressure to articulate mainstream policies, they'd look ridiculous, and political amateurs'.

But Hanson was ready. 'I'm not going anywhere!' she told jeering MPs in the House of Representatives. 'Tell Mr Howard, Mr Beazley and Mr Fischer not to worry, we'll have our candidates there.' One Nation fielded an audacious 139 candidates for the lower house and twenty-three for the Senate. Hanson's 1998 federal campaign is now the stuff of legend: one of the most bizarre, anarchic and shambolic bids for national power Australia has ever seen.

In Canberra, as Howard and Beazley donned their face paint for the slickly orchestrated, small-target TV sound bites that would characterise the major parties' campaigns, an excited Kingston grabbed her field vest, notebooks and brick-sized mobile and hit the road. Her wingman on the Hanson trail was the trigger-accurate crime photographer Dean Sewell – a man adept at high-speed car chases and split-second shooting on the fly.

Sewell's skills were exactly what were required. Hanson's volunteer-run quest to reclaim Australia was quickly dubbed the 'Headless Chook' campaign by the reporters who tried to follow it. 'It was literally a road movie,' Kingston enthuses. 'We were chasing her, running red lights, going at 180 miles per hour, chartering planes, begging her pilot to hold her in the air while we caught up in ours! You had to be wearing everything you needed, because we didn't know what was going to happen from one minute to the next. But that was because One Nation didn't know! She had no organisation. We could do anything we liked with her; we were in total control. It was an honour to be covering such a free-for-all. It was probably the biggest challenge in my reporting life.'

'Hang on a minute,' Hanson interjects crossly. 'Because Margo couldn't get her act together to pack up her stuff and keep up with me – that's her problem, not mine. You have to remember when they talk about speeding cars and planes, the federal police were driving, not me. I was out to get a job done, and the media hindered me so much!'

'Pauline was a simple person out of her depth, a small fish out of water,' Oldfield says wearily of the gruelling weeks he spent wrangling Hanson and the media on the election trail. 'She was a train heading for a cliff all the time, and you had to speed it up and slow it down and turn the corners. I felt like I was directing a movie with a bad cast who can't remember their lines.'

One Nation's chaotic six-week election campaign destroyed the accepted professional boundaries between the media, the politician and the adviser, and locked Kingston, Hanson and Oldfield on a collision course. Hanson, a first-term MP, was the unthinkable pursuing the impossible: an untested far-right populist now forced to justify her policies on the national stage. Oldfield, running for his own seat in the New South Wales Senate, needed to keep Hanson on message. Kingston, keen to test her theory that Hanson's racism stemmed from ignorance, was determined to hold Oldfield to account: positioning him as the manipulative demagogue behind One Nation's extremist views. Hanson, for her part, just wanted to win. Their three-way battle to control the political narrative produced a slow-moving train wreck from which none of them could escape.

The slide to disaster began immediately, with One Nation's first policy launch. At the Barry Jones Auditorium in Ipswich, Hanson unveiled Easy Tax, the revolutionary brainchild of an unknown Brisbane engineer, in which every transaction would be taxed at 2 per cent.

'I tried to explain to her, we can't do this – it's lunacy,' Oldfield groans. 'Australians won't get it. John Hewson lost an unlosable election with this in '93. If you have to explain a policy to voters, you've already lost!'

But Hanson and Ettridge stood firm. 'No-one likes doing their tax every year,' Ettridge says with a shrug. When a visiting CNBC reporter asked Hanson if she was worried how her policies would be received overseas, she retorted cockily, 'Actually, you might learn something and take it back to America.'

Within twenty-four hours, Oldfield's worst fear was realised. Easy Tax lost One Nation 30 per cent of its vote. Howard, in a radio presser, labelled One Nation's financial policy 'one of the most ridiculous economic statements I've ever heard'. When Kingston questioned Hanson on her 'loopy tax policy', the politician snapped, 'Don't call me loopy!' and stormed off. The *Herald* ran a picture of Hanson knocking at the door of an unimpressed voter as a Shih tzu yapped at her feet.

But at the Linville Races the very next day, Hanson, with her trademark unpredictability, backflipped. With a bra-flinging competition in full swing behind her, she drank Ginger Bitches with adoring farmers and casually announced she'd drop Easy Tax if people didn't like it.

'So you have to deal with these journos in your face all the time?' a young bloke asked Hanson with a grin. 'You're causing a shit fight. Great! Wake 'em up! The media gives everyone the shits!' In Hanson heartland, the media, and not Hanson's policies, were to blame for the sliding polls. The baffled Kingston bought an akubra hat that she'd wear for the rest of the campaign. The label on the rim, 'Worn Out West', would prove to be prophetic.

Four days in, Hanson was already fed up with the relentless media scrutiny. She rounded up Kingston and her colleagues in a Gympie paddock full of chooks, told them, 'This is off the record,' and blasted them. 'If I lose my seat, it will be on the basis that people don't want my policies. But there's no way in the bloody wide world I'm going to allow the media to make me lose! All I ask is you report the facts. Let the people judge me. Don't put a spin on that makes me come across as negative, and if it's your boss saying, "Right, let's have a shot at her," then I don't need you!'

As Hanson ranted, a cameraman secretly kept recording.

'The public wanted to see me but the media were in the way,'

Hanson seethes now. 'I said "off the record" and they said, "Yes, Pauline, we're honourable people." The camera was on the floor rolling, and it came out on the ABC, me dressing them down!'

Shortly after, Hanson approached the astonished Kingston and her colleague Helen McCabe in a bar, and invited them to dinner at her farm. 'We thought, "Maybe she doesn't have any friends,"' Kingston recalls. 'We went in her car, followed by the cops. She picked up a roast chook on the way, and we got there and it was very uncomfortable because she was treating us as friends.'

Kingston seized on Hanson's receptive mood to present a different view on the Indigenous debate. 'Her advisers were telling her, "Race is giving you votes," and I disagreed. The economic issue – the country people's scream, the working-class scream – were giving her other votes. I explained that she couldn't abolish native title under the constitution, and that Aboriginal people should really be getting a lot of money. I tried to explain the truth – that Australia was colonised, that there were massacres, that a war was perpetrated on the Aboriginal people. And I think she did listen.'

Kingston ended the night on a couch by the fire, certain that Hanson was not racist or malicious but naive and misinformed – the susceptible pawn of her minders. 'When Oldfield was off the campaign, she softened. She can think for herself if she's given the chance, but she tends to be "in that ear, out that mouth",' Kingston explains. 'She needed someone who was genuinely on her side, who was intelligent and politically sophisticated, and she never had that.'

By the time Hanson's campaign hit Gatton, news of Kingston's sleepover had reached the press gallery. 'The usual shit hit the fan,' Kingston says, wincing. 'You know, "Margo's got too close to Hanson. She's fallen in love."'

Concerned that Hanson was going 'soft' on race under

Kingston's influence, Oldfield dropped his own campaign in New South Wales and flew to the politician's side. 'If Pauline wasn't doing well nationally, the party wasn't going to do well, so the main priority was to keep her on track. I didn't like Margo because Pauline trusted her. She thought she was "fair",' Oldfield says. 'Margo was a dope-smoking drunk. The journalistic code was her pretext for moving into people's lives. She's the ugly side of the media, in every sense of that word.'

The animosity was mutual. 'And now the "professional" comes in, the guy in the black outfit in westerns – oooh, David Oldfield!' Kingston says with camp horror. 'And then it's a totally different drama, because he goes for complete humiliation. You'd ask him something and he'd go, "This is an example of the evil media and they're led by Kingston and she's a fascist." As soon as the Hanson team and the media got into an okay space, he'd come in and destroy it.'

Oldfield quickly made his view of Kingston known to the press: she was the left-wing attack dog of 'The Sydney Moaning Homosexual' and 'The Aboriginal Morning Herald'. But more intriguing to the media was the fact that Hanson and her svengali were no longer a well-oiled team. On the sixth day of the campaign, Hanson sprinted out of One Nation's Gatton office without Oldfield and veered off in her car, with her AFP detail in hot pursuit. Most journalists dutifully headed for a mall, the first stop on Oldfield's itinerary. But Kingston and the jaded veterans of the 'Headless Chook' campaign knew better.

They chased Hanson to a house on the outskirts of town, where she bolted inside, barring the press pack from entering. Minutes later, an elderly woman emerged and begged them to come in. Her husband, a Vietnam vet who'd lost his pension, was dying of emphysema. It had been his final wish to meet Pauline. The woman

THE FALL OF PAULINE

implored Kingston to report the truth: Hanson had dropped everything to be by her husband's side. As the cameras started to flash on Hanson and the dying man, Hanson, always protective of her 'tribe', was furious. What would have been publicity gold to any other politician was, for Hanson, an unforgivable intrusion.

That night, at the Gatton Senior Citizens Hall, an emotional Hanson spoke off the cuff, issuing the most ridiculed sentence of her campaign: 'I care so passionately about this country, it's like I'm a mother, and the Australian people are my children.'

'"I am the mother of the nation!" Ergh!' Oldfield fake-vomits. 'The problem was, you always had people saying, "Pauline, speak from your heart. We want to hear what you think," and you really didn't want to hear that, believe me, because it wouldn't make any sense. They'd say, "My goodness, we're hearing from Pauline's heart!" But they were never going to hear from Pauline's brain. Whenever she did something herself, it turned into a disaster.'

Hanson's enemies pounced on her hubristic brain snap. 'I have always regarded myself as the servant of the nation,' Howard said primly. Kennett labelled Hanson's maternalism 'hideous'. An impassioned Beazley declared, 'My mum's philosophy was there was always room for one more. And the view of Australian mums is you love everybody, but there's always the vulnerable one in the family you take care of. That's motherhood Australian-style. It is not motherhood Hanson-style.' The inaugural chair of ATSIC, Lowitja O'Donoghue, quipped, 'If she's the mother of the nation, I'm suing her for child support!'

Pasquarelli slapped the blame squarely back on Oldfield. 'It's clear Pauline's campaign has been a disaster so far, and if she wants me to come and help her, I will!'

As the One Nation circus rolled on to Western Australia, Hanson's simmering conflict with Oldfield bloomed into full-blown public rivalry. Oldfield introduced the politician as 'just a little redhead from Ipswich', and Hanson threw away his speech in disgust. 'There's this idea floating around there's this puppet up my back and other people running my agenda. Well, it's not. It's me. This is someone else's words and I don't like it!' she announced, to a rapturous cheer.

But contrary to Kingston's hopes, Hanson's problem with her spin doctor was personal, not political. As the politician unveiled One Nation's Indigenous and trade policies, she stuck to Oldfield's ideological script, showing no sign of the open-minded, empathetic listener Kingston had glimpsed at the farm. 'Do we want to be a tourist country, turning down beds for Asians?' Hanson asked an angry crowd in Perth. In York, she slammed the Wik decision in front of 600 cheering supporters, promoting her 'one-point plan' to abolish native title. When a young man interjected that Hanson was falsely assuming Aboriginals and whites were already equal, the politician quietly looked on as a woman threw a coat over the protester's head and a posse of jeering men dragged him from the hall. 'There's a spare seat now, if anyone would like to sit down,' Hanson deadpanned as the crowd guffawed.

At the Stockman's Hall of Fame in Longreach, the site of Howard's broken promise to stand firm on his ten-point plan for Wik, Hanson labelled native title a 'shameless grab for land [that] is not about reconciliation, but in fact an exercise in remuneration'. When challenged by Kingston and the press to justify this claim, Hanson, true to form, attacked: 'Get this *clear*: we are *Australians*, and it makes no difference whether you are from Aboriginality or whether you were born here or whether you were a migrant. We are all Australians together. So *don't* try to divide this nation!' A few One Nation supporters clapped, as a protester called out, 'You're the mother? There are a few fathers around too – Hitler, for one!'

Hanson's 'Headless Chook' campaign lurched southwards, plagued by intensifying criticism, anger and dissent. At a presser in Laidley's Hard Yakka store, a shopper told Kingston, 'She's got a head like a broken arse-hole. If I'd known she was in there, I woulda blown the place up.' In Melbourne, a squawking man in a chicken suit stalked Hanson for twenty-four hours. On a cliff in Davenport, a film shoot for a One Nation campaign ad was disrupted by a surfer, who leapt into the air behind Hanson's head with the words 'The Ugly Australian Doesn't Speak For Me' emblazoned on his board. Resistance protesters sabotaged Hanson's environmental policy launch in Hobart, erecting an anti-racism banner behind her as she spoke. When Hanson's miniskirt blew above her thighs as she alighted from a country plane, the *Daily Telegraph* ran the snap under a derisive headline: 'Forget Policy, I've Got Great Legs'.

Kingston strove to maintain a level of intellectual decency in her popular critiques from One Nation's increasingly crazy front line, but the commercial media was hungry for dirt. *New Idea* decided Hanson's mother-of-the-nation delusions were fair game after she launched One Nation's shockingly skewed family policy, in which welfare would be drastically cut for single mothers while fathers would no longer have to support their children at pre-divorce levels. The magazine paid a large sum to Hanson's son Steven, who was suffering from an 'undisclosed illness', to spill the beans. 'She was never the type of mum who picked you up from school and baked cookies,' Steven obliged. 'I don't speak to her now because she's too busy, but I've often asked her to "please explain" my childhood – so far I haven't got an answer.' *New Idea*'s cover story, 'Hanson's Dying Son: I can't even speak to her', devastated Hanson. She retreated behind her sunglasses, as Oldfield posed helpfully for the cameras with the offending magazine in his lap.

'Oldfield was obsessed with himself rather than with her,' says Kingston, who refused to cover *New Idea*'s story. 'He's a maniac idiot. He thought he was the puppetmaster and she was the puppet, and that's how he treated her.'

Oldfield lets Kingston's gibe slide. 'I can handle feminists. They are just a man in a woman's body,' he says with a shrug. In his view, Kingston and her left-leaning *Herald* readers were out of touch, with 'only 5 per cent of Australians' agreeing that reconciliation, land rights and native title deserved the nation's support. 'The only thing we can learn from Aboriginals is after a nuclear war, they could help us find food in the desert,' he says now.

Seventeen days into Hanson's campaign, her exhausted entourage checked in to the shag-piled time warp of Launceston's Olde Tudor Hotel – and the already tenuous line between the politician, the spin doctor and the journalist finally collapsed. The press pack was abuzz over a statement by One Nation's Queensland MP Jeff Knuth that Indigenous Australians should be returned to indentured labour, as the decades before Labor's reforms 'were a lot happier time for the pastoralists and the Aborigines'. Kingston and her colleagues rounded on Hanson in the lobby for a response, and she stared at them in mute shock. Oldfield was nowhere to be seen.

'He spent that whole night arguing with surfers, when he should have been briefing her,' Kingston remembers unhappily. Hanson disappeared – then sent her bodyguard to summon Kingston to the ladies' room. Deeply conflicted, Kingston found herself doing Oldfield's job for him, and filling Hanson in on Knuth's remarks in the loo. When Hanson returned to the lobby to announce she did not endorse Knuth, the press pack castigated Kingston for helping Hanson get off the hook.

The already bizarre night descended into black absurdity when an upbeat Oldfield joined Kingston and Sewell for a drinking

THE FALL OF PAULINE

session in Kingston's hotel room – alternating between pla puppeteer above Hanson's head on the TV news for Sewell and attacking Kingston for her negative coverage of One Nation's stance on race.

'Does the One Nation race policy entail exterminating the blacks and building a monument to their memory?' Kingston challenged Oldfield.

'Yes, in the shape of a boomerang that won't come back,' he replied cheerfully. 'You're going to stand on your head and spew green vomit when you hear her [next] speech!'

In the last weeks of the 'Headless Chook' tour, Team Hanson's already fractious relationship with the media degenerated into camp farce. With no credible national policies, One Nation was flatlining in the polls. Hanson's surreal adventures on the election trail were being run as a daily comedy fix against Howard's and Beazley's main game.

To the delight of anti–One Nation voters everywhere, Hanson's nemesis, Pauline Pantsdown, emerged on the hustings to run for a federal Senate seat, announcing she wanted 'to be part of the last gasp of Hansonism before it is down to the annals of history. The Strayan people want a candidate with better dress sense and good policies.' Pantsdown even had her own campaign song: the wildly popular Hanson mashup 'I Don't Like It', which soared to the top of the charts as Hanson's political credibility plummeted.

'I saw Hanson as a constructed media character,' explains Simon Hunt, aka Pauline Pantsdown. 'The talk was she was just a natural person, and she was just up there having a go. And I never thought that was true. I thought she was a lot more wily than people gave her credit for, and she knew the effect of constructing herself as an ordinary person.'

In Hunt's hilarious 'I Don't Like It' music video, Pauline Pantsdown fries hot chips in Hanson's 'Bumblebee' suit, hits semi-naked Asian dancing boys with fish and undergoes a lobotomy under a disco ball, while lip-synching mangled Hanson sound bites: 'I don't like it, when you vote One Nation out . . . My language has been murdered . . . Please explain, can't my blood be coloured white?' Hunt's father, Supreme Court Justice David Hunt, advised him that Pantsdown's new song was not defamatory. Hanson may have been able to censor 'Backdoor Man' on the grounds that she wasn't homosexual or a 'very caring potato', but no lawyer would be able to challenge Hunt's depiction of the politician as racist.

With 'I Don't Like It' on high rotation across the country, Pantsdown was mobbed by ecstatic schoolkids and jubilant fans as she promoted herself as the 'best woman for the job'. Determined to undermine the ornery, folksy persona that had made Hanson a media star, Pantsdown stalked her through shopping malls, schoolyards and RSL clubs, intent on replacing the politician with her 'real' drag queen self.

Hanson and her heavily made-up alter ego finally made contact at the launch of One Nation's health policy, which was being held – with the party's counterintuitive logic – in the beery, smoke-filled haze of Sydney's Mortdale Bowling Club. As Hanson and Oldfield walked towards the club, Pantsdown chased after them with 'David Mussolini Mouldfield': a leather-clad character inspired by Oldfield's declaration on the ABC that he was a 'national socialist'. The press pack muscled in to catch the golden two-shot of Hanson and Pantsdown going head-to-head, but burly One Nation minders blocked Pantsdown's path. As Hanson fled inside, the men punched Pantsdown's female videographer in the stomach, and Oldfield mocked the satirist's 'idiot transvestite' make-up.

Inside the club, a boozed-up One Nation crowd shoved and jostled Kingston and the press pack as Hanson's spokespeople, Dr Ray Danton and the Private Doctors of Australia's Dr David Cunningham, announced that One Nation would abolish universal health care, exempting the privately insured from the Medicare levy. The policy was 'basically an annihilation of Aboriginal health funding', recalls Kingston in disgust. When the journalist asked Hanson why One Nation was promoting 'a good health system for the rich, and a poor health system for the poor', Oldfield swiftly shut her down. 'It's a shame that everybody in the media keeps trying to divide Australia into two groups,' he sighed, and ejected the press pack from the meeting. Outside the club, a furious Kingston faced the cameras. 'They don't believe in accountability; they don't believe in democracy,' she said, and joined Pantsdown on the footpath, dancing to 'I Don't Like It' on Pantsdown's boom box.

Four days out from the election, the growing enmity between Oldfield and Kingston made the news. The embattled Hanson had retreated to the safe One Nation heartland of Gatton for her 'official' campaign launch. Annoyed that Oldfield had yet to provide the policy costings he had been promising the media since the beginning of the campaign, Kingston led the press pack in a rowdy sit-in, refusing to budge until Oldfield delivered his documents.

'This is not a uni protest, this is a private meeting,' Oldfield yelled, revving up the violently pro-Hanson crowd. One Nation's webmaster, Scott Balson, snapped pictures of the defiant Kingston and her colleagues for his Reporting the Reporters media hate page. Jeering people began encircling Kingston, many already familiar with Balson's vitriolic online depictions of the reporter as an 'entitled' lesbian leftist. When Oldfield theatrically called the police to throw the media out, all semblance of civility disappeared.

'The more ugly we made the media look, the more useful they

became,' Oldfield explains of his decision to call on state force to stop the media asking questions. 'We turned them into protesters in the people's eyes, and it worked. People thought they wanted to burn Pauline at the stake!'

By the time a squadron of police officers arrived to control the melee, Kingston's sit-in had become the story. A Radio National reporter asked the journalist if she'd become 'too close to this whole campaign', while Oldfield slammed Kingston to the cameras. 'The media are anarchists looking for fights, largely led by Margo Kingston,' he declared. 'They are a pack of mongrels and a pack of dogs. If the Australian public is not going to get an honest press, then it's better to have no press at all.'

Hanson quietly signed autographs in the background, letting her spin doctor eviscerate the journalist who'd helped her back in Launceston. The next day, Kingston's protest dominated the headlines. Hanson froze the journalist out during the final days of her campaign, while an angry press gallery colleague told Kingston she needed 'disinfecting', and should 'consider [her] actions, when Hanson gets eight seats'. It was a rock-bottom moment for the journalist, who had worked so hard to avoid inflaming the divisions One Nation had caused, and had tried to ignite a constructive debate between the 'Two Australias' that Hanson's rise had exposed.

'According to commentators, the media's outrageous behaviour had resurrected One Nation's campaign,' Kingston reflected in *Off the Rails*. 'According to Hanson, we'd destroyed it.'

On 3 October 1998, Kingston, Hanson and 18.7 million fellow Australians went to the polls to deliver their verdict on One Nation's 162-candidate army. The *Sydney Morning Herald* stood by its embattled journalist. 'One Nation has perpetrated the big lie of the federal election campaign,' the paper's editorial said. It 'is not a party, but a vehicle for the cult of Ms Hanson and her delusions of grandeur. Cults become vulnerable when the facts about them are exposed.'

Hanson, encased in her bubble of diehard followers, chose to ignore the message. Rejecting the latest poll, which had her re-election chances sitting at 8 per cent, she posed sunnily with her ballot paper for the cameras, predicting One Nation would win 'twelve to fifteen seats, lower house, and six in the Senate'.

That evening, Oldfield flirted with a blonde reporter in the national tally room, saying he'd 'like to meet any single swinging voters still out there'. And Hanson's dyed-in-the-wool supporters gathered in the '60s-era dance hall of the Ipswich showground. Clutching yellow balloons, homemade lamingtons, One Nation banners and portable TVs, they settled in happily to watch the returns. Kingston remembers Hanson arriving 'dressed for a ball' in neck-to-toe purple taffeta. But the buoyant mood quickly turned to confusion as the major parties' collusion on preferences began to swallow up the One Nation vote. Hanson turned to Kingston, bewildered.

'No-one had briefed her!' Kingston gasps, appalled that, once again, she had to do Oldfield's job. Kingston gently explained to Hanson that despite One Nation winning one million primary votes, no-one was giving its candidates the crucial preferences they needed to convert the support into seats.

'I didn't understand the preferences, and there was no chance of my actually winning the seat. I would've had to get 50 per cent plus one of the vote, and I only got 36 per cent,' Hanson remembers angrily. One Nation's wipe-out was total. The party won a single seat in the Senate. Every other candidate, including Oldfield and Hanson herself, lost. Hanson's Liberal Party rival in Blair, Cameron Thompson, popped champagne and claimed victory. As news of Hanson's devastating defeat sunk in at the Ipswich showground, the media was ejected from the hall. The tearful Hanson refused to share her concession speech with the nation. Instead, she spoke to her shattered supporters behind a locked door, as sixty confounded journalists tried to read her lips through the windows.

In the kitchens, pubs and community halls of multicultural Australia, Hanson's fall from power was greeted with jubilation. Pauline Pantsdown performed 'I Don't Like It' with forty LGBT Asian Australian dancers for a 20 000-strong crowd at Sleaze Ball in Sydney, detonating a papier-mâché effigy of Hanson in a cascade of glitter.

When asked to 'please explain' how he'd beaten Hanson in Blair, Cameron Thompson said he'd simply focused on looking after the local people, while 'Hanson seemed to be running around the country, battling Pauline Pantsdown'.

Chapter 9
Rock bottom

I blame John Howard, Tony Abbott and Peter Beattie for my imprisonment, and nothing will ever change about that.
—Pauline Hanson, interview, December 2015

On a bright summer morning in December 2015, Margo Kingston walks over to the Ipswich showground, site of Hanson's ignominious 1998 defeat.

'This is where I last saw her,' the journalist says, peering through the windows of the modest hall, where Dean Sewell's final image still lingers: an old woman slumped in a chair, a One Nation balloon lolling beside her. 'This was a place of elation, then devastation,' Kingston sighs. 'This is where Pauline Hanson's political career ended.'

She climbs apprehensively back into our van, and we drive through the sparkling Lockyer Valley towards Hanson's farm. Hanson is waiting for Kingston in her kitchen, grumpily whipping up a chocolate mud cake for morning tea. The two women have not seen each other for seventeen years. They last spoke on 4 October 1998, the day after Hanson lost power. 'Our paths will never cross again,' Hanson told Kingston on the phone, and hung up. Judging by the dread, anger and expectation on their faces whenever I mention their impending reunion, the journalist and the politician still have a lot to resolve.

'I'm not nervous, I'm numb,' Margo tells me, as we film her trudging past Hanson's windmill, up the hill to the house. 'I'm wondering why the hell I agreed to do this. Hanson was the beginning of the end of my career. I had a nervous breakdown at the end of it, so I'm keeping detached.' Kingston is wearing her old 'Worn Out West' akubra from the 1998 'Headless Chook' campaign for the occasion, and carries a satchel of photographs from her time on the Hanson trail.

Hanson, in her apron, is tetchy. She impatiently lets Phil mike her up, annoyed the mud cake isn't rising properly. An expert baker, she's working from a recipe in her head. She normally gets the measurements right, but something's off with the butter. When Kingston knocks on the door, she slams her oven shut, wipes her hands and cracks open the flyscreen. She gives Kingston a glacial stare.

'Well, well, well. Been a long time,' Hanson says coolly.

Kingston shuffles, hat in hand. 'You've done a lot to this place – garden, pool, it's a mansion!' The journalist smiles warmly.

Hanson purses her lips. And glares at Kingston, unblinking. 'Yeah. Well, you better come in,' she says finally. Kingston's shoulders slump, and she follows the politician inside.

The two women face each other over the kitchen counter, and suddenly it's as if we're not here. Most vérité documentary-makers have to film people for years to achieve this level of invisibility, but when the history is as deep as it is between Kingston and Hanson, a camera crew is irrelevant.

'I don't know what to say to you. I just . . . I have anger, I'm upset, I'm cranky. I just – I see you as one of the mob that were out there to destroy me!' Hanson flashes suddenly, teetering between rage and tears.

'I, I don't think that's the case, Pauline,' Kingston interjects, but Hanson's on a roll.

'Bloody media! I got ridiculed all the time! It was like a media circus. What was it about me? Because I come from the background of running my own small business, you thought, "This woman shouldn't be in politics, she doesn't have a uni degree, what's she in politics for?"'

'I was never of that opinion,' Kingston soothes. 'I thought a lot of the criticism against you was class-based. I've written this! Did you read my book?'

Hanson angrily shakes her head.

'Here's the situation,' Kingston says. 'You reckon I destroyed your campaign, and the left reckons I was in love with you! Can we just have a cup of tea, or something . . .?'

Hanson smiles at last, and grabs a jar of Moccona. Watching them settle in for a chat, I'm struck by how radically their status has reversed. Hanson, the 'stumbling, gauche' outsider, who fascinated Kingston and the mainstream media with her redneck marginality, is now an A-grade celebrity, midway through a well-funded federal election campaign, paid handsomely to air her political views in a regular slot on breakfast TV. Kingston, once a rising star in the prestigious Canberra press gallery, is now a political blogger with a progressive but marginalised following, and midway through a part-time nursing degree.

'I don't understand why you keep coming back. It's such a dirty game!' Kingston tells Hanson on her verandah. 'You're a celebrity now, why don't you just enjoy it?'

Hanson's suddenly furious again. 'Don't you believe in honesty?' she snaps. Kingston nods. 'So if you don't fight the bastards, we all lose. I couldn't give a damn about being a celebrity. People are crying out for what is happening to them, and all they want is good governance, and peace in their life. I don't see myself as a celebrity,

I see myself as an Australian that got into politics. If I didn't have the belief of the people, I wouldn't keep going. It would be like hitting my head against a brick wall! I know what's going on is wrong, and for me to turn my back on it, and not say, "You are not doing the right thing by me, or my children or future generations" – so you let them get away with it! So many people tell me, "Why do you bother? You're not going to win." I'm sick of that attitude. If I walk away and do nothing, they've won!'

'So it's in your blood,' Kingston prods gently.

'Right! All I want is some common sense, some justice. I want politicians there making decisions based on the wellbeing of our country. I don't want to be there to say, "Oh, look at me, I got a seat in parliament." I don't give a shit about that.'

'You've just given me a personal stump speech. Saw a few of those in '98.' Kingston grins.

Hanson won't acknowledge the joke. 'I haven't changed at all, Margo. I feel the same back then as I do now, because I've learnt so much. I was a new kid on the block, I was naive.'

'So you've hardened up?'

'I've hardened a bloody lot. And I won't have bastards like Oldfield or Pasquarelli around me!'

'Well, you think about Ashby. I've spent three years investigating that story,' cautions Kingston, as the two women wander back inside.

At the time of our shoot, James Ashby, Hanson's current media adviser, is under investigation by the AFP for allegedly stealing the diary of his former boss, Nationals MP Peter Slipper, to support a damaging sexual harassment suit that helped see Slipper's career destroyed. Ashby dropped his suit in 2014, after Slipper was charged with defrauding the Commonwealth in a parallel action and forced to resign as speaker. Ashby has assured me Hanson's 'a very good judge of character' and has nothing to fear from him. Hanson sees Ashby as a son.

'That man is very bad news, and he's likely to be charged,' Kingston mutters to Hanson, on the other side of the flyscreen door.

'Bugger,' Hanson mutters back. Then she sees our camera. 'Well, we're not going into that now,' she orders Kingston.

'Just remember I was right about Oldfield, that's all I ask,' Kingston urges, clearly disturbed by Hanson's uncanny knack for hiring controversial advisers.

Then she moves on to safer ground, Hanson's 'Fed Up' campaign for the federal Senate. 'I think you'd be a lot better off not doing race,' Kingston tells the politician. 'But the problem you've got is, race attracts media.'

'You've got the experience. You want the job?' Hanson asks, just like that.

Kingston laughs, incredulous. 'Gee, um . . . would you take my advice on race?'

Hanson rolls her eyes, and the two women end up side by side, surveying Hanson's well-stocked bookshelf. Kingston is amazed to discover a mint-condition copy of *Not Happy, John* – her 2004 critique of the Howard government and the shady deals that led to Hanson's imprisonment. Hanson, unsurprisingly, hasn't read it.

'You're a maniac! There's two chapters in that investigating Abbott's role in your downfall. Fucking hell!' Kingston exclaims.

'I've got plenty of other books I've been reading, Margo. I find them very interesting,' Hanson says coldly. But Kingston's not letting her off the hook. The journalist spent a year of her life uncovering the truth behind Hanson's demise, as the politician languished in her cell. Kingston grabs the book and starts reading:

> Hanson's jailing pinched a dangerous nerve. It exposed
> Howard's strong-arm tactics and the lame Australian Electoral

> Commission to scrutiny. And opened the door to who really profited from Howard's regime, destroying the myth that he governed for all of us. Many felt Hanson's jailing revealed something rotten in our democracy. Australians laughed bitterly. With Hanson behind bars, Australian politics was beginning to look like a sick insiders' joke.

'Good,' says Hanson simply. There's a flicker of recognition in her eyes. Maybe she understands, for the first time, that Kingston was never the enemy, but a journalist doing her job. Maybe she finally sees how much Kingston sacrificed by insisting on giving the politician a fair go. Or maybe Hanson is just pleased that we've caught her old foe in the 'elitist' media defending her on tape.

'Do you believe John Howard was involved?' Hanson asks Kingston, impressed that the journalist is intimately acquainted with the complex five-year legal battle she fought to defend herself and One Nation, between 1998 and 2003.

'I would be very surprised if he didn't know, but he has denied it,' Kingston replies.

'Yeah, well, he had to.' Hanson glowers.

Hanson's anger against the 'bastards' of big politics runs deep. The events that stripped her of power, credibility and dignity and sent her to Wacol jail remain a political minefield for everyone who took part. Who exactly was behind Hanson's trial; how Terry Sharples, an ex–One Nation candidate of modest means, was able to initiate the costly litigation process that eventually led to Hanson's conviction; why Tony Abbott escaped punishment for his part in the affair; and whether Hanson is, in fact, innocent, are questions with radically different answers, depending who you talk to.

Hanson sheets the guilt to the men at the top. 'I blame John Howard, Tony Abbott and Peter Beattie for my imprisonment.

I should never have been in there. Abbott is a protégé of Howard's and they're both like cut snakes. You can't trust them. When Abbott was asked by the ABC did he fund [Sharples], he lied. He couldn't leave it up to the Australian people to decide at the ballot box whether they wanted me or my policies; he had to undermine me and be deceitful and have me thrown in prison, and this is how much corrupt and lying bastards we have in this country!'

Oldfield, on the other hand, is certain that 'Pauline would've ended up in jail irrelevant to Tony. Pauline was the federal president of One Nation, and the state director, president and administrator in Queensland. Any job Pauline Hanson had didn't get done. So what she signed eventually put her in jail.'

Ettridge, the forgotten man in the saga, has written a damning account of the major parties' involvement in the destruction of One Nation. 'Abbott provided lawyers to Sharples to run the case. One way parties kill each other is to drain them of their money in court, and Abbott and the Liberals have form with this: they did it to the Democrats in Western Australia.' Ettridge leafs through his 2004 book, *Consider Your Verdict*, to a copy of the letter Abbott wrote Sharples on 11 July 1998, one month after One Nation's electoral triumph in Queensland.

> Dear Terry,
> Congratulations on your decision to challenge One Nation's registration, I appreciate the courage it took. As you know there are others taking the risk and putting themselves on the line to stop the Oldfield/Ettridge juggernaut. You have my personal guarantee you will not be further out of pocket as a result of this action.
> Cheers,
> Tony Abbott

Scott Balson believes Sharples was a pawn in a larger Liberal conspiracy. 'Oldfield was a plant, and Abbott was pulling the strings in the background. The Liberals were aware what Hanson's policies were, because Oldfield was romantically involved with Pauline and influenced what she did. The point of the whole exercise was for the Liberals to assess how Australians responded to One Nation policies, which Howard adopted a few years later. Then, when they thought One Nation was gaining a foothold, it was Abbott who brought in the challenge to the party's registration in Queensland. One Nation was their little pet project, and when they'd had enough of it, they closed it down. The prime ministership was Abbott's reward for getting the Liberal Party into power.'

Howard, who has always denied any knowledge of Abbott's dealings with Sharples, finds Balson's claim astonishing. 'That's a ludicrous conspiracy theory. Abbott was acting off his own bat, and certainly had no encouragement or inspiration from me. In any event, that all occurred after the main event. The main event was the '98 [Queensland state] election, and although One Nation was around for a while afterwards, that was where the greatest damage was done electorally.'

Pasquarelli, with old-school gallantry, thinks Hanson was the innocent victim of Abbott's cowardice: collateral damage caused by the Oxford boxing blue's inability to avenge himself against Oldfield's betrayal like a man. 'Tony should've taken Oldfield around the back of the office and went *bang-bang*! That's what he should've done,' Pasquarelli growls. 'You know, don't take it out on an intelligent though poorly educated woman. Don't go and take it out on her, take it out on the bloke who dudded you, mate!'

I approached Abbott twice for an interview. He declined.

The one thing that is not in doubt in this murky tale of megalomaniacal egos and ruthless ambition is that the Troika's decision not to reimburse Sharples the $11 000 he'd spent on his failed 1998 Queensland campaign cost Hanson and Ettridge dearly. By the end of 2003, they had spent over $450 000 in legal fees, endured a personally and politically damaging battle in the courts, suffered eleven harrowing weeks in jail, and seen One Nation collapse. But when I ask Ettridge, Hanson and Oldfield who made the call not to pay Sharples, they all pass the buck.

'That's like asking who wrote Hanson's maiden speech, Pauline or Pasquarelli?' Ettridge smiles, insisting he had nothing to do with One Nation's accounts in Queensland. 'I was running every other state and had trustees who looked at everything before cheques were written. And I was denied access to Queensland, because there were too many people up there who wanted to run to Mummy, because that "nasty man down in Sydney" wouldn't give them what they wanted.'

Hanson is adamant that in a conversation at the Tweed Heads Bowling Club in June 1998, she agreed with Sharples that he should be paid back, and that Ettridge then told her, in Coolangatta, that he'd 'handle it'.

Oldfield will only offer that 'Ettridge and Pauline were involved in all the things alleged. I wasn't. I never signed anything more than I had to. Which is why I didn't go to jail.'

One Nation's unorthodox constitution was the smoking gun in the civil suit Sharples filed against the party in 1998, with Abbott's help. His lawyers used Ettridge's skink-like disposal mechanism, which positioned the Pauline Hanson Support Movement (PHSM) and rank-and-file members as dispensable subsidiaries, to argue that when One Nation supplied 500 names from the PHSM to the Queensland Electoral Commission to register the party in June 1997, it had done so illegally. Under its own constitution, Sharples's lawyers argued, One Nation's only 'real' members were its executive:

Ettridge, Oldfield and Hanson. One Nation was therefore not a valid political entity and its registration was a sham.

To help finance the brutal legal onslaught that followed, Abbott provided Liberal Party lawyers to Sharples pro bono, and set up a clandestine slush fund – which he ironically named Australians for Honest Politics – to which Hanson's adversaries on both sides of politics made anonymous $10 000 donations.

The strategy of eradicating Hanson through the courts, rather than risking the alienation of conservative voters by attacking her political views in public, would prove extremely effective for Howard. The Coalition would go on to win the 2001 and 2004 federal elections on the back of the same hardline, extreme right policies that Hanson had espoused. Meanwhile, Hanson became crippled by controversy, forced to fight a debilitating three-front war in the media, in the courts and inside her own party.

To Hanson's many enemies, her fall from power was deserved and inevitable. To her rusted-on followers, her persecution was a political witch-hunt, designed to eliminate the Aussie Joan of Arc and her battler party for good. The first cracks in Hanson's seemingly inviolable position as the country's most powerful populist appeared in November 1998, shortly after her defeat in the federal election. Hanson promised the one million Australians who'd voted for One Nation that she'd be back: with almost $3 million in the national coffers to fight the major parties at the polls, she was not going anywhere.

But inside the tightly knit Troika, Hanson was under siege. Ettridge, as the national accounts manager, set about paying One Nation's 1998 federal candidates 75 per cent of their election costs, in line with party policy. Hanson, he claims, not only argued that the expense reimbursements were too generous, but exaggerated her own.

'Pauline over-claimed $75 000,' Ettridge says. 'I knew it was nothing like that. I refused to pay. She was getting paid for her campaign out of brown paper bags. She refused to spend even $8000 on mail-outs because she said it was too expensive. I had set up an election account using trustees to approve everything. It was impeccable. Pauline had to accept that the rules were the rules.'

Oldfield, to Hanson's annoyance, sided with Ettridge. He lists a number of random, unaccounted-for donations she had received from supporters during One Nation's 1998 federal election campaign: $1400 from a punter who'd struck it lucky at the pokies; $10 000 from a 'Slovenian in a car park'; a $250 dole cheque from an enamoured young girl. According to Oldfield, Hanson had collected – and pocketed – up to $150 000, but claimed she 'only spent $8000 on her campaign. She wouldn't doorknock. She wouldn't pay for posters and letter drops. "The people know who I am," she said. She thought she'd win anyway. And she was tight.'

Hanson flatly denies these accusations, countering angrily that Oldfield wanted to annex One Nation's electoral riches for his own political advancement: 'He wanted to stand for parliament, and when he went for New South Wales, he spent a million dollars on his campaign, and when he got in, it was, "Thanks very much, see you later." And he worked behind the scenes from then on to get me out of the party.'

In March 1999, after a well-publicised campaign, Oldfield was elected to the New South Wales Legislative Council on a One Nation ticket. The day he delivered his maiden speech, his growing animosity with Hanson became embarrassingly public. Oldfield gave the six VIP invites he'd been allocated to his family and his speech therapist. Hanson, the party leader, was forced to sit with the tourists and look on from the public gallery.

Oldfield's snub kicked off an increasingly conflict-ridden year for Hanson and her party. In August, thanks to the civil action begun by Sharples, One Nation was officially deregistered in Queensland. The party's eleven Queensland MPs quickly defected and established a new entity, the Country City Alliance, to protect their parliamentary seats. Hanson was appalled. On the national airwaves, Queensland premier Peter Beattie crowed, 'We told you we'd get rid of her.'

Meanwhile, within the party itself, damaging allegations about One Nation's undemocratic nature and opaque financial dealings continued to build. When Oldfield told the fleeing Queensland MPs they were 'all idiots and on drugs', Scott Balson promptly circulated the slur to the 10 000 One Nation members now following his increasingly critical online posts.

'One Nation Pty Ltd received millions in the [1998] federal election. All that money just disappeared,' says Balson, recounting his painful realisation that Hanson and her party were not the heroic saviours he'd been led to believe they were. 'I had no idea it was actually a company, and the money was being stolen or embezzled. My belief in running the online newspaper was that integrity was critical. The facts had to be out there, and when the facts became unpleasant, the Davids started having a go at me. I'd spent thousands on One Nation. I travelled to the launches, I covered my own accommodation, I took my photos and put them on the web and I did that willingly, because I thought this was a party that had credibility. I thought it was a democratic party, a people's party, and it never was. It was only a party belonging to the three.'

By November, Balson and the One Nation Troika were at war. Hanson, the woman to whom he'd devoted thousands of hours and had once kissed at a party – the leader he'd transformed into Australia's first 'internet politician', faithfully defending her against media attacks and building her an online army of followers — accepted Balson's resignation without remorse. Ettridge immediately dispatched a letter to One Nation branches nationwide, labelling Balson a 'white ant'.

Balson, like many other intimates Hanson has discarded throughout her career, took years to recover. As he delicately leafs through the party memorabilia and Hanson posters he's preserved in the One Nation archive at Brisbane's Fryer Library, it's clear that Balson's wounds haven't healed.

'The enigma that is Miss Pauline Hanson is not lost to me nor those who have faced her sword,' Balson reads quietly from his 2000 book, *Inside One Nation*:

> While she presents the façade of vulnerability through emotional outpourings to the media, she can lop off long term friendships without batting an eyelid, missing a beat or considering the consequences. Deep down she is a heartless woman who many believe has used and discarded many good men and women. She takes no prisoners.

Balson's final act as the party's webmaster was to alert One Nation members to everything he knew about the Troika's suspect financial and administrative dealings. 'I said, "The whole thing is a lie." And when I hit the "send" button, the party imploded. Within days, branches closed all over the country and that's the power of the internet. That email went out to 10 000 people, and that was the beginning of the end of the party.'

Hanson and the two Davids arrived at One Nation's annual general meeting in Sydney's Rooty Hill to confront a membership close to mutiny. The Troika played hardball, barring Terry Sharples and other dissenters from entering the hall, and using proxy votes to maintain their executive positions. They countered accusations of fascism by promoting themselves as exactly the kind of strong leadership team the party required.

'We can't have democracy because democracy is mob rule,' Hanson declared to her stunned and fractious audience, as the two Davids watched imperiously from the stage.

In the car park outside, a One Nation loyalist punched Sharples in the face, determined to avenge Hanson for her continuing legal woes. The media jumped on the incident as proof of a party ripped apart by internal division, and predicted One Nation's imminent demise.

The beleaguered Hanson fled to America for a holiday with her old flame, President Clinton's bodyguard Steve. But she was no longer immune from the accelerating legal juggernaut. In January 2000, she received a distress call from Ettridge in Sydney. One Nation's Manly HQ was being raided by the AFP, in front of a large, and mysteriously pre-briefed, media pack.

'What we're seeing is Gestapo-type tactics, which are designed to cause maximum political damage. And it is the first time this has happened to a political party in this country,' the indignant Ettridge told the news cameras, as AFP officers filed down the stairs behind him, carrying One Nation computers and files.

With the party deregistered in Queensland, Hanson and Ettridge, as the office bearers responsible for administering the $502 589.74 the party had received in the 1998 state election, were now being investigated for electoral fraud.

Ettridge swiftly resigned from One Nation, securing Oldfield's endorsement to set up a new party, the No GST Party. One month later, the Queensland Electoral Commission sued Hanson for $502 589.74. Abandoned by her financial right-hand man and publicly scorned by Oldfield, Hanson broke down on Sky News, sobbing to broadcaster John Laws, 'I'll have to sell my farm.' The program ran sweeping aerials of Hanson's swimming pool, lush paddocks and extensive house. But the One Nation faithful rallied around the tearful Pauline, and donations began flowing in to the Pauline Hanson Fighting Fund. Hanson, whose business sense never fails her in a crisis, was mining her devoted support base to finance her ongoing battles in the courts.

Behind the scenes, Hanson hired lawyers to wage an all-out assault on Ettridge and Oldfield, who she now suspected were conspiring to take over One Nation and its assets. When One Nation was deregistered in New South Wales in May 2000, she took legal action to prevent the Davids from removing her from the national executive. She also demanded that Ettridge hand over One Nation's tax returns and froze the party accounts. Oldfield fought back, re-registering the New South Wales branch of One Nation as the designated state officer, and telling the party's New South Wales executive that Hanson was illicitly siphoning money from both One Nation and the Pauline Hanson Fighting Fund for her personal use.

'When she started nicking campaign funds, I felt like I'd created Frankenstein's monster,' says Oldfield. 'I needed to destroy what I'd created. The paper-bag donations were Pauline's, as far as she was concerned. They went straight into her pocket and she never declared them.'

But Oldfield's insistence that One Nation's New South Wales powerbrokers get rid of Hanson fell on deaf ears. 'One Nation members had a crazy, latched-on loyalty to Pauline. If she killed their children, they'd help her bury their corpses,' Oldfield groans. 'When I told them she'd misappropriated up to one million bucks, one old guy said, "I don't care what she's done – how do we stop anyone finding out?"'

News of Oldfield's betrayal quickly reached Hanson. On 31 October, when she discovered that Oldfield's parliamentary staffer, Brian Burston, had been named as a company director on One Nation tax documents, she locked herself inside Oldfield's New South Wales office, desperate to find out what he and Burston were plotting. Oldfield called the police, and the officers looked on uncomfortably as the former lovers screamed at each other through the locked door. That night, Hanson expelled Oldfield from the party.

'When I was raising money for the fighting fund, David Oldfield was giving information to the cops, making the charges stick, doing all these things to discredit me,' Hanson flares. 'He never gave us any support whatsoever; he was working strenuously behind the scenes to undermine me. He was running a dirt file on me in his office in Parliament House. He was being interviewed by the detectives all the time. David was out to destroy me, and I've had people who were working with him who told me what he was doing.' Hanson's key informant was Brian Burston himself, who would later earn her forgiveness – and a One Nation Senate seat in the 2016 federal election – for revealing Oldfield's treachery, and apologising for his own part in it.

In early 2001, however, Oldfield had the upper hand. Hanson's political and personal prospects were increasingly under threat. With her former spin doctor serving an eight-year term in the New South Wales Parliament, speculation was rife that the only term Hanson would be serving would be in jail.

On 5 July, while jogging along the road at the bottom of her farm, Hanson was approached by a police car. A detective handed her a summons through the window. The Queensland Office of the Director of Public Prosecutions had amassed enough evidence to prosecute Hanson and Ettridge for electoral fraud. The civil suit

Sharples had kicked into motion had morphed into a full-blown criminal case.

'I was so distraught. I ran to a neighbour's house, and there was this guy, he was media, taking photos. How did they know?' Hanson asks angrily. 'They were informed! I went out the back door and crawled under the wire fences, through the paddocks, and into my house. It was a devastating experience to me.'

Under a darkening cloud of acrimony, Hanson pleaded not guilty to three charges of fraud in the Brisbane Magistrates Court on 31 July, and fought and lost a doomed campaign for a Senate seat in the November federal election. One Nation failed to pick up a single seat in the House of Representatives and were left clinging on to their solitary seat in the Senate.

On 14 January 2002, Hanson's intensifying legal battle finally cost her the leadership of One Nation. A faction of concerned party operatives, encouraged by Oldfield, accepted Hanson's resignation from the role of president and every other office she held.

On her forty-eighth birthday on 27 May, Hanson was committed to stand trial for fraudulently registering One Nation and dishonestly claiming half a million dollars in electoral reimbursements. To add insult to injury, Hanson received a birthday present from Oldfield: a second fraud charge, for illegally taking $25 000 from the Pauline Hanson Fighting Fund to pay back the Queensland Electoral Commission.

Hanson doggedly fought on, just as she'd done when the Liberals disendorsed her in Oxley in 1996. She campaigned as an independent for an upper-house seat in the 2003 New South Wales state election, but her efforts in the political arena were undermined by Oldfield's continuing public attacks and the controversy surrounding her looming criminal trial. 'The concept of One Nation was mine,' Oldfield announced in one damaging email:

I started the party through the use of Pauline Hanson as a vehicle. She didn't have a clue from the start, and as we all know probably didn't care about Australians or any other person other than herself. Put simply, Pauline Hanson's One Nation was effectively destroyed by self-interest and the political errors of amateurs.

'It was just my whole life, since I entered politics. It's been a battle in and out of courtrooms, because they just threw one court case at me after another,' Hanson says as we walk towards Queensland's Supreme and District Court complex in Brisbane in November 2015. In a tight red cocktail dress with matching lippy and heels, Hanson is feeling chipper. A handsome businessman just chatted her up at the lights, telling her she's 'a bloody good-looking sheila', and she's been mobbed by selfie-snapping fans all along the walkway to the Court entrance.

Hanson poses for our camera next to a 'High voltage' sign on an electrical outlet, enjoying the visual riff on the 'red-headed match' label she's worn proudly for twenty years, as the politician who 'set Australia on fire'. The confident femme fatale vamping it up for our camera is poles apart from the dazed and tearful woman who faced the news crews in July 2003, when her electoral fraud trial commenced in the Brisbane District Court.

'If I'm found guilty, I have got no choice but to opt out of politics – I'm finished,' the trembling Hanson told one reporter.

'Do you think they're trying to break you?' another asked.

'I don't think. I know,' she replied, pale with fear.

When Hanson arrived in the courtroom of District Court chief judge Patsy Wolfe, she did so with the full might of the political system stacked against her. Queensland premier Peter Beattie had extended the penalty for electoral fraud from six months to seven years, fully aware that anyone jailed for more than one year would be barred from standing for parliament. Prime Minister Howard monitored the trial from a dignified distance, reminding Australians that 'the reality is that, by and large, politicians who break the law are quite severely punished'.

'The courtroom was much bigger than this,' Hanson notes disapprovingly as we lead her into the empty room in which we have been given permission to film. Hanson's defence team was led by the colourful Queensland solicitor and crime writer Chris Nyst. David Ettridge, facing similar fraud charges in a parallel trial, was unable to afford a lawyer. Estranged from Hanson and denied access to her fighting fund, he was forced to represent himself.

Hanson sits down at the defence benches on the left side of the courtroom, reliving the agonising five weeks she spent watching Wolfe and the twelve-person jury fielding testimony from a string of hostile One Nation witnesses. Her eyes take on that glazed, flinty sheen that indicates a major meltdown is imminent.

'The jury were absolutely bamboozled with the whole process of the whole lot!' Hanson snaps. 'And when we had the people on the stand who just lied through their teeth, it was a sham! The whole thing was an absolute political witch-hunt to destroy me! Of course I'm not guilty! Definitely not guilty!'

Angered and bewildered, Hanson watched people she'd worked with since the beginning of One Nation enter the witness box to discredit her: Terry Sharples, the man who was never paid; Andrew Carne, the man who came to fix the computers, then allegedly sold One Nation's membership lists to the press; Jack Paff, one of Hanson's eleven Queensland MPs, now happy to sink the knife into his leader.

'Jack Paff, the evidence he gave was so untrue. His character was slayed in the court, and I remember with Sharples, he perjured himself and no-one did anything and it was accepted,' Hanson snarls.

'And the day they brought the sentence down, [Detective] Newton was sitting in the back of court, and he said, "It was never meant to go this far."'

On 20 August 2003, Hanson and Ettridge were found guilty on all three counts of fraud. Each charge carried a term of three years. Hanson was sentenced to nine years in jail, to be served concurrently over three.

'I was devastated. I couldn't believe it, and neither could Ettridge,' Hanson recalls. 'There was mayhem in the courtroom. It was a shock that we'd been found guilty. The room was packed with friends and family. People were amazed. No-one – my friends, the media – could believe it. Everything was going through my mind. And I said, "Where's David Oldfield?" I turned, and the kids were there, and they all gave me a hug and I took off my jewellery and gave it to my son Tony, because I didn't want to take my jewellery into prison.'

Tony, who had worked as a prison guard, told his mother the golden rules of survival behind bars: do what you're told, and don't ask anyone what they're in for. The police then led Hanson downstairs, handcuffed her, exchanged her clothes and her handbag for prison fatigues, photographed her, and locked her in the watch house. The next day, she was driven to the Women's Correctional Centre at Wacol, eighteen kilometres south-west of Brisbane.

'That first night, my son Adam stayed in the car park all night, until the cops asked him to move on,' Hanson says softly, as she looks out our van window at the low-slung buildings of Wacol jail. Spiky surveillance pods cluster ominously along the towering razor wire that encircles the sprawling complex in concentric rings. The intersecting fences are so densely barbed, the inmates loading laundry trucks in the yard beyond appear splintered and out of focus.

Hanson, or Prisoner C70079, as the system now knew her,

spent her first nights at Wacol on suicide watch, refusing to eat for three days. She seems to age visibly as she recounts her experience, lurching between grief, humiliation and deep, untempered rage.

'Here you are, accused of something you've never done,' she tells me. 'You've been set up, found guilty, handcuffed, thrown into a cell, and taken into a maximum-security prison. Everything was stripped away from me. I felt ashamed, embarrassed. I've always been upfront, and what would the public think of me, as if I'm a liar, and it was horrific. And what was more important than how people perceived me was what my kids went through. Here I am, fighting for my beliefs and the country, and the major parties had to get rid of me. And because of that, my kids went through it, my siblings, my close friends. My dad was devastated. It's very hard for anyone who's never been to prison to understand what I am expressing. I've gone from highest point of life to lowest, being a criminal. I just sort of shut down. I was put into the hospital ward, and when I watched the news that night and saw my daughter give this interview, I broke down. And it . . . it wasn't so much the word for word I could hear, it was . . . no, enough. Give me a break.'

Hanson walks out of our interview, fighting back tears. It is impossible not to empathise with this proud woman who worked so hard to pull herself out of a dead-end life in the 'burbs, winning a coveted place in the corridors of power – only to see the system she believed in destroy her. That it was the legal system, and not the political one, that dealt the final blow seems to hurt Hanson the most. Jack's obedient youngest daughter, the 'reliable and industrious' student at Coorparoo State who dreamt of being a police officer, has always had a passionate respect for the law.

When I ask Hanson in the Brisbane courtroom to explain why she was found guilty, she finds the story too painful to finish. She flees the camera, and I find her in the dark alcove between the double doors of the courtroom, sobbing.

'I'm not a liar, Anna! I don't like people thinking I am a liar! I am an honest person! I didn't do anything wrong!' she whispers through her tears, and I believe her. Hanson and Ettridge may have been flouting the rules when they used PHSM members to register the party in Queensland, but I have no doubt that Hanson had no conception that what they were doing was wrong.

Later, we break for lunch at a Middle Eastern restaurant under the Supreme Court building, and Hanson's tough, take-no-prisoners front returns. She eats her first ever Arabic meal – lamb and rice – with wary suspicion, convinced I've chosen the restaurant to goad her about her bigoted stance on Muslims. I assure her I didn't, and steer the conversation back to her time in jail.

'You're not getting anything more out of me. I'm over it,' she says firmly. 'Some things you leave in your past. When I'm old and on my verandah and in my rocking chair, I want the good memories. I'm not interested in all this. No-one wants to look back at the horrid – you look at the up. I'm a positive person.'

True to form, Hanson hasn't read the diary she kept in prison until I ask to see it, twelve years after her release. She lends it to me one night when I am staying in her guest cabin at the farm. It's a standard A4 notepad, off-white paper with thin blue lines. Hanson's looping, orderly hand flows across the pages with perfect symmetry, doing little to convey the anguish and hurt behind her words. Her daily routine is described with workmanlike precision, her emotions restricted to Hallmark generalities. The matter-of-fact prose would make the reading experience monotonous, if it wasn't for the fact that these one hundred pages were written by Pauline Hanson, the far-right populist who once so frightened the Big Party machine that it had her thrown in jail.

'The system I believed in had failed me,' she reads from diary, sitting on a beige leather recliner next to a pot-belly in her guest wing. 'Life deals us blows, but the blow I received the twentieth of August 2003 at 2.45 p.m. is something I will never come to terms with. In my heart, I am innocent of all charges. My ambition in life is to prove to my peers my innocence. My family must be able to hold their heads high, and not carry the burden of my conviction.'

On her third night at Wacol, Hanson was discharged from the hospital wing and moved to a high-security surveillance cell, where the lights were left on all night and a ceiling camera recorded her every move. A male guard told her he didn't agree with her politics but didn't think she should be in jail. He handed her a sanitary pad through the grille in the door, so that she could cover the camera and shower in private. The next day, Hanson ventured into the dining hall for her first prison meal. It was fish and chips. The irony was not lost on the snickering inmates of Wacol. Hanson promptly returned to her cell.

'I thought, "Too much. I'm out of here,"' Hanson remembers bleakly. 'Then three girls came in, and I was just sitting on the bed staring at the wall, and the first one said, "Oh my God, you look bloody awful," and she gave me some make-up and I thanked her. The next one came and said about the procedures and the meals. And the third came to the door and said, "I suppose you know who I am," and I said no. And she said, "I'm Fay Cramb." And I shrugged. And she said, "I just want you to know, I don't like politicians." And I said, "Neither do I."'

Cramb, a top dog at Wacol, was impressed by Hanson's chutzpah. Also known as Valmae Beck, she was a mother of six and a lifer, having brutally murdered a twelve-year-old girl, Sian Kingi, in 1987. Hanson would share many meals with the powerful Cramb, undaunted by her history. One night, with her trademark conviction, Hanson told her dining companion, "If you ever harmed a hair on my daughter's head, I'd press the button myself."'

As Hanson settled in to her strange new life behind bars, politicians were polarised by the harshness of her conviction. Liberal Party stalwart Bronwyn Bishop declared that Hanson was a 'political prisoner', while Democrats senator Natasha Stott Despoja announced that Australians deserved a 'please explain'. New South Wales Labor premier Bob Carr observed righteously, 'Prison should be there for the people who commit violent offences or who sell drugs.' Independent MP Bob Katter was outraged: 'This person is being put in a steel cage, like an animal!'

But many of Hanson's political enemies were satisfied that justice had been done. 'Mrs Hanson spent the last New South Wales election campaign campaigning for tougher penalties. And now she's got one,' rising Labor star Mark Latham gloated. 'Make sure that she is in protective custody, particularly given that a lot of Indigenous people are in Wacol prison,' Indigenous Democrats senator Aden Ridgeway cautioned.

Oldfield seized the opportunity to bury Hanson's political credibility. 'Yes, I did call the shots. Pauline didn't know what she was doing! She outgrew her usefulness. She thought she was some kind of political messiah. I'm quite sure she toyed with the idea of being prime minister,' he told *New Idea* on 23 September.

The thinking media, led by Margo Kingston, refocused the debate on the thorny issue of Abbott's involvement in Hanson's legal destruction. A week into Hanson's incarceration, Abbott was grilled by Kerry O'Brien on the ABC, and denied for a second time that he had provided any financial assistance to Terry Sharples to bring the politician down in the courts.

'I jumped on it very hard,' says Kingston of the investigation she conducted into Abbott's Australians for Honest Politics fund, through her online *Sydney Morning Herald* column, 'Web Diary'. 'Abbott lied to the ABC about the indemnity to Sharples, then he lied to the *Sydney Morning Herald*. He just rang his mates in business and got a hundred grand like that, ten grand a pop, to destroy her in the courts!'

Kingston hounded Abbott to disclose the names of the Honest Politics donors, enlisting her 'Web Diary' readers to uncover and share information. 'It was the first crucial case of a journalist and readers working together to design and discover news, and I can't tell you how exciting it was to do this, when the official system was closing down and the mainstream media in Canberra was literally protecting Tony Abbott,' she says.

Abbott batted Kingston off, telling her, 'There are some things the public has no right to know,' and stressing that his donors had 'done a good thing for Australia'. When Kingston asked Abbott why he felt the need to keep the donors' identities a secret, he attacked. 'You're Hanson's best friend. You'd be delighted about her coming back,' he said, and hung up. But Kingston's online exposés of Abbott's connection to Hanson's imprisonment inflamed the controversy, forcing Howard to weigh into the debate.

'It's the job of the Liberal Party to politically attack other parties. There's nothing wrong with that,' the prime minister said calmly, and told the media to take a cold shower.

Behind the razor wire at Wacol, Hanson was oblivious to the battle Kingston was fighting for her. With hundreds of letters arriving daily from fans as far away as Russia, she was busy. The messages of support eventually numbered over 4000. They gave Hanson strength, as did the candlelit protests her friends staged outside the jail, and her son Adam's song, 'Innocence', which the outraged Alan Jones played to his staunchly pro-Hanson listeners on 2GB.

Hanson still keeps a ringbinder of her most treasured prison letters. Carefully pressed into the plastic sleeves are a handwritten card and a photo from a ten-year-old Aboriginal Irish girl, Nellie Dargan. Dargan, a budding musician from Campbelltown, wrote to Hanson offering to perform a duet with her when she was freed. 'I think she will hold a very special place in my heart for the rest of my life,' Hanson said in 2004, when she and Nellie finally sang together in Tamworth. The song they chose was one of Dargan's favourites: Bruce Woodley's 'I Am Australian'.

Hanson made another Indigenous friend during her jail term, whom she still cherishes. Rosie was a 28-year-old Wacol inmate with six children on the outside and a seventh baby on the way. Hanson wrote to the Queensland Housing Commission to help Rosie secure a safe home for herself and her growing family when she reached the end of her sentence.

'She was a great kid. We had a laugh,' Hanson says, smiling. 'I told her when we get out, we should do a tour of Australia speaking about prison and call ourselves The Black and White Inmates. She was really sad when I left. She missed me. She wrote me a letter saying I was an angel in her eyes, and "You helped me so much". I'd love to catch up with Rosie and see where she is now.'

I wonder if Hanson's longed-for reunion springs from a genuine place, or if she sees it as a useful PR opportunity: a chance to disprove her racism, like the photo she posted to her Facebook page of herself with Thanh, the Vietnamese owner of her old fish shop. When we track Rosie down through the crime pages of a local Queensland paper, I have my answer. Rosie is alleged to be battling an ice addiction and has been involved in a number of petty thefts. I relay this news to Hanson, and she is sad and disappointed. She immediately shelves the reunion idea, insisting that Rosie deserves her privacy.

Hanson's diary reveals how close she and Rosie were in the eleven weeks they lived together. When Rosie got caught up in a violent fight with another inmate, guards threatened to cancel the women's visitation rights, and Hanson intervened to calm the inmates down. When Hanson had an angry outburst about the 'discriminatory' policies of the prison store, Rosie supported her.

Wacol inmates were allowed a 'buy-up' once a week, when they could purchase items directly from the store, or order things in from pre-approved lists. Hanson was allowed to buy knitting needles, mascara, moisturiser, lipstick, a clock and a hairdryer – but was furious to find herself barred from one list designated 'For Asians only'.

'It applied to a store in Darra that supplied Asian products,' Hanson rails. 'Whether or not I wanted to buy Asian products was not the issue for me. Here I am, an Australian in an Australian prison, told I can't buy from a store in Australia because I am not Asian. Talk about discrimination! Who are the bloody idiots who make up these rules and probably have the hide to call me a racist?'

Despite these skirmishes, Hanson adapted to the prison routine with her usual tenacity. She defied the guards when ordered to sign up for an educational course or a job in the laundry, explaining – to the amusement of her fellow inmates – that she was too busy replying to fan mail. When two young psychiatrists suggested she take psychological counselling to help her 'come to terms with her crime', Hanson countered that she hadn't committed any crime, and if they thought she was going to go back out and try to register another party, they were crazy. To tackle the ongoing back pain caused by her hard cell mattress, Hanson attended Wacol's weekly volleyball and aerobics sessions, writing with pride, 'I am the fittest woman on the block even though the youngest here is 19, and I am 49.'

Hanson's approach to survival in a world where 'every day tends to blend into the next and soon you lose track' was to stay active, and not to agonise over the events that had led her there. But when the outside world intruded, her confidence evaporated and the humiliation of her conviction plunged her into black despair. Two visitors in particular rocked Hanson's fragile equilibrium. The first was her lawyer, Chris Nyst, who had to relay the distressing news each time her costly bail applications and sentence appeals were rejected. When the court turned down her first appeal, Hanson told Nyst, 'No matter what happens, I am not doing three years.' The prison psychiatrists staged an intervention, asking Hanson if she could 'see any future'. Devastated, Hanson said she couldn't, and was promptly thrown into the neon-lit hell of the observation cell.

Hanson's second visitor caused her even deeper pain. To have a contact visit with her devoted father, Jack, Hanson had to be strip-searched. This involved taking off her clothes, bra and underwear in front of two guards, allowing herself to be patted down, and then squatting on the cold cement floor to cough, so they could check she wasn't hiding drugs or weapons inside her body. She was so mortified by the experience, she couldn't repeat it, and was forced to see her beloved father from behind a glass wall.

'It was extremely hard for me to actually do it,' she says. 'I didn't want to be strip-searched, it upset me that much. I felt my privacy was invaded. I was there, but I was totally innocent of any crime. I had to go through that experience even though I would never smuggle anything in. It's humiliating and embarrassing and I hated it.'

Eight weeks in to her sentence, after her second unsuccessful appeal, Hanson's battered spirits were buoyed by unexpected news. On 16 October, her old friend Bronwyn Boag organised a noisy and well-publicised rally outside Queensland's Parliament House against the legitimacy of Hanson's sentence.

To the dismay of Hanson's enemies, the controversy around her imprisonment refused to die. With Kingston asking questions in the media about Abbott's alleged slush fund, and public suspicion mounting about the credibility of the witnesses at Hanson's trial, the Beattie government was besieged by angry constituents demanding to know why 'innocent Pauline' was still stuck behind bars.

An unlikely new financial angel had also entered Hanson's orbit. Michael Kordek, a besotted German-born Sydney property developer, stumped up over $250 000 for the politician's third appeal.

'Public opinion was red, red hot,' says Kingston of the heady days leading up to Hanson's final attempt to challenge Judge Wolfe's nine-year verdict. 'My journalism helped direct public opinion to finding a way to get the truth out. And the appeal court got the major parties off a major sharp political hook with its decision.'

On 6 November 2003, the wheels of justice finally turned in Hanson's favour. Following a forensically detailed argument by Nyst and his team that the DPP's initial case against Hanson had been plagued with inconsistencies and unreliable testimony, the Queensland Court of Appeal finally quashed all charges against Hanson and Ettridge. Hanson discovered the news on the TV in her cell.

'Hanson! You've got half an hour to get your things packed!' a screw yelled down the corridor. Hanson distributed her make-up to Rosie and the girls. Then she carried her small bag of possessions to the loading bay, changed into a simple white T-shirt and waited for Wacol's big grey roller door to open.

It would be nice to think that Hanson emerged from jail a more open-minded and compassionate politician. That her time inside taught her that the similarities between people are greater than their differences, and that the most productive response to societal discord is driven by wisdom and kindness, not fear and division. That prison changed her for the better.

But that – as Hanson would be the first to agree – is a wet leftie fantasy.

Footage of the thinner, blonder Hanson walking out of Wacol in the golden Queensland light, arm in arm with her beaming sons, shows a woman who is physically drained but ideologically unbowed.

'I said the truth would set us free,' she told Ettridge, embracing him warmly. Then she fronted the clamouring press pack, no longer a political pariah but a rolled-gold celebrity. Prison redeemed Hanson in the eyes of mainstream Australia. No matter what they thought of her politics, most voters felt Hanson's jailing had little to do with justice and a lot to do with her enemies. When Hanson was asked if she'd ever go back into politics, she giggled. 'I'd have to have bloody rocks in my head.'

As it turns out, that was the only political view she would change. Hanson wore her post-prison martyrdom like a well-cut suit, embarking on a five-star celebrity junket that fourteen years later shows no sign of ending.

'She took off – she was runner-up in *Dancing with the Stars*, even though she was the worst dancer anyone had ever seen on television!' Kingston muses to me as we travel to Hanson's farm in 2015. 'I've said since 1998 that I didn't think she'd be elected again, and I've been right so far. I think the no side for me about meeting her again is feeling she has changed or hardened. That would be a disappointment, but for her to keep coming back into politics, well, maybe she's just another politician. That feeling of power, once it's in there, it's hard to lose.'

I remember Kingston rummaging in her satchel in Hanson's kitchen and triumphantly holding up a faded red T-shirt. Hanson had lent her the shirt during her 1998 federal election campaign, the night Kingston slept over at the farm.

'Did you ever think you'd get that back?' Kingston asks with a grin.

'You can keep it,' Hanson replies, smiling.

'Really? In that case, can you autograph it?'

Hanson sighs and goes off to find a pen, and Kingston slumps on a bar stool, exhausted.

'So what are we doing here?' Hanson asks, returning with a Sharpie.

'Depends on what mood you're in. You've been in a fair few today . . .'

'It does. I have to think.'

Hanson frowns and stares at the shirt, and Kingston looks at the floor.

'You've been very influential in my career,' Kingston says quietly. 'You helped me realise we had lost touch with what people were feeling. This thing about the media versus you, it's really complicated, and I know I did my best, and you did your best, and I certainly didn't seek to demonise you.'

Hanson doesn't seem to be listening. 'Want to read it?' she asks suddenly.

Kingston walks over to the shirt. '"Life has its ups and downs",' she reads, and chuckles. 'Fair enough.'

Hanson is done chatting. She has a live cross with Channel 9 to prepare for, and a federal election campaign to win. She ushers Kingston to the door.

'I will acknowledge you tried to offer me advice,' Hanson tells the journalist in a conciliatory tone. 'And I do appreciate that, but overall it was so new to me, and to be thrown into it from the deep end . . .'

'Thrown in from the deep end – and now you're a good celebrity,' Kingston replies.

'A good or a bad celebrity,' Hanson shoots back, with a flinty smile.

She thanks her old foe for dropping by, and waves her off down the hill.

Chapter 10
The rise of Senator Hanson

We are in danger of being swamped by Muslims who bear a culture and ideology that is incompatible with our own.
—Pauline Hanson, Senate maiden speech, 14 September 2016

It's September 2015, and Pauline Hanson is sitting patiently under our Kino Flo lights as we glide across her flat-planed face with a macro lens.

'With the nose I've got, I could make an Aboriginal claim,' she whispers, with a smile.

I ask her to repeat this so we can get it on tape, but she's astute enough to refuse.

'We've become too precious, we can't say anything, and that's what I'm saying: I don't like my nose,' is all she'll offer. Then she stares down the barrel in silence.

We're filming Hanson at a volatile time. The image of a lifeless Syrian toddler, Alan Kurdi, lying facedown on a Turkish beach has just ricocheted around the world: shocking proof of the devastating refugee crisis now sweeping Europe as the six-year civil war in Syria intensifies. What began as a peaceful uprising against the policies of Syrian president Bashar al-Assad has exploded into a bloody global battleground, as the United States, Russia, Iran and Saudi Arabia jostle for military supremacy in the so-called war on terror.

The death toll in Syria is 300 000 and rising – but Hanson refuses to engage with the tragedy of little Alan and his five-year-old brother, also drowned. 'Their parents shouldn't be bringing them out on boats to put them in that situation,' she says flatly. 'I see a lot of little children who need help here. Young kids, homeless on our streets in Australia; old people can't get the operations they need. We have diggers and aged pensioners living off baked beans. I'm not a bleeding heart – my job is to look after the people here first and foremost. You can't save the world. It's time these countries got their acts together.'

I point out that Alan Kurdi's family were not fleeing their homeland willingly: that they, and millions of Arab asylum seekers like them, have been forced to seek safe havens in the West since 2001, when the United States kicked off the bloody destruction of the Middle East with its illegal invasions of Afghanistan and Iraq.

But Hanson's not remotely interested in cause and effect. Her hardline anti-Muslim stance is paying off handsomely in her 'Fed Up' campaign for the federal Senate. She's hotly sought after on *Sunrise* and *Today*, and each time she slams Prime Minister Abbott for allowing the global outcry over Alan Kurdi's death to shame Australia into accepting 12 000 Syrian refugees, her Facebook 'likes' spike dramatically. On Channel 7 this morning, she railed at her sparring partner, Derryn Hinch: 'Why aren't the Muslims taking them? Can't you see the problems that's going to happen in Australia? You better be prepared, because a lot of people are going to suffer if we open the floodgates to let them in. We have never had such problems as with the Muslims. I warned Abbott – there are millions of Australians that are concerned. They're protesting at mosques, in the schools, everywhere.'

Within minutes of her prime-time outburst, Hanson received 690 comments on the 'Pauline Hanson's Please Explain' Facebook page. She reads them for our camera with quiet pride: '"Thanks for saying what every Australian is thinking." "Hinch's arguments do not pass the pub test." "Onya Pauline, if we must bring in refugees, let them be Coptic Christians who embrace our Christian way of life." "Pauline for PM." "Australia is a soft target. Importing Muslims is risking the future of our children. Refugee today, Jihadist tomorrow. Shut the gate, we are already full."'

Hanson scrolls through the anti-Islam slogans that she and James Ashby regularly post on her page, under One Nation's pristine orange, white and blue logo. Hanson's dyed bob has been tastefully graded in a matching shade of tangerine. 'Nearly 72 000 people reached already,' she says contentedly. 'I did a post on this in May: we reached four million. When you clean up your own backyard, then maybe you can help others.' She shuts her laptop and picks up her mobile to continue her anti-Muslim crusade on talkback radio.

'The Syrian refugees coming here – are they ISIS cells?' she asks angrily. 'They destroy their passports, some have criminal records, 90 per cent don't have their papers. Why? Are they jihadists? They're refusing to be fingerprinted, and you're not going to be able to stop them; they're getting on the trucks and buses. But how are the UK and Australia going to provide for thousands of people who want to move to another country? How do we know these are genuine refugees and not plants? The world has become a horrible place, and just because we're the biggest island and the smallest continent, we can't solve the world's problems. It's time we demand these countries take care of their own destinies, instead of us trying to bandaid things.'

Hanson rings off, having galvanised another few thousand

voters with her trademark cocktail of uncorroborated hate speech, righteous patriotism and fear. As usual, her tirade has been utterly without artifice.

I ask her why she's replaced the Asians in her crosshairs with Muslims, and whether she thinks Australia has indeed been 'swamped by Asians', twenty years on.

Hanson is unequivocal. 'You still have problems, whether they are Asians living here or foreign investors. And you turn up to auctions and the majority are Asian bidders, and Australians are flat out trying to buy a home. So you ask Australians what they feel about it. Or the Shenhua coal mine. Or the ports up in Darwin that are Chinese-owned.'

'So why do you think Muslims are a bigger threat?' I prod.

'Because with Muslims you have a lot of people who are extremists and they hate us Westerners with a vengeance. It's been filmed on the streets in Sydney, the hate for us. They were out celebrating after 9/11. Do you feel safe in this country?'

'Yes,' I reply, remembering the peaceful streets of the mainly Muslim suburb of Lakemba in Sydney, where we filmed last week. In the marbled serenity of the local mosque, Hanson's 1998 Unity Party foe, the 38-year-old writer Randa Abdel-Fattah, persuasively dissected the politician's anti-Muslim rhetoric. The only threat to our safety was a banana peel, dropped by a woman in a coral hijab who was buying pomegranates at a halal grocer. The peel was quickly picked up with a smile.

'Well, I'm happy for you that you feel safe, because lots of Australians don't,' Hanson snaps. She has never been to Lakemba and refuses to go there now – even when I assure her that she'll survive the experience unharmed.

'With their belief to kill those who are nonbelievers, do you honestly feel that you can trust every Muslim out there?' she continues, annoyed that I am not buying her line. 'If they follow a religion that's under a totalitarian ideology that hates the Western way of life, can you trust them? Even with these ones who are born overseas, they still follow the Qur'an. So you ask the people around the world who've lost their loved ones, ask them how they feel about it!'

'The vast majority of people who have been killed by Muslims are other Muslims,' I reply, astounded by Hanson's hypocrisy. The politician has always claimed she is 'happy to talk with whoever' and is 'prepared to answer the tough questions', as long as she's given 'a fair go'. But Hanson, who now expects Australians to endorse her for the federal Senate, does not extend a fair go to Australians who disagree with her. So far, she has stubbornly refused to meet any of the distinguished multicultural commentators I have interviewed for our film. With three months left on the shoot, I am determined to change her mind – hopeful that if she sits down with Helen Sham-Ho, Linda Burney and Randa Abdel-Fattah, she will be forced to see the issues that so terrify her in a more rational light, and her nasty rhetoric against Asian, Indigenous and Muslim Australians will soften.

A month after our interview, I try to get Hanson to meet Abdel-Fattah's father-in-law, the Parramatta Mosque chairman Neil El-Kadomi. The idea has been prompted by Hanson herself. In early October 2015, a radicalised Muslim teenager shoots an accountant, Curtis Cheng, outside a police station in Parramatta, and El-Kadomi tells his worshippers, 'If you don't like Australia, leave.' Hanson is so pleased with El-Kadomi's remark, she enthuses to Karl Stefanovic on *Today*, 'Exactly right, good on him. I'd like to meet the man and shake his hand.' She adds that she'd also like to see Australian imams denounce 'section 4.882, I think, or 89 of the Qur'an,' which she claims instructs Muslims to kill nonbelievers.

El-Kadomi, unsurprisingly, has zero interest in discussing Islam with Pauline Hanson. But his niece, Abdel-Fattah, is willing to step up to the plate. I tell Hanson it will be an invaluable opportunity to air her concerns with an actual Muslim Australian, and arrange to film the conversation in the women's section of Lakemba Mosque, away from prying eyes. As someone with Muslim friends in Palestine and Jordan, I confess that I am driven by more than the filmmaker's desire to observe. Unless Hanson realises how wrong she is to lump the moderate majority in with minority extremists under the same threatening banner of 'radical Islam', she will continue to hurt and divide.

But Hanson has an election to win. She is quite prepared to say one thing to *Today* and another in private. She tells me she will not do a face-to-face with Abdel-Fattah, El-Kadomi, or any other Muslim, under any circumstances. Instead, I have to play her an excerpt from Abdel-Fattah's interview on my laptop. Even this is a hard sell: Hanson won't watch the clip until I turn off the camera and assure her that Abdel-Fattah is not some gun-toting, journalist-decapitating terrorist from an ISIS video but an Australian-born, tertiary-educated, Muslim mother with two kids in Sydney.

'Moderate Muslims are a bit like lapsed Catholics,' I tell Hanson. 'They want a peaceful life for their kids, don't treat their religion as gospel, and have no desire to kill infidels on sight.'

Deeply suspicious, Hanson watches Abdel-Fattah's clip in tight-jawed silence.

'What Pauline Hanson has done is the same as what Muslim extremists do, which is to treat the Qur'an as a literal document,' Abdel-Fattah begins calmly, seated cross-legged on the cool stone floor of Lakemba Mosque.

'When she takes out the verse that seems to permit Muslims to kill people, she is completely taking this verse out of its historial context. The fact that she presumes to have the intelligence to know what the majority of Muslims think and feel, that's news to me. If we believed this verse encouraged us to murder, we would be seeing murder by Muslims every single day, because apparently we are all programmed to suddenly go out and kill. The frustration is having to be situated in such an inane debate, where you are arguing the validity of a verse in a book that is holy to you, with somebody who absolutely has no clue about it. I'm not going to reassure Pauline about my humanity. I'm through with telling white people I am not a terrorist threat. I am sick of having to reassure the racism anxieties of a privileged majority. If I met Pauline, I would say that I feel sorry for her. She is missing out on all Australia has to offer. She is working herself into a frenzy of anxiety and paranoia, and in the process she is damaging the very country she claims to love.'

'She's dressed like you and I. She's not wearing the burqa,' Hanson observes with mild surprise, halfway through the clip.

'That's because she's a moderate Muslim!' I say, appalled by her ignorance.

'I'll compliment her on the fact that I don't find her confronting, which is what Australians want, so let's get rid of the burqa,' Hanson adds with conviction.

'So nothing she said changed your mind about Muslims?' I ask, incredulous.

'I know we've got a big problem in Australia and people are finding it in their schools and their swimming baths. They are fed up with being told they have to be tolerant. So no, I'm sorry, they are in our country. This is a Christian country and they must be tolerant of *our* society and stop trying to change it.'

'Are you a Christian?' I ask, exasperated that she's playing the religion card when I already know, from David Oldfield, that she's an atheist.

'My beliefs are my own business. I don't go out there wanting to cause people harm or murder. I'm not answering your questions of what I believe in, that's a different topic,' Hanson glowers. Clearly, one political tactic Oldfield taught her in the 1990s has stuck – by concealing her own faithlessness, she retains the Christian vote. I decide to target Hanson's genealogy instead. The Irish-Catholic and Anglo-Protestant roots the politician is so proud of are, in fact, far from pure. In 2009, a DNA test revealed that Hanson is of 9 per cent Middle Eastern descent.

'There was a lot that went on back in those centuries long ago. Who knows?' Hanson says crossly, when I point out that she has Arab blood. 'Does it worry me? No. It's part of who I am. I am not going to go into it. This is a short documentary, you can't fit it all in.' Subject closed, for now. Hanson is proving increasingly obstructive whenever I stray from the safely retrospective territory of her first political rise, from 1996 to 1998. She's not going to let my little documentary expose the fallacies behind her vote-winning depiction of Muslims as the evil destroyers of the Strayan way of life.

Satisfied that she's shut me down, Hanson shoots a dazzling smile at Luke and steers him over to a potted palm nestled under the 'Serendipity' sign on her deck.

'Have a look at this. It's a refugee bird, a brown honeyeater that built its nest outside my front door,' she coos, delicately parting the palm fronds so Luke can focus on a tiny featherless chick, clocking the camera through one puckered eye. 'Yesterday you look at it and it's an egg, and today it's a hatchling chick, so that's life. It doesn't take them long, they grow so fast, and it's beautiful to watch. I just love it. I can go right up to the nest and she doesn't feel threatened,' Hanson beams, pointing out the mother bird hopping from foot to foot on a flowering vine. 'I'll walk in and out and they're not frightened by me. So you see, I'm not a threat to everything! I look after things. I love my animals, my birds, and the kangaroos that's around here. And of course she's always welcome at my house.'

Hanson shoots me a friendly 'told-you-so' smile. It's an eerie sensation, trying to reconcile this beguilingly empathetic woman with the vitriolic nationalist who drove late 1990s Australia to the brink of a pseudo civil war; the virulent crusader who labels Islam 'a disease' that we need to 'vaccinate ourselves against' and is boycotting Cadbury Easter eggs because they are halal-certified; the vindictive enforcer who believes that victims of domestic abuse 'make it up' to rort their ex-husbands, and who once locked up three Indigenous children in a detention centre over Christmas, for spitting at her in Ipswich.

'It was caught on camera. I got the cops to look into it,' Hanson explains of the controversial case that won her international condemnation in December 1996 for potentially violating the UN Convention on the Rights of the Child. 'One was thirteen, one eleven and one ten. I pressed charges, but the ten-year-old I couldn't because he was under-age,' she says with a frown. 'The other two were put in detention, and I heard they had a wonderful time playing games, because they didn't get it at home. I wanted to take it further but the cops wouldn't. They were allowed to get away with it, and later I heard one of them was involved in a murder!'

In the blinkered cloisters of Hanson's mind, causality and evidence have no place. The possibility that her punitive treatment of the young boys kickstarted a pattern of anti-authoritarian anger that bloomed into full-blown criminality in adulthood is something she refuses to contemplate: a pointless intellectual exercise. Prison is for punishment. The fact that Norway has proven that a humane approach to incarceration can reduce recidivism rates to as low as 20 per cent, compared with Australia's 44.3 per cent and the Unites States' massive 76.6 per cent, is irrelevant.

Confoundingly, Hanson cites her own time in jail to argue that Australian prisons are not punitive enough: 'You have air conditioning, a clean cell, hot meals, access to education, a gym instructor, so many benefits. Hang on a minute, they've committed a crime against society! And I thought of the elderly. Where's their heating, their air conditioning? What about the homeless? They don't have a roof over their heads and three square meals a day!'

I suggest that the rage and pain Hanson felt, at being punished for a crime she 'didn't commit', is perhaps very similar to what a lot of innocent refugees are feeling on Manus and Nauru right now, and she shoots me daggers. I am being a smart-ass for even making the parallel. The filming is over for the day.

We pack up our gear, and I retreat to Hanson's guest cabin to read the anti-Islamic pamphlets she receives from an alt-right group in America. They are written with the same lunatic absolutism as One Nation's anti-Indigenous, anti-Asian 1997 manifesto, *Pauline Hanson: The Truth*. The dense typeface is crammed with hysterical invective and unsupported 'facts', allegedly drawn from the Qur'an. The dominant message is that Muslims are primitive and sub-human – a malevolent force intent on annihilating the Free World. I wonder if the authors belong to some shady CIA-sponsored propaganda operation to win 'hearts and minds' over to America's ongoing wars in the Middle East; the attributions are disturbingly vague. Even more disturbing is the fact that this is the 'research' that Hanson regularly regurgitates on the airwaves, transforming half a million peaceful Australian Muslims into a national scourge, to solidify her populist appeal.

'Mohammed was a prophet of Allah. He lived in Medina in about the fourteenth century and for the first twelve years he preached peace and had 150 followers,' Hanson tells me with scholarly diligence as we drive to Yeppoon, to shoot the second leg of her

'Fed Up' campaign. 'And after that, Mohammed created viciousness and attacked the caravans and murdered those who didn't believe in him, and forced people to join him through murder, and that's where it actually grew. It was only a religion of peace for twelve years. It's quite evident that the Qur'an states that Islam is the submission of women and to behead the nonbelievers of it. And all I'm saying is to have a better understanding of the teachings of Islam.'

Saraya Beric, Hanson's social media manager, chimes in. 'I have spoken to some Muslims in Sydney who are very moderate and Aussie, and they've said the majority of Muslims in Australia support ISIS! That's scary when you have the government and the media saying it's only a minority. A few years ago, *Today Tonight* asked Muslims if they wanted sharia law here and they said yes. Look at women and homosexuals, and what happens to them under sharia.'

'We're not saying every Muslim is a terrorist,' Hanson adds reasonably. 'But if they are allowed to get control, they'll welcome it. So have we educated you?'

'Um, what happens under sharia, Pauline?' I ask, dreading where this irrational hotchpotch of anecdote, hyperbole and myopic generalisation could possibly lead.

'They lose all their rights with it. There are Muslim women that still have circumcision, they are sexual slaves, the property of the husband, if they get raped they get blamed for it, they cannot walk alone without a male, they have no rights over the children, and they're treated like dirt. And a lot of women convert to it, because they're the type that want to be dominated by men.'

I thank Hanson for the explanation. Last time I looked, the oppression she's describing was happening in remote pockets of Afghanistan, not cosmopolitan Sydney. I'm as fascinated by the reductive absurdity of Hanson's Islamophobia as I am repulsed by the support it is winning her wherever she speaks. The conundrum of Pauline Hanson is that she is perfectly pleasant company — self-deprecating, playful, solicitous and oddly astute — until she gets started on Islam. Then she morphs into a flame-spitting medusa, full of invective and bile. Oldfield's description of the politician as 'the worst combination of stubbornness, evil and ignorance' is playing on my mind. I cannot keep allowing her to air her obnoxious views unchallenged. Unless she engages with an adversary on camera, I will have to confront her myself. I resolve to do so during our final shoot in Canberra, when it will no longer matter if she spits the dummy and walks. Until then, I will document her without comment and let her bigotry speak for itself.

The intensifying friction between Hanson and my camera is worlds away from the relaxed banter we enjoyed ten months ago, when we started filming in January 2015. Back then, she was campaigning for the rural seat of Lockyer in the Queensland state election. I was pleasantly surprised by Hanson's focus on environmental issues, and the way her economic views seemed closer to those of democratic socialism and old-school Labor than the lunatic, neo-con right. She was pro free health care and education; against the privatisation of electricity, transport and telecommunications; and hell-bent on protecting the Great Barrier Reef and the Great Artesian Basin from the ravages of coal seam gas and coal mining. With James Ashby not yet officially in the picture, Hanson was running her own campaign — and those of her eleven One Nation candidates — by herself.

I still have the A3 map she printed for us in her little office by the snooker table at her farm, showing the land that has been marked for coal seam gas exploration around Lockyer. 'It makes no difference to me what country the mining companies are from — American, Chinese or Indonesian,' she said solemnly. 'I'm just going to say no, right across the board. The whole fact is, CSG damages our water, and we can't risk it. It's so important to farming, and we don't need it here for environmental reasons, for the safety of the soil and the agricultural land. We can't let the multinationals come in here, rip the guts out of the land and take the profits out of the country!'

Hanson folded the map into her purse and drove at a brisk clip to Rosewood, to debate the Labor, LNP and Greens candidates running for Lockyer at a community meeting. In the car, she launched into another passionate concern, a proposed Chinese-backed open-cut coal mine covering 9000 hectares from Rosewood to Thornton in the Lockyer Valley. 'To have it in this area would destroy it. It's beautiful farmland here, and it's quality of life. And who wants trucks thundering up and down here? Or maybe coal trains? We've got to protect our standard of living and the environment, and we can't keep selling out our country to foreign interests for the almighty dollar. It's gotta stop!'

At that moment, with her no-name sunglasses, modest cotton frock and defiantly tilted chin, Hanson seemed truly heroic. The fact that she had poured $100 000 of her own money into her campaign underlined her apparent selflessness. 'Twenty years ago I was fighting for all this,' she said wearily, gesturing at the fertile plains. 'I fought for the dairy industry, against deregulation. I fought for the orange growers, they were ripping out the trees, and now it's all gone. And the water issue – water is going to be so important, and I warned them and I didn't get the support, and now, twenty years on, they're saying, "Gee whiz, Pauline was right!" Can I turn it all around? Can I make a difference? I don't know. That's twenty years of destruction we've had with our major political parties, and it's going to be a battle. I'm getting good feedback, but the only true polling day is in the polling booth, and every election I'm faced with the fearmongering or there's corruption or the nude photos or vote rigging. I've won it on primaries so many times and lost it on preferences. And that's why I've got to work so hard. I've got two weeks left to prove to the people I'm their best representative. We don't get the donations the other parties have. It's run on a shoestring budget all with my money, because I put my money where my mouth is and I believe in what I'm doing.'

Hanson arrived at the Rosewood Uniting Church to discover that the candidate debate was well under way. The little audience was a cross-section of Australia's hardworking rural poor: men in patched drill shirts and workboots ground down to the leather; women in decade-old frocks with Chinese-made plastic flats. A handful of tree-changers in pastel linen with optimistic haircuts rounded out the tableau. Hanson's opponents from the Labor, Greens and Bob Katter parties were there, but the florid pro-mining LNP incumbent, Ian Rickuss, was a no-show. There was a ripple of recognition as Hanson took her seat; national icons don't often come to Rosewood. But the politician was genuinely contrite. She humbly apologised for her lateness and waited for her turn to speak.

'John Howard separated the water from the land in 2004, and he sold fifty billion worth of international water rights in Australia. Keating in 1992 signed Agenda 21 with 178 countries, and part of that is privatisation of water, so unless we can get on the floor of parliament to reverse whole thing, we can't even put in our dams,' Hanson began with Brechtian conviction, under the church's slow-moving fans. 'And they have satellite surveillance on us, yet CSG can have unlimited water to do their mining, and a farmer can't even feed his livestock. I don't trust the political parties – I have not seen one of them stand up. And we've got to get back to government for the people! So let's unite and fight for our rights, because we don't have democracy anymore. They control us. I don't want to make policy on the run, I want the true facts, and if I am elected, I intend to fight for you. This is not about One Nation, it's about informing the people so we are not led like sheep to the slaughter by the political parties, who are led by the multinationals, who want to rip the guts out of this country. And that's not what I stand for. So there.'

Hanson's audience erupted in applause. Even I wanted to clap. When she speaks about something she actually understands, Hanson is utterly compelling. We followed her over to the Rising Sun Hotel, a magnificently decrepit 1908 pile facing the rail lines on Rosewood's main drag.

'Hi there. Did you know there's an open-cut coal mine going in this area?' Hanson asked two young men pleasantly, as they nursed XXXX beers on the verandah.

'Really?' the darker man replied, more confronted by the fact he was talking to Pauline Hanson than by the imminent threat to the clean air of Rosewood.

'If you scull a schooner, I'll vote for ya,' his mate leered, blearily raising his beer.

Hanson, hands on her hips, scolded him with the unruffled ease of a woman with three brothers and three sons. 'No way, no way, no way. Ladies don't scull schooners, especially not for blokes! If you vote for me, you'll vote for me on my policies,' she teased. Then, with an expert pivot on her shiny stiletto, she sashayed off to the car park. The young bloke held up his schooner in mock salute.

That night, back at Hanson's farm, I felt like Margo Kingston felt at the start of her eye-opening journey through far north Queensland with Hanson in 1998. I was certain the media was wrong to focus exclusively on Hanson's racism and ignore her other policies; that the politician was not, in fact, intrinsically racist, but grossly misinformed. If it were not for her conservative, self-serving advisers, I mused, Hanson might even be persuaded to become a fighter for the left: the humane, climate-focused crusader that Australia so desperately needs. I remembered Hanson's prophetic warnings from the 1998 campaign trail: 'We will lose all Australian-made products by 2005. All our major products will have been sold off'; and her anti-capitalist salvo in her maiden speech: 'If this government wants to be fair dinkum, then it must stop kowtowing to financial markets, international organisations, world bankers, investment companies and big business.'

'That's the kind of message I can agree with,' I told myself. 'Hanson's not a puppet or political idiot savant, she's a working-class hero, with the true leader's gift for prophecy.'

I wallowed in Hanson's tepid swimming pool under the starlit sky, and she handed me an expertly mixed Ginger Bitch in an icy glass – a delicious testimony to her long years cocktail waitressing on the Gold Coast.

'I'm going to convert you, by the end of this shoot,' I told her happily, pointing at her sweeping roofs. 'I'm going to convince you to cover your whole house with solar panels!'

But the next morning, Hanson was decidedly frosty. And I'd come to my senses. We set up our camera without comment as she breezed past us to the front door. She was not wearing make-up. She seemed more childlike without it, and strangely vulnerable. Her visitor was an avuncular seventy-year-old named Viv – a loyal supporter since the late 1990s. Viv had been busy, canvassing the pubs and paddocks of Lockyer.

'You're in, I'll stake me life on it. You're home and hosed. I was at the saleyards at Blenheim yesterday, and if you had a dollar in your pocket for every time they mentioned your name . . .' Viv beamed.

'I hope so, Viv. I've been working so hard,' Hanson said, listening hungrily.

'And I was up at Espy six weeks ago and there were a dozen sitting round having a beer and they all asked about you. Your name's good up there – if you stood against Newman, you'd knock him off. And the *Queensland Times* is good to you – you get free ads!'

'No, I paid for that ad in the *QT*. I pay my way. That was over $900, that ad,' Hanson insisted, and guided her old mate outside. 'But I still gotta get out there and work for the seat, and I appreciate what you're saying, but anything could happen. I don't trust them, what they could come out with.' In deference to Viv's age, Hanson went the extra yard and unlocked her gate for his ute.

Later, she settled into her crimson armchair to heckle the news. Scientists had identified 2014 as the hottest year on record. A Queensland Greens candidate spoke urgently of the need to ban CSG and coal and commit to solar.

'She's not the only one standing against CSG!' Hanson grumbled. 'But these Greenies go too far. They want high tax and all the rest of it, but they're flying around in their planes with aircon! You've got to find a balance. Why won't the Greens work with us? Because One Nation is a threat. And the majors won't acknowledge the minors have any significance in this election. It's not a level playing field. The whole lot of them are so dogmatic in their politics, it's all about me, me, me. Not working together, for what is right for the country and the people!'

We flew back to Sydney and tracked Hanson's progress on the news. On 31 January 2015, the politician lost Lockyer by a minuscule 114 votes. She'd picked up 13 116 against the LNP's Ian Rickuss, who received 13 230 after preferences – driving a 14.7 per cent swing against him, and proving that 49.8 per cent of Lockyer's predominantly rural constituents believed in her. Lockyer was Hanson's eighth straight election loss since her federal defeat in 1998. As the media was quick to point out, the former member for Oxley had failed to win political office for seventeen consecutive years. Hanson, incensed, demanded a recount, claiming preferences and postal votes had not been properly allocated and verified. 'I think it needs a full investigation into this. It's wide open for corruption,' she raged in the *Brisbane Times*. The Electoral Commission of Queensland rejected her demand.

I did not see Hanson again until 16 July 2015, when we flew to Rockhampton to capture the triumphant unveiling of her bespoke Jabiru two-seater, piloted by her new spin doctor, James Ashby. With her eye-catching 'Fed Up' logo, glossy corflutes produced by Ashby's company, Coastal Signs & Printing, and an anonymous, deep-pocketed donor on board, Hanson had recovered from her narrow loss in Lockyer and was raring to start her eleventh campaign – for a seat in the federal Senate.

As the trim, doe-eyed Ashby gently chaperoned Hanson through the cattle auctions at Gracemere, we followed her with our camera. The fierce environmentalist we'd glimpsed on the Lockyer campaign was nowhere to be seen. In her place was a vigilant, money-focused nationalist, with rapacious Chinese investors and satanic Muslim invaders firmly in her sights. With Ashby by her side, it was obvious that Hanson's platform had been carefully honed to inflame the populist resentments that were most likely to win her votes.

'The farmers are suiciding, four a day. They can't pay the mortgage and the banks move in. And the Chinese are lining up to buy our land, purely to feed their own country!' Hanson told an old cockie, surveying a pen of Brangus-cross steers.

'In fifteen years' time, we won't have any feed for us,' he agreed.

'Exactly right. The Chinese have poured a lot of products in, which is why we've lost a lot of our industries, and they don't have the same health standards. And water's going to be the big issue,

I'm telling you now. If we don't stop the water restrictions that are going on, we won't have farming in this country at all!'

'Do you remember Cathy Freeman?' said a second farmer, sidling up to Hanson with a naughty grin. She flashed him her most welcoming smile. 'Well, she turns up at your fish shop, and you say, "We don't serve your sort of people round here. There's a fish shop down the road, ten minutes." And she says, "Do you know who I am? I'm Cathy Freeman." And you say, "In your case, five minutes."'

Hanson looked uneasy.

'Do you spread that one round?' The jokester nudged her.

'I wouldn't dare!' Hanson rolled her eyes at our camera and laughed.

Ashby steered her down the walkway, to spruik her rural bona fides to a matronly grazier and her two sons. 'I've got 150 acres. I've had it since 1991, outside of Amberley air force base,' Hanson told the little family proudly. 'We've got to protect our land. I'm sick of these greedy corporations coming here and not paying their taxes. Australians need to wake up. Young kids are being brainwashed into a way of thinking they don't understand. Once the older generations go, they will have no idea what this country was like. Even all this climate-change stuff, that's all BS! The scientists have been bought off by these companies, and then they brainwash the kids. I was saying flying up here, the amount of trees we've got is amazing, and yet they'll have you believe we don't have a tree left in this country!'

'So much for Hanson's nascent environmentalism,' I think, as we set up our tripod in the bleachers of Gracemere's empty Rodeo pen for our first interview with James Ashby. With the rabid climate-change denier Malcolm Roberts now on the One Nation Senate ticket, Hanson can no longer critique the damaging environmental impact of coal seam gas without appearing seriously unhinged. But it is also clear from the way the farmers snapped up the politician's campaign cards down in the cattleyards that the new improved Hanson is racking up serious support.

'I'm excited about it,' Hanson tells our camera, as Ashby texts quietly by her side. 'I'm speaking to people that say, "Hey, we're not the forgotten ones. She's taken time to get out here to meet us!" And that's our slogan: "Never give up, we won't".'

'I've seen it only in a few other politicians,' Ashby adds. 'Hawke was one of them, Rudd was another, and Pauline is the only other politician that gets the crowd reaction. And they flock to her! I think they see that she is real, and people love it.'

'What made you want to work with Pauline?' I ask him. The political rumour mill is buzzing with speculations that Hanson's new minder is a Liberal Party plant, sent in to 'manage' the politician after he successfully persecuted his ex-boss, former federal speaker and LNP turncoat Peter Slipper. Ashby entered Hanson's orbit in late 2014, when he offered to print the election materials for One Nation's 2015 Queensland campaign at cost. His only request was a face-to-face meeting with Hanson herself. They clicked immediately. One Nation's former Queensland treasurer, Ian Nelson, would later label Ashby 'the Antichrist of every politician' and 'as cunning as a boarding house rat'. But the pleasant, easygoing man seated next to Hanson now seems every inch the devoted surrogate son she claims he has become.

'I met Pauline at the Queensland election and she clearly needed help, and the prospect of getting round the state came up and I said, "I'm a pilot, you just need the plane."' Ashby smiles easily. 'I saw similarities with Pauline and my own self. We've both been through tough times, doing what we love, working in an industry that's supposed to do good for people. And when you look at Pauline, for

Christ's sakes, she went to jail. I went on a tough road, but it was nothing like Pauline.'

'They've taught us a lot,' Pauline says, nodding gravely.

'Yeah, to play by their rules. It's made us cluier,' Ashby agrees. Openly gay, Ashby wears his crimson Broncos windcheater like armour as he follows his boss through the redneck wilds of Hansonland. He continues to maintain he was the innocent victim of Slipper's relentless sexual abuse, crucified by the media when he dared to speak out. It's clear that Hanson's bought his story.

'James and Saraya, they're young, they're entrenched in the campaign, and these two guys are my driving force.' Hanson glows. 'I'll write posts for the Facebook page, and they work behind the scenes to clean it up. Saraya is an office worker and James wears many hats – he's in the marketing of the party, he does the printing and he's also a good friend. He's a very talented young man.'

Beric joins the happy couple at the Campdraft carnival at Paradise Lagoons, a sprawling Rockhampton cattle station owned by the Acton family. The Actons are central Queensland royalty: staunch supporters of Anglo-Australia's rural traditions, and 'the richest ones in cattle here', according to the awe-struck Hanson. The ingenuity and skill of Rockhampton's cockies is on full display as we stroll past the rodeo, the mustering pens, the whip-slinging jackaroos lassoing heifers from galloping steeds.

A middle-aged woman selling hand-carved rocking horses tells Hanson she's 'the only bloody pollie who says it like it is!' A young bloke nursing a bourbon by the gelato truck urges her to 'Give 'em heaps!' A patrician gentleman in head-to-toe RM Williams approaches her outside the saddler's stall to offer his heartfelt support: 'I've often felt sorry for you. You keep speaking your mind and you get bashed and you keep on going.'

'You dust yourself down – doesn't the older generation look at things that way?' Hanson demurs, chuffed to have received this rare nod of patriarchal approval.

She ducks into a dress shop to sift through a brightly coloured sock bin, and reels back as if she's been bitten. 'Cor, everything's made in China,' she snarls, dropping the socks in disgust. Then word comes down from the members' stand that the Actons themselves would like to meet Hanson, and she brightens, traipsing up the stairs to nibble freshly baked scones with Campdraft nobility. 'If they didn't have respect for me they wouldn't invite me up,' she tells me excitedly. 'I may be born in the city, but the country's my thing. I love it. People are coming out of the woodwork now, they're saying "you were right". Because they can see the changes that were happening.'

Hanson's audience with the Actons is a successful exercise in low-key Queensland PR. She sips hot tea and slams CSG mining and the Greens with equal conviction, making sure the laconic graziers gathered around her know that One Nation's anonymous, cashed-up backer is a disgruntled Nationals voter, who donated to Hanson's Fed Up campaign when he realised she cared more about country people than Barnaby Joyce and the LNP.

That night, flushed with her support on the hustings, Hanson and her new Troika sit down to a celebratory counter meal at a rodeo-cum-pub. A one-man band plays easy-listening '80s hits on a synthesiser as pub hands sweep the ring for the next bucking bronco. Ashby shoulders up to the bar, and waits beside four other men in Broncos windcheaters to order Jack Daniels UDLs. Hanson quietly salts her chips, and a drunken woman interrupts her with an adoring monologue. 'My 98-year-old dad died loving Pauline Hanson. God you're a wonderful woman!' she raves. Hanson, clearly hungry, patiently waits for her fan to finish, thanks her politely for her support, then tucks in to her fish and chips. Surrounded by these gently inebriated, hardworking, defiantly monocultural people of the bush, Hanson is in her element. This is her tribe. After dinner, a limping bloke with a speech impediment begs her for a photo, and she complies warmly, gracious and at ease. The vitriolic Muslim-baiter from *Sunrise* and *Today* could be a different woman.

At 9 p.m., when we return to Hanson's budget motel to watch the late news, there's a palpable sense that she's riding a Zeitgeist – a slow-moving wave that seems set to sweep her to power, while the political status quo look blindly the other way. Hanson may be flying under the national media radar, but every report relates in some way to her Fed Up campaign. At Paradise Lagoons, Prime Minister Abbott is singing the praises of Campdraft to the press pack, trying to shore up the Coalition's shaky reputation with country voters. On Great Keppel Island, where Hanson is due to campaign tomorrow, the destruction of cyclones Maria and Dylan continues to wreak havoc on the tourist trade, as the state government vacillates over who should foot the clean-up bill. The nationwide Reclaim Australia rally, at which Hanson is speaking on Sunday, already has riot squads preparing for violence.

'They're trying to focus the Reclaim rally to be about racism. It may be with other speakers, but it's not with me,' Hanson tells Ashby and Beric as they lounge on the motel room beds with their iPhones. 'I go back to foreign ownership, the land, suicide, and why is this country not the one I grew up in? And the media put me into this box that I am anti-Muslim. I'm not, I'm anti-Islam, there's a big difference. They introduce me as a "controversial politician". Well, if I'm controversial, then nearly 10 per cent of Australians are in same boat as what I am.'

'If they're getting it wrong, you need to redirect them,' Ashby says nonchalantly, busy with a text.

'It's the media, James. It's always been like that. They've always bypassed the policies I put out, and the big parties pick them up, and they get a pat on the back.'

'The media has changed. A lot of these journos are young. They're on thirty k a year. They'd get more at a Woolies servo,' he replies with a smirk.

Hanson sighs and walks over to the mirror to touch up her lipstick. 'These young journos are so opinionated and left-wing that when someone comes from the centre, like me, they focus on one issue – immigration and multiculturalism.'

'Yep,' Ashby mumbles.

'I will get on the floor of parliament.'

'Slowly,' he purrs.

'I can't wait to give another maiden speech!' Hanson blurts, doing a happy little spin. Then she glances at the TV. The news has cut to the weather. 'It's going to be cold tomorrow,' she says, feigning a shiver.

'So much for climate change.' Ashby shrugs, and shuts off his phone.

Ashby has never given me his email address – all of his communication appears to be done by text. Several times, I've noticed him briefing an unknown caller on the campaign's progress. His approach to media management has none of Pasquarelli's combativeness or Oldfield's showy erudition. Instead, he is unobtrusive, pragmatic and relaxed. This has earned him a thing that largely eluded Hanson's former spin doctors: her unalloyed trust. Ashby briefs the politician in private, and prefers to interview her on his own camera for Facebook, rather than controlling what she says to mine. He has been a generous helper, rigging a GoPro in the cockpit of the Jabiru to film Hanson in the air for us, and only intervening when Hanson becomes so annoyed by my questions that he needs to calm her down.

Ashby's conviction that Hanson needs to 'redirect' the media is put into action the next day, when he ferries the politician over to the cyclone-smashed dunes of Great Keppel Island. In a breezy wooden bungalow overlooking a line of shattered huts, Ashby introduces Hanson to Zed, the resort manager, and steers the conversation to Great Keppel's contested gaming licence. Hanson is incensed to hear that the Queensland government has denied Zed's boss permission to install casino tables in his bold redevelopment plan for the island, while Chinese Australian developers on the mainland are apparently allowed to expand their casino operations with impunity.

'A lot of the Asians, they like their gambling,' Hanson tells Zed supportively.

'Yeah. There's a tourist market coming up from Asia, and this is going to boost the economy. And all we're asking for is thirty-five tables!' Zed shakes his head.

'If a Chinese investor owned all this, would they be hesitating?' Hanson asks as the two of them stand side by side, looking out over the apocalyptic splendour of Great Keppel's glittering coves and undulating white sands, strewn with the mangled wreckage of what was once a bustling beach resort. Two huge tractors trawl up and down the beach, pushing the broken dunes back into place.

'Five years ago you couldn't see the water. There were beautiful, massive trees, and now it's all gone. We just sat and watched it; we couldn't stop it. In two years we had two cyclones, on the king tide, at the same time. It all turned to hell.'

'Good fishing?' is all Hanson will venture. Zed talks enthusiastically of the redthroat emperor, the sweetlip, the coral trout. Ashby says the place reminds him of Jurassic Park. No-one mentions climate change.

Ashby ends Hanson's excursion under the coconut trees of a crumpled cafe, propped up against some twisted bracken. Making sure that Hanson's facing the afternoon light, he films her writing a letter to Queensland's new premier. 'Dear Ms Palaszczuk, Great Keppel needs your assistance in granting a gaming licence,' Hanson reads obediently. 'Fifteen hundred jobs will be created. You are a reasonable woman, now be a good leader. Sincerely, Pauline Hanson.'

Hanson does the scene for Ashby from three different angles, not at all annoyed at having to do retakes when her surrogate son is in charge. Ashby directs her to mime posting the letter in a red metal postbox sitting quaintly on the sand, and an elderly woman in a lurid yellow sun visor wanders over to inspect the action. To Hanson's surprise, she has no idea who the politician is. An avid techno geek from New Zealand, the woman has come to Great Keppel with a video club from Auckland. She is fascinated by our cameras.

'They're filming for TV, we're filming for Facebook,' Ashby explains politely. 'We're taking a smart approach to something about which most other politicians don't care. It's different to what everyone else has done, and hopefully we'll get attention.' Ten grey-haired members of Auckland's video club watch Ashby approvingly, as he expertly films Hanson and Beric sipping coconuts through straws.

Early the next morning, on a crisp, sunny Sunday, the 'Fed Up' Troika join seventy concerned patriots at the Reclaim Australia rally in Rockhampton's Central Park. Modestly dressed Anglo and European Australians of all ages stand around under gracious oaks on the dewy lawns, waiting for something to happen. Someone has spray-painted a German shepherd with the Union Jack; a young mother has clad her two red-headed toddlers in

Aussie-flag patterned onesies. Several people hold up vintage One Nation banners. A squadron of octogenarians sit stiffly on camp stools, clutching plastic Australian flags on little sticks. Facing the crowd under an impressive pair of loudspeakers, five strapping members of the Patriots Defence League stand in a militaristic line, their fists clasped over their crotches.

'You expecting any protests here?' Hanson asks a young cop idly chatting with his colleagues under a tree.

'No intelligence of that, no. We get a good regular crowd. We'll make sure everything is fine,' he reassures her.

'If you hear of anything, you just give me the nod, because I'm not here to create any violence,' Hanson urges, and walks over to greet her people. The speakers crackle to life with the national anthem, and Hanson bestows hugs and handshakes on the enamoured crowd as the rally's guest of honour. She sings along to 'Advance Australia Fair', totally out of tune and utterly committed. The crowd claps politely when the anthem ends and Hanson steps up to the podium to face her audience, framed by two gently billowing flags.

'Hello, you make me feel proud as I see you today. It's actually twenty years ago I was elected to parliament. I came out from a fish and chip shop. I thought it was important to speak out. John Howard thought differently. He wanted to quieten me. He chucked me out. I still ran, and I won in the biggest swing in the nation. From that time to this day, I believe in being truthful and standing up for what you believe in. Australians feel forgotten, and as I've travelled this country far and wide, speaking to people of all ages, they feel they are not represented by their parliamentarians. To me, the Reclaim Australia rally is to get back the country that I grew up in. Multiculturalism is not the way to go. I'm sorry, this is my country. If you're not happy here, then go back to where you want to come from!'

Hanson's riveted audience lets out a lusty cheer.

'Actually, you know, I've got my own plane now. I can take them back personally myself!' she says with a grin, and the crowd bursts out laughing, waving their flags in delight.

The banality of the scene is momentarily horrifying. Eighteen years ago, Hanson would not have been able to appear at an event like this, let alone address the crowd from the stage, without an armed security escort, snipers on the roofs and a battalion of riot police holding back thousands of anti-racism protesters. I wonder what's more frightening: the civil violence that Hanson's words once caused, or the fact that twenty years on, she is so embedded in the mainstream that no-one considers her offensive enough to heckle.

Hanson, for one, is not surprised that her views no longer incite mass anger. Her enemies have given up bussing in protesters to attack her, and the media no longer slams her as a racist, she tells me, because it simply isn't true.

'This whole thing about me being racist is absolute rubbish. People do it to discredit me. The politicians don't want to answer the questions, so what's the best spin to do? Let's call her a racist. I'm not in fear of foreigners. My grandparents migrated to this country. I married a Pole. I employed a Laotian. I rented flats to an Aboriginal woman. My kids grew up with Aboriginal kids. I'm just a patriotic Australian who wants to protect our way of life, as any people do. I meet cabbies and ask if they're Australian, and they say yes, and I say, "Good, because if you're not, I'll put you on a plane and send you home." I'm connected with these people. They understand it's as important to me that they give this country their loyalty as it is to them to become Australians, so we're sharing this loyalty together.'

Maybe. But Hanson's definition of racism is deceptively narrow – a 1950s-era construct that restricts the word to a purely genetic assumption of superiority. To the people who feel the effects of Hanson's hate speech daily, like Helen Sham-Ho, Professor Marcia Langton, Dr Thiam Ang and Randa Abdel-Fattah, the politician's racism is undeniable.

'It is about refusing to allow people who come from particular faith or ethnic backgrounds the same nuance and complexity that we do with the majority of white Australians,' Adbel-Fattah explains. 'You impute to one group this homogenous identity, this idea that everyone is thinking and acting and feeling in the same way. Hanson says you can't be racist to Muslims, because Muslims aren't a race. But racism can stand in for religion, and it can stand in for race. There are 1.6 billion Muslims in the world: that's 1.6 billion ways of living and understanding Islam. She's denying us the complexity that we afford to other majority groups.'

Sham-Ho prefers to laugh Hanson off as an 'opportunist who should just pack up'. Dr Ang sees her damaging rhetoric as like 'a virus. And viruses are difficult to get rid of.' Tracey Curro, the journalist who famously asked Hanson if she was xenophobic, is astonished that her 'script hasn't changed for twenty years', and says the politician is incapable of feeling empathy for people she doesn't understand. Langton is blunt: 'Pauline Hanson is a hardened racist from Ipswich.'

Filming these comments in the lead-up to my final shoot with Hanson, I am increasingly frustrated by her stubborn refusal to confront her ideological critics. I don't just want to contrast her views with theirs in the edit suite – I want to put her in the same room as them, to see if they can change her mind. If I didn't believe in Hanson's underlying humanity, I wouldn't care so much. I am beginning to suspect that beneath her dogged stonewalling, the politician is scared. With a federal election to win, and still only halfway through her campaign, Hanson cannot afford to be caught out. She does not want another nude photo scandal, a 'Please explain', or some other embarrassing brain snap that will undermine the dignified, stateswoman-like image she and Ashby have been so successfully cultivating on Facebook and breakfast TV.

I'm also sure that if 'racism' can encompass culture and religion as well as biology, then Hanson most certainly is racist. On the lawn outside her front deck one morning, as she faces the satellite truck for her regular paid spot on *Sunrise*, I accidentally capture proof of this racism on tape.

Hanson, in a jungle-print blouse, is in a sparkling mood. The Brangus are grazing, her little honeyeater is nesting, and Ashby's Facebook videos of her sipping coconuts and posting a letter to Premier Palaszczuk on Great Keppel Island have been trending remarkably well.

Hanson smiles at the dark-skinned, neatly dressed camera assistant, James, and adjusts her earpiece to listen in to the control-room chatter at Channel 7 as she waits for the producers to beam her in.

'It's my favourite topic – refugees,' she says through gritted teeth. 'You're not going to tell me you're a refugee, James, are you?'

'No. Aboriginal,' he replies.

Hanson blinks at him, momentarily flummoxed. 'Really? Wouldn't have picked it. Good to see that you're actually, you know, taking up this, and working . . .'

'Twenty seconds,' says the Anglo-Australian satellite guy, and Hanson unleashes her daily tirade against Muslims and Islam, and how every single patriotic, red-blooded Australian should be very afraid.

'It's nothing to do with refugees, it's Islam,' Hanson mutters to herself when the live cross finishes and the satellite guy takes off her wire. Then she fixes James with a determined smile.

'Look, I'm Indigenous to this land, same as you – and when people tell me I'm an immigrant, I get annoyed.'

'You were born here,' James says agreeably.

Hanson nods, her eyes flashing. 'And all I hear is what people said to me when I was in parliament. You know: "Go back to where you come from!" I went to Palm Island, and the Aboriginal women told me the kids are always behind. And people tell me I'm the only honest one.'

'You're the only politician out there speaking your mind, that's for sure,' James replies.

'If you're Aboriginal, you can live your way of life. If not, live the white man way of life,' Hanson flashes. She looks like she's about to stamp her foot.

'I like to say "the Australian way of life",' James answers softly.

Hanson shakes James's hand and offers him a casual job plastering her house.

'I'm Aboriginal too,' the satellite guy pipes up.

'Well, don't you go and claim any benefits,' Hanson says with a grin, and disappears inside.

Later, we film Hanson kvetching about the price of avocados in the vegie aisle at Coles, and she suddenly invites me to dinner. She's making a Thai chicken curry. 'You get coriander, I'll get coconut milk. I got lemongrass in the garden and kaffir lime in a plant, so save your money,' she tells me, with brusque satisfaction.

Back in her kitchen, Ashby and I wolf down Hanson's surprisingly exquisite curry as she sips tea and scrolls through old posts on her Pauline Hanson's Please Explain Facebook page. She usually eats one big meal in the middle of the day, and snacks or fasts at each end. 'That one there. That one had almost 75 000 shares within twenty-four hours,' Hanson says contentedly, pointing at a photo of an Islamic man with a red cross through his face, under One Nation's orange and blue banner. 'It was about the jihadist being allowed back into the country. When I went back to it, it was up to 4.2 million.'

I have a déjà vu flash to Margo Kingston sitting at this same table in 1998, trying to persuade Hanson to see Indigenous issues in a more humane light. 'My responsibility is Muslims,' I think grimly – and launch into what I hope is a congenial, easy-to-follow spiel: about how my time in Jordan, Qatar and Oman has taught me that Muslims are individuals first and a religious group second; how the Lakemba shops are safe and pleasant, with some of the best Turkish delight in the country; how until she takes the time to meet the diverse and overwhelmingly gracious people of Australia's Islamic community, she cannot possibly judge them en masse. Shamelessly repurposing Daniel Patrick Moynihan's famous quip, I remind Hanson that everyone is entitled to her own opinion, but not to her own facts – and suggest that relying on hearsay and anecdotes to attack Islam not only makes her look stupid, it is morally irresponsible. I am curious to see how Ashby will react; so far, he has shown no signs of Oldfield's ideological fervour or Pasquarelli's unapologetic brutality.

Ashby smoothly takes Hanson's side: she's right to be worried, we can't trust these people, they are lying when they say they want peace. But what's surprising is that he does so without a trace of emotion. The startling sense is that Ashby's stance is purely political: if Hanson's Islamophobia is winning her votes, then why should she stop? I'm not sure what's worse – Ashby's clinical opportunism or Oldfield's racial malignity. When I ran these same arguments past Oldfield back in November, he told me I wouldn't feel like standing up for Muslims when they sliced off my clitoris. Pasquarelli just thought I was an idealistic idiot.

On 10 December 2015, Hanson and I walk into Parliament House in Canberra for the last day of our shoot, and I'm done with being polite. Sham-Ho and Abdel-Fattah have both been willing to fly down to meet the politician for a civilised debate. In a restaurant, in a hotel, on the steps of the Australian War Memorial – wherever Hanson feels most comfortable. She has rejected them both. I sit the politician down on the mezzanine on the second floor, and in full view of passing journalists I confront her.

'You say you're for the fair go, yet you won't meet these people. Why?'

Hanson's glacial. 'It's not happening, Anna. Why the hell doesn't the media just report the facts and let the public judge us? You're all so opinionated. If you feel that way, get into politics yourself. This is what pisses me off about the media: you keep going and going until you get what you want. Well, you're not doing it to me. I don't give a shit about your bloody documentary. You've asked your questions, I've answered it. I am not meeting these people.' She stands and starts walking away. Luke follows and she turns on us, furious.

'No! Put the frigging camera away. My main aim is to get back into parliament, and I am *not* going to trust you to get anything there that is going to destroy that, so get that into your head! I've been done over too many bloody times!'

'Let's have lunch,' I say, rattled. It's the first time I've felt the full blast of Hanson's rage. It's a force field of hatred – like running head-on into a concrete wall.

We break for an hour in the cafe, and have a carefully restrained chat about Hanson's ever-increasing Facebook 'likes'. Then, on Parliament House's rolling lawns under the soaring Australian flag, I try to break through to her, one final time. I pull up some 1990s archive on my laptop and take Hanson back over her legacy: the violent protests she incited as the leader of One Nation; the bloody spike in attacks on Muslim and Asian Australians after her maiden speech; a frightened Eurasian toddler holding a 'Why do you hate me?' sign at her night-time rally in Ipswich. I show her the oppressive trajectory she began in 1996 with her demand 'to have a say in who comes into my country', a trajectory that Howard expanded to '*we* will decide who comes into this country, and the circumstances in which they come' in 2001 and that Rudd, Abbott and Turnbull cemented with the horrific brutality of Nauru and Manus and 'Stop the boats'. I end with an old clip of a man in Hong Kong telling *60 Minutes*'s Emily Lau in 1997 that there's no way he's visiting Australia while that 'crazy woman' Pauline Hanson is there.

'Good. I've done my job then, haven't I? Go home, mate, we don't want you here! Forget it!' Hanson laughs derisively. 'Am I responsible for it? Look, I hate seeing this division. Who you are – American, Aboriginal, Chinese, whatever – we are all Australians together. My maiden speech said "swamped by Asians" and I stand by that to this day. This is a debate we have to have. We have a right to have a say. Even today, you have areas heavily dominated by Asian migration, and Australians are fed up with it! They don't want it! Exactly the same would happen if that many Westerners went to these Asian countries. They wouldn't like it either. So I'm not apologising to anyone.'

'Is that why most of your supporters are white?' I ask.

Hanson rips off her mic.

'That's it. You know that's a load of bullshit. You want to go into race and all the rest of it, forget it.' She angrily shakes out the cramps in her legs, her red hair flaming against Parliament House's soaring white walls and the blue summer sky. Luke turns off the camera for the last time. We drive to Canberra airport, and I buy Hanson a

Ginger Bitch, to toast the end of our gruelling journey – in which no-one changed. We're all relieved it's over.

Seven months later, on 2 July 2016, Australia's elite political and media establishment finally woke up to the wave of populist resentment Hanson had been steadily surfing online since her Lockyer defeat in 2015. After eighteen years in the political wilderness, the One Nation leader was back in the big house with a shocking six-year term in the federal Senate and three new One Nation senators in tow.

SBS screened our film, *Pauline Hanson: Please Explain!*, four weeks later on 31 July 2016. The documentary almost didn't make it to air: twenty-four hours before its 8.30 p.m. broadcast, I received an alarming text from Senator Hanson's new chief of staff, James Ashby. The senator wasn't happy that a promotional clip of her asking James, the Indigenous camera assistant, if he was a refugee had gone viral, reaching 1.8 million viewers. Hanson's normally supportive fans had been flooding her Facebook page with negative comments. Ashby told me the clip was 'defamatory' and accused me of showing it 'out of context'. He warned me that unless we pulled it off SBS's site, 'something terrible' would happen.

I rang my commissioning editor, who immediately ran Ashby's threat by SBS's top lawyers.

Their reply was swift. The clip accurately represented what Hanson said, and Ashby was right. The clip *was* defamatory:

Pauline Hanson had defamed herself.

Epilogue

Pauline Hanson always sensed she would win the 2016 federal election.

When we started filming her in January 2015, we, like almost everyone in the mainstream media, thought she was deluded. But after a year inside Hanson's 'Fed Up' tour, tracking the adulation she inspired throughout Queensland's deep north with her trademark mix of righteous patriotism, authentic rage and blunt message that 'ordinary' Australians were being screwed at both ends – by multicultural minorities at the bottom and by the 'political elites' at the top – we knew Hanson was destined for power.

In early 2016, over six months after Hanson started her under-the-radar quest to conquer the hearts of rural Australia in her bespoke Jabiru, analysts began to quietly flag the possibility of a Hanson resurgence. Under the new Senate voting laws, the serial politician was no longer threatened by the major-party preference deals that had stymied her re-election bids since 1996, and with double the number of Queensland Senate seats up for grabs, she only needed 7 per cent of the vote.

Hanson's prospects were the strongest they had been in decades, and commentators reluctantly faced the music. On 29 June, just days before Australia went to the polls, the *Sydney Morning Herald* grudgingly positioned the One Nation leader as a contender for the twelfth spot on the Queensland Senate ticket, alongside Greens candidates Andrew Bartlett and Larissa Waters, and Palmer United Party senator Glenn Lazarus. Asked how he felt about a rebooted Hanson gatecrashing the citadel a second time, Prime Minister Turnbull declared she would not be a 'welcome presence on the Australian political scene', reminding voters that the Liberal Party had 'chucked' her out years ago.

In the bowels of our Sydney edit suite, editor Nikki Stevens and I confronted the truth. The 'happy ending' we'd planned for our film, in which Hanson's tenth tilt at power would be dashed by a sophisticated electorate determined not to let One Nation divide Australia all over again, was fiction. We rejigged the cut and screened *Pauline Hanson: Please Explain!* to our astounded collaborators at SBS, ending with Hanson nibbling fish and chips in Parliament House and gloating about what she would say in her new maiden speech. Then we cut to a card announcing her six-year term in the federal Senate. When the film finished, the suite was filled with silent despair.

Hanson has always been up for a cheeky metaphor. Three weeks before her historic return to power, she climbed into a monster truck in Brisbane's Doomben Racecourse and ran over two utes painted red and blue to represent the LNP and Labor. With impressive agility, the 62-year-old then straddled the flattened wrecks and gave Ashby's Facebook camera the thumbs up. 'It reflects the public sentiment . . . that the major parties are not indestructible,' she said with a grin. On 2 July 2016, Australia's most famous right-wing populist was back in parliament.

Hanson did a live cross to Channel 7 from her election party, surrounded by cheering supporters waving glossy posters that James Ashby had printed for the occasion. 'My Office or Yours, Malcolm?' they blared, above Hanson's tangerine crop. Labor's Muslim senator Sam Dastyari offered to take the newly elected senator out for a halal snack pack in Sydney's western suburbs. 'Not happening,' Hanson retorted. Before the revelry ended, Hanson was whisked away by Ashby – now her increasingly powerful chief of staff.

Ashby has played gatekeeper to Hanson ever since, according to Saraya Beric, One Nation's former social media manager. Beric is one of many Hanson insiders to have been disposed of under the party's new regime, as it divides up its $1.6 million in electoral spoils, fields candidates in successive state elections, and hires new staff. According to sacked One Nation treasurer Ian Nelson, Ashby's control over the new senator and her party is absolute.

I haven't spoken with Hanson since our film aired in July 2016, when she declared, somewhat frostily, that she'd still have a drink with me, despite the fact that *Please Explain!* was anything but a puff piece. With some relief, I've traded my front-row seat to the Hanson circus for the distant sanity of Google Alerts: tracking the senator's volatile progress, and the fluctuating fortunes of One Nation, through the stories that flood my email feed. I've watched Hanson's entrée as a legitimate powerbroker with fascination, revulsion and a strange sense of déjà vu.

Just as she had in the late 1990s, Hanson has again become entangled in a web of political controversy, personal rumours and financial acrimony.

In 2017, the Australian Electoral Commission began investigating claims the party had not properly disclosed a 2015 donation by

Hanson's 'mystery' backer, Victorian developer Bill McNee, which allegedly enabled the purchase of the campaign Jabiru. The AFP dropped their investigation into Ashby's involvement in the Peter Slipper affair, but Ashby is now battling heat for suggesting One Nation candidates purchase $3500 corflute 'starter packs' through his company, instead of using less-costly rival printers. One Nation's mercenary attempt to induce its Western Australian candidates to pay a $250 000 'exit penalty', should they defect from the party once successfully elected, was abruptly dropped after an angry outcry.

Candidate-wise, One Nation is attracting an even more extreme line-up than it did in the late 1990s. Contenders endorsed for the 2017 Western Australian election included Richard Eldridge, whose Twitter posts advocated the killing of Indonesian journalists, attacked 'poofters' for wanting to link marriage to 'poo games', stated that only 'ugly blacks' complain and labelled Muslims 'sheet heads'. A second candidate, Michelle Meyers, described the LGBTI+ push for marriage equality as a Nazi-style 'mind-control program'. A third, David Archibald, declared that single mothers are 'too lazy to attract and hold a mate'. In welcome proof of the humanity of Western Australian voters, One Nation failed to win a single seat in the legislative assembly – although it did pick up three in the council.

Despite the dubious company it continues to keep, One Nation, with the clickbait-attracting Hanson at the helm, still poses a significant threat to the embattled major parties in Queensland. The senator insists she wants candidates 'with a bit of mongrel in them', and is fielding over ninety in her home state. Those initially endorsed, then subsequently dumped, by One Nation include Andy Semple, whose Twitter feed describes vegans as 'miserable people'; Shan Ju Lin, who believes homosexuals should be treated 'like medical patients'; and Peter Rogers, whose website linked to blogs claiming the photos of drowned Syrian toddler Alan Kurdi were fake, and that the Port Arthur massacre was fabricated to push through tougher gun laws.

Policy-wise, the populist senator has repurposed the strategy she developed under Oldfield and Pasquarelli: that of maintaining an ultra-conservative ideological platform, while lurching occasionally and unpredictably to the left.

She has called for a ban on the burqa, a royal commission into Islam, and an end to Muslim immigration. She remains a steadfast climate-change sceptic, wants a national ID card to battle welfare fraud and terrorism, rejects the need for a national sugar tax to combat obesity, and has slammed a pro-diversity Australia Day lamb ad for 'suppressing who we are as Australians'. She has repeatedly backed Coalition policies that gut support for the struggling battlers she claims to represent, voting for cuts in penalty rates and welfare for single mothers, and for the halving of government-funded childcare for Australia's poorest children. She has praised Donald Trump and Vladimir Putin as 'strong leaders', and in early 2017 appeared to fat-shame three million protesters in the global Women's March against Trump, describing them as 'clowns' in need of 'a bit of exercise'.

In stark contrast to these ultra-right moves, Senator Hanson, with characteristic contrariety, has also come out swinging for causes more often associated with the extreme left.

She's supported the push for a pardon for exiled Wikileaks founder Julian Assange; backed moves to legalise euthanasia and medicinal cannabis; worked to protect a large swathe of Queensland farmland from being annexed by the Australian Defence Force for its expanding military drills; challenged the generous government funding slated for the Adani coal mine in the Galilee Basin; opposed a Chinese-consortium bid to build a mega-casino on a pristine strip of the Gold Coast; and, true to her form in her 2015 Lockyer campaign, continues to be an outspoken critic of the environmental threats posed by coal seam gas mining.

And that's where the flashbacks to 1990s Hanson end. Something is very different this time around, and I find it alarming. Hanson Mark II, with three One Nation senators on the crossbench, 9 per cent of Australian voters behind her, and a popular platform on commercial TV, is no longer being treated as a minority voice. She is being given the attention and status of a major political leader.

Helping drive this radical change in perception is the government itself, which has assiduously courted Hanson to push its reactionary measures through the Senate. When Prime Minister Turnbull struck a preference deal with One Nation in Western Australia, he attracted none of the widespread condemnation and vitriol that John Howard endured when he refused to rule out preferencing One Nation in 1997. Liberal minister Arthur Sinodinos has been quick to leap to the Coalition's defence, claiming that One Nation is a 'very different beast' now, and that Hanson is 'a lot more sophisticated'. Even Hanson's old foe, the deposed prime minister Tony Abbott, insists she is a 'better person today than she was twenty years ago'.

But Pauline Hanson has not changed. She is just as politically and culturally divisive as she was in 1996 – it is Australia, itself, that has shifted. When the senator speaks in public these days, she does so free from violent mass protests, and is more likely to be interrupted by selfie-seeking fans than by hecklers. She is no longer a heretic, but part of the centre. Her working-class persona, which once mesmerised the media with its unmediated rawness, is a carefully maintained facade. Hanson is now a polished politician, playing the game. Her wealth has made her part of the establishment. Footage of government MPs falling over themselves to congratulate the senator in September 2016 following her shockingly Islamophobic maiden speech speaks volumes. The aspirational fish shop lady, who dreamt of a greater destiny over her fryers, has arrived.

I no longer feel the sympathy I felt for Hanson when she cried about her 'people' during our first meeting in Sylvania Waters in 2009. Back then, she was a fallen star, and her compassion – at least for those with whom she identifies – obfuscated the harshness of her views. Now, with Hanson's words in black and white, and without her childlike charisma to distract me, I sit in sad and furious judgement. The damage she continues to inflict on this once openhearted and proudly multicultural country, and the platform she's been allowed to wield, are, to me, both unforgivable and horrific.

And she's impossible to ignore. In St Kilda recently, while downing a quiet plate of cannelloni in Leo's Spaghetti Bar, I glanced up at a wall-screen TV to see Hanson arguing with Tracy Grimshaw on *A Current Affair*. The senator was wearing the same red and blue frock she'd worn on our last day in Canberra, when I accused her of hypocrisy for not engaging with Muslim commentator Randa Abdel-Fattah on camera.

'Where are the good Muslims leading quiet lives? Why aren't they standing up and saying something?' Hanson railed, having conveniently forgotten the hours I'd spent trying to persuade her to sit down with exactly these people in Lakemba.

Grimshaw expressed surprise that Hanson was so extreme. 'Where am I extreme? I'm suspicious of them. Many Australians are!' Hanson flared.

'You don't discriminate between individuals?' prodded Grimshaw.

'I find it very hard. They have a word, *takea*, which is to lie. And that's what they do,' Hanson answered, in her apparently acceptable new role as a national authority on Islam.

The senator was not attacked for these remarks. *A Current Affair* was not taken to task by its viewers for failing to invite a Muslim commentator to present a rebuttal. The Coalition, always happy to play the 'bias' card when the ABC dares to feature a pro-Muslim voice on *Q&A*, was silent. *A Current Affair* was running Hanson because she rates. The accuracy of what she says, it seems, was – and remains – irrelevant.

Hanson's new 'legitimacy' captures the world we now live in. The pendulum of public opinion has swung 180 degrees – from the humane and left-leaning 1990s, when Hanson was a voiceless battler selling Chicko Rolls in Ipswich, to the reactionary, minority-baiting 2010s – where the One Nation senator, with no understanding of Islam, is allowed to rail against Muslims unchecked. 'Facts' are no longer about veracity; they are about what sells. Politics may have always been show business for ugly people; but in the fracturing silos of digital media, the 'truth' has officially jumped the shark.

So why should we care? Because in 1996, when Hanson first exploded onto the political landscape, hundreds of thousands of progressive and culturally diverse Australians rose up to protect the tolerant and inclusive values we once shared from being obliterated by Hanson and her chief enabler, John Howard.

The protesters may not have entirely succeeded, but the memory of the nation they fought for – an Australia far greater and kinder than the Australia Hanson is selling us now – lives on. And unless we cherish this memory, and see through the darkening fog of alt-facts and fake news to push back, Hanson and her divisive, far-right contemporaries – the Trumps, the Le Penns and the Wilders – will win.

Acknowledgements

Over a year ago in a bar filled with sewing machines, I floated the idea of a Hanson book to the good folk of Penguin. I blew many deadlines stitching it together. Massive gratitude to my wise, insightful and supportive publisher Cate Blake, and to editors Penelope Goodes, Amanda Martin and Kevin O'Brien, lawyer Briony Lewis, sales manager Louise Ryan, designer Alex Ross and publicist Chloe Davies for believing in it. Your insights, encouragement and patience have been invaluable. I'm sure I drove you all mad, and thanks for never letting me know.

A heartfelt thank you is also due to the contributors, on both sides of the Hanson debate, who generously participated in our 2016 SBS documentary, *Pauline Hanson: Please Explain!* and helped make this book a reality. The Hon. John Howard OM AC, Alan Jones, David Ettridge, David Oldfield, Scott Balson, John Pasquarelli, Barbara Hazelton, James Ashby, Saraya Beric, Professor Marcia Langton AM, The Hon. Linda Burney MP, Neville Roach AO, Pat O'Shane AM, Dr Thiam Ang, The Hon. Helen Sham-Ho OAM, Tracey Curro, Randa Abdel-Fattah, The Hon. Emily Lau JP, Jacqueline Leong QC SC, James the satellite assistant, Bruce Woodley AO, Greg Jennet, John Cook and

ACKNOWLEDGEMENTS

Thanh Huong Huyhn – your observations have been prescient and illuminating.

I'm deeply indebted to fearless commissioning editor Joseph Maxwell, John Godfrey and the legal eagles at SBS, my wonderful lawyer Caroline Verge, and incredible collaborators Michael Cordell, Toni Malone, Matt Campbell and the team at CJZ – with whose kind permission I have included many behind-the-scenes moments from the film. To the talented creatives who worked on it – DOP Luke Peterson, soundie Phil Myers, editor Nikki Stevens, archivist Naomi Hall and everyone else on the crew – thank you for helping inspire this book.

Grateful hugs and respect to the kick-ass feature film producers Leanne Tonkes and Steve Kearney, who introduced me to Senator Hanson, and started me on this strange journey: not at all surprised you both got to Cannes!

For being an astute and always nurturing agent, thank you Fiona Inglis. For your brilliance and some excellent nights, thank you, Margo Kingston – *Off the Rails* is still the best Hanson road trip ever – and the incomparable Pauline Pantsdown, aka Simon Hunt. You are an artist and angel. Anthony Green, thank you for calling me back. Lisa Duff and Sally Regan, thank you for those dubs. David Marr, thank you for the wine and encouragement – there's a stack of vintage *New Ideas* here for you any time.

For ignoring my tunnel vision and writey-pants and just being there, love to the family of my 'hood: Sonya, Susie, Caroline, Damian, Aline, Flavia, Brett, Arlene, Catherine, Grace, Jesse Rae, Rachel Vincent, Rachel Landers, Scotty, Snakeman, Beckley, Mel, Ravi and my nearests, Alison, Richard and Ava.

Finally, a personal thank you to Senator Hanson. You won't like this book if you read it. But you listened when I tried to change your mind, and you were a humorous, courageous and

ACKNOWLEDGEMENTS

gracious host. You shared your time and your life with us during a long and demanding shoot. For staying the course, even when it was clear we'd never agree, sincerely, thank you.